THE EVENT OF DEATH: A PHENOMENOLOGICAL ENQUIRY

MARTINUS NIJHOFF PHILOSOPHY LIBRARY

VOLUME 23

For a complete list of volumes in this series see final page of the volume.

The Event of Death: A Phenomenological Enquiry

by

Ingrid Leman-Stefanovic

1987 **MARTINUS NIJHOFF PUBLISHERS**
a member of the KLUWER ACADEMIC PUBLISHERS GROUP
DORDRECHT / BOSTON / LANCASTER

IV

Distributors

for the United States and Canada: Kluwer Academic Publishers, 101 Philip Drive, Assinippi Park, Norwell, MA 02061, USA
for the UK and Ireland: Kluwer Academic Publishers, MTP Press Limited, Falcon House, Queen Square, Lancaster LA1 1RN, UK
for all other countries: Kluwer Academic Publishers Group, Distribution Center, P.O. Box 322, 3300 AH Dordrecht, The Netherlands

Library of Congress Cataloging in Publication Data

```
Leman-Stefanovic, Ingrid.
   The event of death.

   (Martinus Nijhoff philosophy library ; v. 23)
   Bibliography: p.
   1. Death.  I. Title.  II. Series.
BD444.L44  1987      128'.5      86-23494
```

ISBN 90-247-3414-2

Dedicated to the
memory of my mother
Katya Grib Leman

TABLE OF CONTENTS

PART TWO:
DEATH AS AN ONTIC E-VENT:
Coming to terms with the phenomenon of death
as a determinate possibility.

PART THREE:
ONTIC/ONTOLOGICAL IMPLICATIONS

THE EVENT OF DEATH: A PHENOMENOLOGICAL ENQUIRY

I N T R O D U C T I O N

> "Before he is 'cast into the world', as
> claimed by certain hasty metaphysicians, man
> is laid in the cradle of the house.. A
> concrete metaphysics cannot neglect this
> fact..."1

In this quote, Gaston Bachelard points to a most common sin
of philosophers: a sin of over-generalizing and abstracting to
the point that their grand systems become irrelevant to the
concrete facts of daily existence. Before I can be seen to be
simply "thrown" in-the-world, let us remember that I am thrown
within a definitive Situation, among essents, among significant
Others, "in the cradle of the house", as Bachelard notes; let us
beware of our over-intellectualizing existence to the extent that
we lose sight of the concrete, lived moments which, explicitly
and implicitly, make our lives meaningful.

This book is on the topic of death, not as it relates to
grand metaphysical schemes of the ultimate purpose of the uni-

---

1   Gaston Bachelard, <u>The Poetics of Space</u>, p. 7.

verse, but as it relates to the concrete, ontic realities of the phenomenon of death, as it appears to human consciousness.

This is not to say that the book commits no sin: in fact, it commits a most serious "sin" of attempting to address more than one audience; an audience of those well-versed in the phenomenological thought of Martin Heidegger, as well as those who approach the Heideggerean ontology for the first time or with little background!

Let me speak first, to the latter group.

Heidegger's central conviction and essential objective was to "raise anew the question of the meaning of Being". At first glance, this appears to be the most serious sort of abstraction and generalization one could imagine, but in fact, as this book attempts to show, this is not necessarily so.

In Part One, we deal exclusively with Heidegger's Interpretation of the phenomenon of death, specifically within the context of his ontological quest for the meaning of Being. We describe how it is that man is the only one who can ever be engaged in this quest, how his individuation is defined by Being, and how it is that the phenomenon of Being-towards-death reveals the authentic temporal roots of man as essentially finite. While there are a number of excellent books already in print summarizing Heidegger's views on death, Part One of this book is meant to not only introduce these views once again in a somewhat different form, but it is also meant to set the foundation, particularly through the discussions of individuation, transcendence and temporality, for a firm understanding of Heidegger's ontology, without which subsequent chapters lose their significance.

Those "well-versed" in Heidegger's work, however, may wish to pass immediately to Part Two, where we go-beyond Heidegger, hopefully yet remaining faithful to his central Thought, to unfold the special signifiance of concrete, determinate ontic events of death as revealed to the terminally ill patient, and to those who survive the death of someone whom they love.

It should be clear that we are heading in Part III to a re-thinking of the meaning of the Ontological Difference itself. Part of the incentive to do so came to me in the form of a chal-lenge posed a number of years ago by Thomas Langan2 in his ar-ticle on "Transcendence in the Philosophy of Heidegger": a chal-lenge (quite inadequately addressed to date) to explore the factuality of contingent existence in such a way as to "fulfill the basic program of a concrete, phenomenological philosophical structure outside of all arbitrary metaphysical limits".3

---

2   I am grateful to Professor Langan for his review of major
     portions of this manuscript, for his suggestions, and for
     his support of the entire endeavour.

3   Langan, Thomas, "Transcendence in the Philosophy of Heideg-
     ger", in New Scholasticism, Vol. XXXII, 1958, p. 60.

In this unique article, Professor Langan suggests that only if concreteness is explored without being understood as simply equivalent to limiting particularity, "this development will be the unmistakeable indication that the philosophy of Heidegger has at last become the fundamental ontology by rooting itself firmly in Being."4

Citing Levinas' criticisms to be "basically just", the article points out how:

> "Side by side with the awareness that every phenomeno-
> logical analysis must arrive at an encounter with the
> brute existence of the things that are, another current
> of Heidegger's thought manifests a conception of being
> as a general form, vague as the Plotinian One, as
> indefinite as the Platonic Good, a kind of Great Light
> which spreads its illumination over the things that are
> and, while being none of them, while being no-thing,
> while, properly speaking, not being at all, brings all
> to be...
> -Not that this conception is without value. It mani-
> fests a vivid awareness of the fundamentalness and
> transcendent mystery of the ontological fundament of
> all things... But does the fundamentalness of being and
> its transcendent mystery, to avoid being identified
> with a particular Seiende, have to be expressed as
> something grounded in non-particularity?"5

Professor Langan proposes then, that "what is lacking in Heidegger's philosophy is a fundamental phenomenological analysis of the conditions of Seiendheit in relation to the unlimited existence of its ontological ground, das Sein", and therefore,

---

4   Ibid.

5   Ibid, p. 53-54.

"the very foundation of Heidegger's thought becomes anti-parti-cularistic before the conditions of particularity have been submitted to a thorough phenomenological investigation."6

The specific challenge, then, in response to which this book was written, was brought home by Professor Langan when he wrote:

> "...the assertion that das Sein 'hides itself', that it transcends in its essential nature our direct know-ledge, does not justify the assumption that das Sein cannot be explored phenomenologically through the partial revelations of the Seienden. The question should be rather how."7

That question, of course, was the crux of the matter. How was one to begin to explore the essence of "concreteness" in such a way as to remain faithful to the rich Heideggerean insights, and therefore avoid the representative limits of metaphysical structure?

The advice of Heidegger was helpful here. He is reported to have said in the Der Spiegel interview that even for him, "the greatness of what is to be thought is too great. Perhaps we might bring ourselves to build a narrow and not far-reaching footpath as a passageway."8 The clue, then, as I saw it, was to explore one particular, concrete event, the event of death, in

---

6   Ibid, p. 55.

7   Ibid, p. 57.

8   Heidegger, M. "Only a God Can Save Us", p. 284.

the hope of providing some "passageway" to the general problem of the essence of concreteness, as posed by Professor Langan, and as required, in my view, by the original Heideggerean enterprise.

Perhaps one of the most startling revelations to me has been how very fundamental (-even more than I initially expected) the description of the ontic moment can be for an understanding of the ontological. Not only is Time seen to pervade the structures of mourning the ontic event of the death of the Other, and of eventual Recovery. What also emerges is how Dasein's transcendence as a happening or a coming to pass of ontological comprehension is essentially modified by virtue of the ontic event: in fact, if primordial Time is, as Heidegger describes, "forming in advance the pure aspect of succession which serves as the horizon", this book uncovers how an ontic event can change the very form of the "forming in advance". Certainly, Time remains the transcendental horizon, but for the terminally ill patient, that horizon now has an end in view; and that end is going to change the meaning of the horizon itself.

This book, then, is a book about Death; but it is also a book which raises some fundamental questions about the meaning of the relationship between ontology and the concrete, determinate ontic event, as much more than simply an inauthentic covering up of Being, but rather, as a revelation of Being itself.

PART ONE:

ONTOLOGICAL ROOTS
OF THE PHENOMENON OF DEATH:

A Heideggerean Interpretation

INTRODUCTION

Building upon the "preliminary conception of Phenomenology"
introduced by Heidegger in Section II of the Introduction to Sein
und Zeit,1   one may say that a phenomenology of death would
mean: "to let death, as that which shows itself, be seen from
itself in the very way in which it shows itself from itself."

Does this mean then, that a properly phenomenological description of death may reveal to us what death as a factical event
is like "in the very way in which it shows itself from itself"?
Although I cannot experience my death in order to describe it,
may some kind of phenomenological inference or "extrapolation"2
be the condition for a unique and privileged revelation of what
it is like to be dead?

There is an important element of phenomenological description which renders such an extrapolation implausible, and it
involves what Husserl originally called the reduction to significance or meaning. It can never be true for the phenomenologist,

---

1   Heidegger, Martin, Sein und Zeit, p. 34. e.t. page 58.

2   Henry W. Johnstone Jr. thinks that while one cannot extrapo-
     late from the experience of sleep to the experience of
     death, it may be possible to extrapolate from the phenomeno-
     logy of sleep to the phenomenology of death. Cf. H.W. John-
     stone Jr., "Toward a Phenomenology of Death", in Philosophy
     and Phenomenological Research, Vol. XXXV, No. 3, 1975, pages
     396-7.   Cf. also Joseph Galloway's interesting rebuke of
     such a theory in Philosophy and Phenomenological Research
     Vol. XXXVIII, No. 1, September 1977, p. 107-113.

as it was for Epicurus, that death "means nothing to us...because so long as we are existent, death is not present and whenever it is present, we are nonexistent"!3   On the contrary, death is present for me insofar as it is meaningful for me, i.e. insofar as I am aware that death will necessarily be present for me at some indeterminate time as a factical event, and indeed, as we will see, inasmuch as it defines my being-in-the-world as a being-towards-death.

To whatever extent we may wish to avoid facing death as a phenomenon of life, it is nevertheless clear that the human being is quite well aware, though perhaps only initially at a pre-reflective level, of his own vulnerability and consequently, his own finitude. The so-called "survival instinct" incorporates an unthematic acknowledgement that we are, each of us, temporal beings, fighting for survival, yet susceptible to the demands of time and a granting of Being beyond our control and manipulation. In this sense, death is present for me, is meaningful for me, even if it is not explicitly acknowledged in a determinate, ontic event, for as we shall see, the phenomenon of death defines the finite, human condition in all the manifold structures of its existence. One cannot begin to understand the question of the meaning of Being if one ignores the ground of temporality which is the condition of the possibility of understanding the world

---

3   Epicurus, Letter to Monoeceus, L26.

into which we are "thrown"; consequently, one cannot begin to understand life if one ignores the phenomenon of human finitude and death.

Realizing this to be the case, a phenomenology of death will not seek to uncover what it is like to be dead, or what the singular event of death is like, but, as a description involving a reduction to meaning, it will be intimately related to a "phenomenology of life", exploring the ways in which death penetrates human understanding as a necessary condition of being-in-the-world.

As Heidegger himself has said, death is "in the widest sense, a phenomenon of life".4   Some may insist that "life is only life; death is death and only death. But life's being is also death. Everything that enters into life also begins to die, to go toward its death, and death is at the same time life."5

Thus, any analysis of death must remain in a very strict sense "this-worldly", rooted in the lived-world and taking precedence over any ontical other-worldly speculation of what may be after death; similarly, a phenomenological description of death must take precedence over any ontic understanding of death which would define it in terms of a mere perishing, which factually comes to an end despite all attitudes or relation to such

4   Heidegger, Martin, SZ, 246. e.t. 290.

5   Heidegger, Martin, EM 100, e.t. 111.

cessation in a <u>Sein zum Ende</u>. In contrast to any ontic meanings, an existential-ontological understanding reveals death to be the very structure of being-mortal, an <u>existentiale</u>, the mode of Being of man himself in his structure of existing as Being-towards-death.

Despite Epicurus' suggestion that my death as an event cannot, empirically speaking, be present while I am present, ontologically speaking, death is a way to be which belongs to man as soon as he is, and therefore, it is an <u>ever-present</u> element in the ontological structure of man and a determination of his very existence.

But while I can say that I can be <u>aware</u> of death, or that my death can indeed have a <u>meaning</u> for me even though the event of my death is not-yet here, it seems that a writer like Heidegger presumes something more when he writes how Dasein 6 in fact "<u>is</u> already its 'not-yet', and is its 'not-yet' constantly as long as it is."7   The ontological depth of the question of the "meaning" of death reveals something quite distinct from one more ontic meaning among others.   Dasein not only possesses an ontic awareness of its death as an end, but, writes Heidegger, Dasein

---

6   Martin Heidegger chooses to describe man as a "Dasein", as "there-Being", thereby stressing the ontological (<u>Sein</u>) roots of human being.

7   SZ 245, e.t. 289.

"is already its end too".8   How _am_ I my end?   How is this ontological depth of "meaning" going to reveal death to be an element of my very constitution as a Da-sein?   If death is not-yet present as an ontic occurrence, how indeed is it "ever-present" in such a way and to such a degree that I must say not merely that "my end awaits me", but in fact that somehow I am my end, insofar as I am at all?

In order that we at all adequately ask this question, let alone attempt to answer it, Martin Heidegger suggests that we must guard against any ontic re-presentation and inauthentic objectification of the factical event of the death of the Other. If _I am_ my end, then an enquiry into the meaning of death must begin with the recognition of death as that most unsurpassable, non-relational and the most _personal_ of life's potentialities.

Therefore, taking Heidegger's example, we shall begin by exploring the meaning of individuation, _Selbstheit_, (Chapter One), in order that its significance for the problem of Being-towards-death itself (Chapter Two) be resolved.

The central position of temporality as related to individua-tion and also as the meaning of Being-towards-death, will in turn prepare the way for the discussion of time with regard to the meaning of ontological difference (Chapter Three).

---

8   SZ 245, e.t. 289.

CHAPTER ONE

INDIVIDUATION AND TEMPORALITY

A. Transcendence as the Key

That death is to be conceived as the "ending" of human
existence seems to be inconsistent with the ontological meaning
of care: defined by Heidegger as the "ahead-of-itself", the
phenomenon of "care" reveals that it is essential to the basic
human constitution that there is always something-more to accomplish, something is always outstanding.1   Human existence is
never to be seen as a static phenomenon of the present: unlike
simple material objects, human beings always have .plans and
projects which, on a fundamental existential level, orient them
towards a futural horizon of possibilities. A human being is
never to be seen as a completed, defined thing or essent: so long
as one is, one's being is directed toward a future which is-not-
yet.

The lack of totality in one's potentiality-for-Being signifies that there is always eine ständige Unabgeschlossenheit
which would seem to preclude both the practical, existentiell

_____

1   SZ 236

possibility of standing outside of myself to objectively analyze my potentiality-for-Being-a-whole, as well as the existential possibility of discerning the state-of-Being of "totality" and "end". As Thomas Browne reminds us, "the long habit of living indisposeth us for dying"2; it seems that in practical terms, to really accept my death as the termination of my existence, the genuine end, is made all the more difficult because for as long and inasmuch as I exist, there is always something yet to be accomplished in the future. Inasmuch as we are, we are as temporal beings, possessing a future. Can we ever come to terms with the reality of death as the end of all my futures?

Heidegger offers that it is precisely insofar as Dasein understands itself in being-ahead-of-itself by projecting itself against the futural horizon of its possibilities, that Dasein stands before the most ultimate possibility, i.e. the possibility of the impossibility of any existence at all, and is thereby "fully assigned to its ownmost potentiality-for-Being".3

To understand how this is so, one must interpret "end" in a special way, remembering that death as "ending" does not signify for Heidegger, man's Being-at-an-end (Zu-ende-Sein), and so it is not to be understood in an ontic sense of disappearance or even

---

2   Cited in Slinger, J., "Going Against the Flow", in Quest
     (Comac Communications Ltd., Canada), Sept. '84, Vol. 13,
     Issue 5, p. 60.

3   SZ 250.

fulfillment.4   A   plant   ceases   to   be;   an   acorn fulfills its
intrinsic purpose of existence when it matures into an oak tree;
but the ontological meaning of care shows the finitude of human
existence to mean something much more.

Death as "end" is not a Zu-ende-Sein but a Sein-zum-Ende,
understanding that death, as the most extreme possibility of
existence, is a way to be5, that is, as the possibility of possibilities, it limits and determines all other possibilities,
engulfing man's total Being-in-the-world. Death as "end" is much
more than another present-at-hand or even ready-to-hand
possibility among possibilities which are still "outstanding":
the issue is nothing less than "no-longer-being-able-to-be-there
(Nicht-mehr-dasein-können)", which means in the existential-
ontological sense that insofar as death belongs to the very
constitution of man as the possibility of the impossibility of
every way of comporting himself towards anything, of every way of
existing,6 -then death must be seen to lay claim to the very
totality of man's own unique, irreplacable and incommunicable
being - in short, all that is most "personal" to human
understanding.   "By its very essence, death is in every case

---

4   Cf. SZ 242-5.

5   SZ 245.

6   SZ 262.

mine, insofar as it 'is' at all",7 because Being-towards-death as Dasein's ownmost (eigenste) possibility "discloses to Dasein its ownmost potentiality-for-Being in which its very Being is at issue."8 According to Heidegger, this ownmost possibility is also non-relational (unbezügliche): that potentiality-for-Being in which its ownmost Being is at stake must be taken over by each Dasein alone.   We must each die our own deaths; no-one can do it for us, which means that "end" as a Sein-zum-Ende does not represent a mere end-point which is-not-yet, but it is the mark of each individual's life; it is that which defines us in our temporal, finite being-in-the-world. Insofar as death is "unüberholbare",9 it can only be so as mine, which is why Heidegger believes that when someone else dies, his Being-in-the-world is still a Being "in the sense of Being-just-present-at-hand-and-no-more of a corporeal thing which we encounter...- The end of the entity qua Dasein is the beginning of the same

---

7   SZ 240.

8   SZ 263.

9   Suggesting the "unüberholbarkeit" of death, the first chorus
       from the Antigone of Sophocles is quoted by Heidegger in
       his Einführung in die Metaphysik (page 112, e.t. 123-4):
           "Everywhere journeying, inexperienced and without
           issue,
           [Man] comes to nothingness.
           Through no flight can he resist
           the one assault of death,
           even if he has succeeded in cleverly evading
           painful sickness."

entity qua something present-at-hand10, so technically, one can overtake and recover from the death of the Other and in so doing, death as an "unüberholbare" possibility remains undisclosed.11

Thus the certainty of death demands more than a merely special behaviour toward death, it "demands Dasein itself in the full authenticity of its existence"12, because the mark of finitude is the mark of the humanity of each individual human being. Coming to authentic existence requires that man come to an awareness that his own being is at stake, so death does not just belong to Dasein in an undifferentiated way: "Death lays claim to it as an individual Dasein. The non-relational character of death ...individualizes Dasein down to itself".13

That it is not possible for the individual Dasein to "transcend" these limitations of Selbstheit in approaching the existential-ontological significance of death by way of the death of the Other, is evident in the very meaning which Heidegger attaches to the transcendence of Dasein's Being, a transcendence which is distinctive precisely in that "it implies the possibility and the

---

10   SZ 238.

11   This claim of Heidegger's will, of course, be examined in later parts of this book, and the limits of the claim discussed.

12   SZ 265.

13   SZ 263.

necessity of the most radical <u>individuation</u>".14   In clarifying
the meaning of such "individuation" with regard to the problem of
transcendence, it should become clear in what way death is mine
in much more than superficial terms; it should also become clear
how it is impossible to transcend one's "I-ness" in any authentic
understanding of death by way of the Other.

(i)   <u>The Necessity (Notwendigkeit) of Individuation as
Revealed in the Meaning of Transcendence:
Lessons from Kant</u>

Inasmuch as transcendence is no longer to be conceived
within the context of a meta-physical striving toward a transcendent (highest) entity or domain, the term itself is to be understood in a non-metaphysical sense, which means that rather than
be re-presented by way of any metaphysical priority of some-
thing-beyond-me,15 its very meaning and essence will be sought
elsewhere, i.e. within the futurally pro-jecting and transcending
activity of <u>human understanding</u>.   Somewhat reminiscent of Kant,

---

14   SZ 38.   In the original: "Die Transzendenz des Seins des
      Daseins ist ausgezeichnete, sofern in ihr die Möglichkeit
      und Notwendigkeit der radikalsten <u>Individuation</u> liegt."
      Lost in the English translation is the sense that individua-
      tion is not so much implied in Dasein's transcendence,
      as it is seen to <u>lie</u> therein, eventually to be <u>laid bare</u>.
      Also important is the <u>Not</u> of the <u>Notwendigkeit</u> - but we
      shall return to this.

15   Heidegger's main criticism of the metaphysical tradition
      was that philosophers in the tradition consistently made
      the mistake of interpreting the meaning of Being in terms
      of <u>a being</u>, so that Being as the ground of the emergence
      of essents remained forgotten.

Heidegger will (initially at least) make the idea of transcendence an ontological problem of man's Being16, by identifying transcendence as the fundamental constitution of the selfhood (<u>Selbstheit</u>) of Dasein and condition of any comportment within a world. In the words of the <u>Grundprobleme der Phänomenologie</u> volume17, "das Dasein ist das Transzendente".

But there is an immediate problem: if the very notion of Da-sein implies that the essence of man's ontological constitution as care is a being-ahead-of-oneself in a transcending activity of understanding, what is the significance of this relationship between being-ahead-of-oneself on the one hand, and "Selbstheit" on the other? What is the significance of saying that my very "selfness" is a being-<u>ahead</u>-of-myself?

What this cannot mean is that initially man is in essence "ein Ich-Selbst" which only then possesses secondarily an openness to the world within an ontic activity of transcendence.18 On the contrary, "Existieren besagt immer schon: Überschreiten, oder besser: Überschrittenhaben",19 and this is so because Dasein, as "das Transzendente", is as such "offen für... Die Offenheit

---

16   Cf. SZ 49.

17   GP 426. These Marburg lectures "thematisch im Umkreis von <u>Sein und Zeit</u> stehen." (cover).

18   GP 425.

19   GP 426.

gehört zu seinem Sein. Es ist sein Da..."20; which in turn
leads Heidegger to conclude that the original essence of
transcendence reveals itself within the fundamental state of
Being-in-the-world: "In der Grundverfassung des In-der-Welt-
seins bekundet sich das ursprüngliche Wesen der Transzendenz."21

　　But even so, our problem remains, albeit in a re-worded
fashion. We may now ask: What is the significance of saying on
the one hand, that the very "individuality of Dasein is grounded
in its transcendence"22, and on the other, that the essence of
transcendence is revealed within a Being-in-the-world, and that
the question of transcendence can in fact be "answered by
recourse to the transcendence of the world"?23

　　While the meaning of transcendence will normally be sought
within the question of what it is that transcends the entities
which are present to us, yet even within the context of such a
question, a reasonable reply is that we ourselves are "transcending", within an understanding appropriation and intentional
consideration of any tode ti, and that even the transcendence of
the world is meaningless apart from the transcending activity of

----

20   GP 426.

21   GP 426.

22   GP 425.

23   SZ 366.

the Dasein. Heidegger makes this clear in his <u>Vom Wesen des Grundes</u> volume, where he tells us that:

> "Transcendence means surpassing... the surpassing that
> makes anything like existence and thereby movement in
> space possible in the first place."24

But while transcendence is said to signify what is unique to human existence, not as one among other possible types of behaviour, but as a basic constitutive feature of being-human that happens prior to all behaviour; and while it is for this reason that "transcendence constitutes selfhood",25 on the other hand, writes Heidegger, "not only transcendence but also surpassing touches on a kind of Being that Dasein 'itself' is not".26 Significantly,

> "the being that Dasein surpasses is not a random aggre-
> gate of objects, but however it may be defined and
> articulated in any particular case, is always surpassed
> in a totality... Surpassing occurs totally. It never
> merely occurs 'sometimes and sometimes not', as might a
> theoretical knowing of objects. Rather, surpassing is
> there with the fact of Being-there [Dasein]... How-
> ever... that towards-which Dasein transcends, we call
> the <u>world</u>, and we can now define transcendence as
> Being-in-the-world. World goes up to make up the
> unified structure of transcendence..."27

To understand transcendence as Being-in-the-world means more than the trivial realization that Dasein is found amidst other

---

24   WG 35-37.

25   WG 39.

26   WG 39.

27   WG 39-41.

essents, because "world" itself is more than the sum of all that is immediately present at hand. It is no particular being, but rather that by and in terms of which Dasein is able to understand particular beings: "That Dasein gives 'itself' to understand in terms of 'its' world means then, that in approaching Being through the world, Dasein makes a _self_ of itself...World belongs to selfhood."28

Yet to say, as Heidegger does, that "Weltverständnis als Daseinvertständnis ist Selbstverständnis"29 once again returns us to the problem of the meaning of such an apparent identification of "Selbst" and "Welt". Could it be that the meaning of such an "identity" is to be sought within the middle term of the proposition, that is, within the "Daseinverständnis"? Heidegger seems to suggest just that: "Selbst und Welt", he tells us, "gehören in dem einem Seiendem, dem Dasein, zusammen."30

But once again, we have come full circle, back to our original problem: wherein lies the _necessity_ of the "individuation" (_Selbstheit_) of this very Dasein, which as "das Transzendente", is in essence, in-the-world?

---

28   WG 85.

29   GP 422.

30   GP 422.

The insights   offered by   Heidegger's own Kantbuch may be of some help; here we are told that transcendence   as such "consists in a precursory act of orientation":31

> "In this primordial act of orientation, the finite being pro-poses to itself an area of free-play [Spiel-raum] within which something can 'correspond' to it. To hold onself in advance in such an area of free-play and to form it originally is nothing other than transcendence which marks all finite comportment [Ver-halten] with regard to the essent."32

Again, it is clear that "Selbst" and "Welt" are not two "things" (Seiende) like subject and object,33   and consequently, the "problem of transcendence" cannot be interpreted in tradi-tional metaphysical terms of how a subject encounters the world as an "object" or as an aggregate of "objects". Rather, the following question emerges: "what makes it ontologically pos-sible for entities to be encountered within-the-world and Objec-tified as so encountered?"34

The question of transcendence in the Kantbuch really centers around that very problem of the possibility of ontological know-ledge, although in its final formulation, the basic unity of the structure of transcendence (or ontological knowledge) finds its expression within the "supreme principle" that "the conditions of

---

31   KM 88, e.t. 96.

32   KM 70, e.t. 75.

33   GP 422.

34   SZ 366.

the possibility of experience in general, are likewise conditions of the possibility of objects of experience."35   If ontological or transcendental knowledge is to be concerned not with the essent as such (Gegenstände und Dinge sind nie transzendent"36) - but with the condition of the possibility of a prior comprehension of Being, then the structure of transcendence itself is revealed (according to Heidegger) to Kant, within the unity (expressed in the above principle) of experience and objects of experience.   Such a unity, however, requires precisely that "act of orientation" or "turning oneself toward" the object, which is the condition of experiencing an object at all,37 and which constitutes the transcendence of Dasein in bringing into being a horizon or Spielraum for essents to manifest themselves in.   Such an act of orientation which lets something "take up a position

---

35   Kant, I., Critique of Pure Reason, (hereafter CPR), A-158, B-197.   Cf. Heidegger's remarks about this principle in Die Frage nach dem Ding, p. 143: "He who grasps this sentence, grasps Kant's Critique of Pure Reason. He who grasps the latter, knows not just a book in the literature of philosophy, but has a grasp of the basic attitude characterizing our historical existence, which we can neither circumvent, nor leap over nor disavow in any other way.   We must, on the contrary, by appropriating and transforming it, bring it to a decision in the future."

36   GP 426.

37   "Ontological knowledge... is the condition of the possibility that an essent as such can, in general, become an object for a finite being. All finite beings must have this basic ability, which can be described as a turning toward.. [orientation toward...] which lets something become an ob-ject." (KM 69-70, e.t. 74.)

opposite us...forms as such the horizon of ob-jectivity in general. The going-beyond to.., which in finite knowledge is necessary in advance and at every moment, is accordingly a constant ex-position [Hinausstehen] to... [Ekstasis]. But this essential ex-position to... in its position [Stehen] forms and pro-poses to itself a horizon. Transcendence is in itself ecstatic-horizontal."38

The transcendental object, therefore, is not an essent behind the phenomenon, but rather requires Dasein's own "turning-oneself-toward" and "holding itself suspended in Nothingness" for the "object in general", for the Kantian "X", for the correlate of the unity of apperception - which is to say, for the pre-given horizon of objectivity itself, in and through which the Being of essents manifests itself a priori. This projection into Nothing is the overcoming of what-is-in-totality: in short, Transcendence.

Indeed, according to its essence, the Nothing appears as pure horizon of all objectification, as the ontological condition of the possibility of an encounter with "things". Projecting itself in-the-world, in anticipation of a future of possibilities, the transcendence of the human understanding opens up a world within which particular essents are encountered. Thus, "ontological knowledge 'forms' transcendence and this formation

_____

38   KM 111, e.t. 123.

is nothing other than the holding open of the horizon within which the Being of the essent is perceptible in advance."39

How ontological knowledge "forms" transcendence is revealed in further detail, suggests Heidegger, in Kant's discussion in the Critique of Pure Reason of the role of the transcendental imagination, although the elucidation of the structure of transcendence in terms of the unity of experience and the objects of experience (Kant's own "supreme principle") as constituted through the synthesis of the pure imagination, shows as much (and perhaps more) about Heidegger's own convictions as it does of Kant's. It is, suggests Heidegger, the transcendental imagination which for Kant renders possible ontological knowledge by projecting, prior to all experience of essents - the pure schema of a horizon of objectivity or "constant presence" within which the essent may manifest itself as present. It is the transcendental imagination which is the root of transcendence40, and the transcendental condition of an encounter with a world which is in fact never fully revealed to understanding. More specifically, the unique Heideggerean interpretation and "destruction" of the original insights of the Critique and the hidden motivations behind the evolution from the first to the second editions, reveals the transcendental imagination to be the a priori basis of knowledge

---

39   KM 116, e.t. 128.

40   KM 129, e.t. 147.

and original, unifying source of sensibility and understanding-
a source later relegated to a subordinate position of an activity
(Wirkung) of the understanding on the sensibility.41   Eventually
turning away from his original insight, initially however Kant
was to uncover an important truth: if intuition and thinking are
essentially related and hence cannot be understood in isolation
(since "the more radically one attempts to isolate the pure
elements of finite knowledge, the more apparent becomes the
impossibility of such isolation and the more evident becomes the
dependence of pure thinking on intuition"42) - then neither of
these elements can explain their essential unity; which then
leads to the function of the transcendental imagination as the
ground of such synthesis and true source of experience, bringing
into conjunction the "two extremes" of sensibility and
understanding43, and providing the a priori basis of all
knowledge. But such a priori "knowledge", Heidegger adds, has
less in common with traditional epistemological conceptions of
knowledge than it has with Heidegger's own ontological notion of
man's Being-in-the-world, for it recalls the hiddenness which is
the source of all knowledge and out of which awareness arises;
and it is precisely that "unknown root" from which Kant will

---

41   Cf. Kant, I. CPR B-152.

42   KM 58, e.t. 61.

43   Kant, I. CPR A-124.

shrink   in   the   Second   Edition,   recognizing the transcendental imagination to   be "das   beunruhigende Unbekannte..."44, oriented not   towards   beings   as   an   empirical imagination must be - but rather, towards that   presence   which   is   the   condition   of the possibility for anything to be in the first place.

While the   Kantian treatment of the problem of transcendence remains too subjectivistic for   Heidegger,45   yet   the inherent need (Not) of individuation is reflected in Kant's very grounding of the "innermost essence" of transcendence46   in a pure imagination which   is itself necessarily oriented towards an ontological presence.   This need of individuation, we must remember, is not a need   of   subjectivity   in   its   objectifying   encounter with the world, and the very meaning of the Not as a need of   the truth of Being,   tells   us   why   it   is   not.   "Need" for Heidegger is the

---

44   KM 148, e.t. 169.

45   Heidegger's final evaluation of the Kantbuch   is that Kant's thought is   ultimately an anthropocentric project, revolving around man as the   absolute foundation   and perfectly suffi- cient ground   of all   truth and Being, and therefore in fact running the "constant risk of concealing from us   the neces- sity   of   developing   the   question   of man as a problem and of connecting this problem with a   laying of   the foundation of metaphysics."   (KM 225).   What takes place in the Kantian laying of   the   foundation   is   that   "the   establishment of the   intrinsic   possibility   of   ontology is accomplished as the   disclosure   of   transcendence,   i.e. the   subjectivity of   the   subject"   (212-13);   however, "the insight into the transcendental essence   of   pure   imagination... was   not in itself   enough   to   permit   the   subjectivity of the subject as a whole to   be seen   in a   new light."   (172-3).   Cf. KM, Section Four.

46   KM 133, e.t. 152.

thirst for Being of a finite Seinsverständnis: extending itself towards the Nothingness of the future, the urgency of Dasein's ontological need is to fill itself up, to open a horizon of interpretation in which meaning will be created. This exigency reveals a Not which is not a mere lack, but if anything is a lack that lays claim to my Being, that beseeches and entreats me, that invites and in fact, lays a demand on me, in my need of an understanding of Being itself. Heidegger's proposal of a "need" of individuation is more than an ontic need for a subjective foundation, because it is Dasein as a Selbst, and not as a Subjekt which is the "location of the truth of Being" itself. To quote from Sein und Zeit, "only if we are oriented phenomenally by the meaning of the Being of the authentic potentiality-for-Being-one's-Self are we put in a position to discuss what ontological justification there is for treating substantiality, simplicity, personality [and subjectivity!] as characteristics of Selfhood".47 In short, the human essence "shows itself here to be the relation which first opens up Being to man. Being-human, as the need [Not] of apprehension and collection, is a being-driven [Nötigung] into... the sapient embodiment of Being."48

What we arrive at then, is an ontological interpretation of the "I" which is neither an I-substance, nor an I-subject, but on

---

47   SZ 323.

48   EM 130, e.t. 142.

the contrary, is to be understood in terms of Dasein's authentic potentiality-for-Being.   The notion of "Selbst", therefore, is not a delimiting, ontic notion of "mineness", or mere subjectivity; on the contrary, it indicates an openness to Being, and a "releasement" (Gelassenheit) in the sense of both an attentive as well as receptive hearkening to the offering of Being, to which "Selbstheit" essentially belongs.49

In an ontological pro-jecting toward a future which is-not-yet, Dasein engages its existence in a surging, surpassing Being-

---

49 It is incorrect to suggest, as Michael Zimmerman does, that this concept of the self as a "vehicle" for the unfolding of Being is found only in the "New Concept of Authentic Selfhood" of the later writings of Heidegger. Zimmerman contends that the notion of "mineness", the understanding of "authentic existence" and the conception of Dasein as a temporalizing activity which is the principle condition for encountering, -are all subjectivistic notions of Being and Time, and that it is only in the later works that the "self is not personal, but is the ground of personality", inasmuch as Heidegger is introducing a "new concept" of the self which "belongs not to 'me' or even to Dasein, but to Being itself".(p.205).

There is nothing fundamentally "new" in the later thought to take us "beyond the subjective elements of Being and Time", in a "new" revelation of the relation and belonging of man to Being; after all, page 1 of Sein und Zeit states that it is only "fitting that we should raise anew the question of the meaning of Being"; the Introduction is an "Exposition of the Question of the meaning of Being" which enquires first about "The Necessity, Structure and Priority of the Question of Being", and only then proceeds to consider "The ontological analytic of Dasein as laying bare the horizon for an Interpretation of the Meaning of Being in general." (II.5) Finally, Heidegger stipulates (page 12) that it is Dasein (Being-there!) which is ontically distinctive in that it is ontological. "Understanding of Being is itself a definite characteristic of Dasein's Being".

in-the-world. Transcendence then signifies "sich aus einer Welt verstehen",50 which then means that all individuation is itself already partly characterized by the world that stands over a-gainst it; and this is why individuation is never subjectivity, but rather, a creative and vibrant participation in life itself.

That is also why there is no contradiction in saying, as we did above, that Dasein's very "selfness" (Selbstheit) is a being-ahead-of-oneself, or that the individuality of Dasein is grounded in a transcendence, the essence of which is revealed in a Being-in-the-world; because to be present as an individual (Selbst) has the character even of self-forgetfulness,51 and being-outside-of-oneself as the positive possibility of being wholly with some-thing else. So "in saying 'I', I have in view the entity which in each case I am as an I-am-in-the-world".52 It was the accom-plishment of Kant that he was able to sense (though, we must re-member, incompletely,53) that transcendence itself is rooted in a pure imagination which, in its primordial "act of orientation"

---

50   GP 425.

51   "As something which keeps silent, authentic Being-one-self is just the sort of thing that does not keep on saying 'I'". (SZ 323.)

52   SZ 321.

53   While one positive aspect of Kant's analysis is that he "holds fast to the 'I' as 'I think'", and while Heidegger allows that the "'I think' gives Kant a genuine phenomenal starting point, he cannot exploit it ontologically and has to fall back on the 'subject', that is to say, something substantial". (SZ 320-1).

reveals the fundamental ontological comportment of the structure
of man ("In transcendence, Dasein manifests itself as need of the
comprehension of Being"54), and a finite freedom and spontaneity
which is nonetheless fulfilling a certain necessity as well.

(ii)   The Meaning of Transcendence as Temporality

     That the transcendental imagination recalls the "disquieting
unknown" means therefore, that it will serve the unique function
of a unity of receptivity and spontaneity both - not in the sense
of an "äusseres Band" of simply a passive sensibility and a
creative understanding, but rather, as an original unity,55 it
must allow that the receptive and spontaneous elements which it
unites will each reveal distinct traces of the other. In short,
we must recognize a certain spontaneous element in sensibility,
and a receptive element in thought. Inasmuch as reason is not a
merely arbitrary imposition of understanding, but in fact is
characterized according to a "faculty of rules" and governed by
"laws",56 it is in this sense essentially passive with regard to

---

54   KM 213, e.t. 244.

55   The transcendental imagination, Heidegger explains, "is
      originally unifying, i.e. it is the specific faculty which
      forms the unity of the other two, which faculties themselves
      have an essential structural relation to it." (KM 126,
      e.t. 144.)

56   Kant, I. CPR A-126.

its object as given,57 with regard to the transcendental ideas of God, self and world as ultimate sources of these rules,58 and with regard generally to the architectonic demand that all our knowledge be regarded as belonging to a possible system59; and more, in its practical employment as well, reason in its receptivity is revealed in reverence for the moral law. "In having respect for the law, I submit to it. This specific feeling for... which is characteristic of respect is a submission."60

---

57   Kant, I. CPR A96, A105.

58   Kant, I. CPR A643-45.

59   Kant, I. CPR A474.

60   KM 145, e.t. 165. Heidegger is, in other words, suggesting here that if the transcendental imagination is to be an original unity, there will be revealed a receptivity of thought in "respect" (and, as we shall see, a spontaneity of sensibility in the form of time). Professor Thomas Langan's analysis of this aspect of the development of the Kantbuch emphasizes the fact that "Kant pointed to the pure image of 'respect'.. as the counterpart of Time in the verifying synthesis", and then suggests that "in so doing, he discovered the truth, very central to the Existentiale, that ontology and ethics are rooted in a deep unity within the one concrete existent." Quoting Heidegger, Langan continues: "'The immediate gift... is pure receptivity, but the free act of primordially giving oneself a law is pure spontaneity; the two are originally, in themselves, ONE'. The 'one' considered ontologically is Time; considered ethically, it is Respect." (Langan, Thomas, The Meaning of Heidegger, p. 79).

If the practical (ethical) employment of reason reflects a genuine "respect", does this not suggest:

-      that the ontic realm can be more than just an inauthen-
       tic mode of re-presenting reality, i.e. it can involve
       a "receptive submission" in the face of some sort
       of given?

Similarly, Kant's "ursprüngliche Vorstellungen", space and time, are revealed as the spontaneous element in sensibility. As the pre-formative forms (Formen der Vorbildung) in pure intuition, space and time "form in advance the pure aspect which serves as the horizon of that which is intuited in empirical intuition."61 By not being visible themselves ("one says summarily that 'nothing' is intuited in pure intuition"62) they are the condition of the possibility of the very visibility of things, and since it is the ens imaginarium which "pertains to the possible forms of 'Nothing' - to what is not an essent in the sense of something actually present", therefore, "the act of pure intuition is essentially pure imagination."63

But while Kant sees both space and time as pure intuitions, he nevertheless adds a qualification, indicating that time takes precedence over space. Kant writes: "Time is the formal condition a priori of all appearance whatsoever."64 All our knowledge

---

        and
-     that if this is the case, then the condition of the ontic event is not simply the ontological, but the ontic and the ontological are, in some sense, "themselves one"?
We shall return to this kind of consideration in the final chapter of this volume.

61   KM 131, e.t. 149-50.

62   KM 131, e.t. 149-50.

63   KM 131, e.t. 150.

64   Kant, I. CPR A34, B50.

is "subject to time, in which all objects of knowledge without exception must be ordered, conjoined, and brought into relation with one another. This is a general observation which is fundamental to everything which follows".65 As universal pure intuition, adds Heidegger, it "must be the dominant and essential element of pure knowledge and hence of transcendence as well, since it is pure knowledge which makes transcendence possible.66

That Heidegger agrees that transcendence has a temporal foundation, is clear. In Sein und Zeit, we read: "...if Dasein's Being is completely grounded in temporality, then temporality must make possible Being-in-the-world and therewith Dasein's transcendence";67 and in the Grundprobleme der Phänomenologie volume, it is equally evident that Dasein can only be seen as transcendental inasmuch as "die Seinsverfassung des Daseins ursprünglich in der ekstatisch-horizontalen Zeitlichkeit gründet".68 We are told that "time is the primary horizon of the transcendental science, ontology, or briefly put, the transcendental horizon."69

---

65   Kant, I. CPR A99. Heidegger agrees. Cf. SZ 335 and 369.

66   KM 50, e.t. 52.

67   SZ 364ff; cf. also 350ff and p.389.

68   GP 447.

69   GP 460.

There is a necessity of individuation revealed in the meaning of transcendence, and this necessity is ontological, insofar
as it points to a transcending activity of a spatializing Dasein,
and an original, pretheoretical capacity for intentional involve-
ments with entities within the opening of a specific Spielraum;
but what does it mean now to say that such a primary comportment
toward the world and the opening of a transcendental horizon is
itself grounded in temporality?   What does it mean to say that
"the essence of transcendence is based... originally on time"?70

In Vom Wesen des Grundes, Heidegger tells us that Dasein's
transcendence is a "happening" (Geschehen) or a coming-to-pass of
ontological comprehension.   To say then, that "'Dasein transcends' means: the essence of its Being is such that it 'forms the
world' in the sense that it lets the world happen..."71 History
too is said to be not merely the past, and much less the merely
contemporary, but it is a happening - an "acting and being acted
upon which pass through the present, which are determined from
out of the future, and which take over the past. It is precisely
the present that vanishes in happening"72; and similarly,
transcendence is not something which accompanies ontological
understanding, not something which is merely present in all such

---

70   KM 219, e.t. 252.

71   WG 33.

72   EM 34, e.t. 36.

instances, but on the contrary, inasmuch as it is an achieving (Vollziehen) rather than a completed achievement, it is a temporal oc-currence in the process of being achieved; it is a dynamic and a continuing coming-to-pass, and therefore not a domain which is an ever-present possession.

It is precisely as such a coming-to-pass transcending comprehension that it is perspectival, receptive, finite and therefore essentially temporal: as perspectival, Dasein's transcendence is the openness of an understanding pro-ject which is never fully achieved and therefore can never completely and finally comprehend and control entities or the world; moreover, inasmuch as transcending Dasein can never achieve total mastery over objects, it is therefore referentially dependent on them and in an important sense, receptive in the face of their givenness.73

Such perspectival limits and referential dependence is that which in turn constitutes the very finitude of understanding. To quote Ricoeur,

> "Primal finitude consists in perspective or point of view. It affects our primary relation to the world which is to 'receive' objects and not to create them. It is not exactly synonymous with 'receptivity' itself, which consists in our openness to the world. It is rather a principle of narrowness or indeed, a closing within the openness. Neither is this finite openness synonymous with corporeity which mediates our openness to the world. It consists more in the role of the

---

73   Cf. KM 172, e.t. 195, where the finite self is defined as a "being dependent on receptivity".

body's zero origin, in the original 'here' starting from which there are places in the world."74

But recall that Heidegger has said that temporality is prior to the spatial ordering of "places in the world", and it then becomes evident how Dasein's primary transcendental comportment in the world must be essentially temporal, and how temporality in fact is at the very center of man's Being.‾

To say this, however, is to understand the phenomenon of time differently from traditional conceptions where time was seen to consist of a flow of "nows", having been interpreted basically as being the present. Alternatively, Heidegger understands the phenomenon of time not in merely ontic terms of presence only, but in terms of the integral unity of past, present and future; for even when emphasis is placed on the future-oriented character of time, time's continuity is not thereby denied but in fact it is stressed: "As authentically futural, Dasein is as authentically 'having been'."75 This means that the future "is not later than having been, and having-been is not earlier than the Present. Temporality temporalizes itself as a future which makes present in the process of having been."76 As with Heidegger's interpretation of the Kantian transcendental imagination, this ecstatical unity of temporality is the condition of

74   Ricoeur, Paul, Fallible Man, page 37.

75   SZ 326.

76   SZ 350.

the possibility of there being an entity which exists as Dasein's "there" - which is the justification for Heidegger's identifying the transcendental imagination with primordial time, as the condition for ever considering time in terms of a series of present "nows".

For, as we shall see, neither primordial time nor the transcendental ego - the Kantian "I think" - are "in time" themselves, but in fact are the same in constituting the very horizon in which anything can appear as present. In the language of the Kantbuch, "Time and the 'I think' are no longer opposed to one another as unlike and incompatible; they are the same".77

B.   Temporality as the Meaning of Individuation

I have already noted Kant's "highest principle" of synthetic judgments: "the condition of the possibility of experience in general are at the same time conditions of the possibility of objects of experience." In paragraph 24 of the Kantbuch, Heidegger asks: "What does this 'at the same time' signify?" - and he quickly responds: it expresses the essential unity of the complete structure of transcendence which is in itself ecstatic-horizontal.

David Starr has an interesting remark regarding this "unity" of the temporality of transcendence, when he speaks of tempora-

---

77   KM 173-4; e.t. 197.

lity   as   the   "unified   and   unifying   order of the transcendence
whereby Dasein   'steps outside   of' the   mere fact   of his conditioned involvement   with a given set of circumstances."78   Rather
than speak of an "order", I   prefer   the   term   "ordering"   - but
still the question remains: What is the nature of this "ordering"
or "unity" of temporality which will root the   meaning of individuation?

Since the   primordial temporality   of which Heidegger speaks
is not of   a   derivative   categorial   nature,   and   therefore its
ordering is   not itself a time-series, yet neither is it so vague
as to be opposed in any   sense to   intelligibility.   Paul Ricoeur
suggests that   "to know   being is not merely to let it appear but
is also to determine it intellectually,   to order   it, to express
it."79   That   is   why,   he adds, a philosophy of finitude (even
transcending finitude) is not sufficient, and why a philosophy of
synthesis (of   finitude and rationality) is required.   He implies
how Kant was   more   perceptive   than   Heidegger,   inasmuch   as he
"could   not   be   satisfied   with   a vague, formless transcendence
which would be a   simple field of appearances   but by   no means an
intelligible order.   Consequently, he   could not draw this order

---

78   Starr, David, Entity and Existence, p. 39.

79   Ricoeur, Paul, Fallible Man, p. 67.

from time itself, but on the contrary, had to determine time by the category."80

That Heidegger would not wish to speak of temporality itself as an intelligible order or series determined by a category, does not mean however, that the only alternative which he must accept is a merely "vague" and "formless" conception of the temporality of transcendence. In Sein und Zeit, he explicitly states that "if we are enquiring about the meaning of Being, our investigation does not then become a 'deep' one [tiefsinnig] nor does it puzzle out what stands behind Being. It asks about Being insofar as Being enters into the intelligibility of Dasein."81   Indeed, ontological knowledge is said to "'form' transcendence"82 and while the reference is to Kant, this formation is for Heidegger nothing less than the holding open of the horizon within which the Being of the essent is perceptible in advance. To be sure, temporality is not a category, and so this is not the meaning of temporality as "ordering"; but nor is temporality a vague condition of letting-appear within a formless transcendence. On the contrary, as an ecstatical unity, temporality fundamentally regulates the unity of all Dasein's existential structures;83 it

---

80   Ibid, p. 68.

81   SZ 152.

82   KM 115, e.t. 128.

83   Cf. SZ 350, 365.

is "ecstatico-horizontally constitutive for the clearedness of the 'there'"84 and consequently, while it is true that Heidegger will be reluctant to rely on a philosophy of "synthesis", perhaps because of the Hegelian metaphysical implications of the word which he will deny, and therefore while he will not speak of a synthesis of finitude and rationality, yet he does not deny that the notion of finitude and therefore temporality, essentially belong to the notion of an understanding Dasein.

Heidegger realizes that the alternative to a "vagueness" and "formlessness" of transcendence is not to understand the temporal ground in terms of a Kantian category, but it is rather to uncover the condition of both - a condition which though not a static and thoroughly intelligible structure itself, nonetheless is in some sense "primarily regulating"; and indeed, as regulating or ordering, temporality makes no sense apart from the understanding pro-ject of man - all of which is why Heidegger can say with Kant that time is neither present-at-hand, nor outside us: it is that which constitutes something on the order of a line of orientation, a directedness toward the world, so that, in short, time "forms the essential structure of subjectivity".85 This is not to say that time is to be found "in the mind", "beside" pure apperception; on the contrary, time is already included in pure

---

84   SZ 351.

85   KM 172, e.t. 194.

apperception, as the condition of the possibility of selfhood. In other words, "the pure finite self has in itself a temporal character."86

The primordial identity of time and the Kantian "I think" can be traced back to the initial identification which Heidegger makes (as implicit in Kant) between the transcendental imagination and temporality which constitutes and generates time in the three modalities (past/present/future) through the operation of the three-fold synthesis. As the transcendental imagination was seen to be the unity of spontaneity and necessity both, so too primordial time "spontaneously pre-forms the aspect of succession and, as an act both receptive and formative, pro-poses this aspect as such to itself."87

While Kant was certainly "alive in his philosophizing to the problem of the possibility of metaphysics as no-one before him or since", Heidegger sees an ultimate subjectivism in Kant, and therefore, will not identify temporality specifically with a Kantian transcendental imagination;88 temporality will still be

---

86   KM 173, e.t. 197.

87   KM 171, e.t. 194.

88   Heidegger suggests that inasmuch as the a priori condition of the possibility of objects is the objectivity (standing-opposite) of objects for Kant, this conception of objectivity (seen to constitute the Being of all essents) is an objectivity only for a rational subjectivity. Therefore, objectivity is the form of "Being as presence" which could only arise in the age of subjectivity. "That Kant demands any proof at all for the 'Dasein of things outside of me'

seen to be the meaning of individuation, but "existentiality, as
constitutive for care, provides the ontological constitution of
Dasein's Self-constancy"89 and therefore, temporality as the
meaning of individuation will be presented by Heidegger as the
ontological meaning of care.

(i)   Heidegger's understanding of Individuation as Grounded
         in Care:

   Kant's analysis, admits Heidegger, certainly had its positive aspects: for one thing, it reflected an awareness of the
impossibility of ontically reducing the "I" to a substance; and
for another, the "I" was understood to be an "I think" which was

---

   shows already that he takes the subject - the 'in me'-
   as the starting point for his problematic." (SZ 204.)
   Kant's own "supreme principle", then, implies in the final
   analysis that Being is representedness, that is, a kind
   of being handed over so that the re-presenting Self can
   be certain of what is thus presented or brought to stand
   (which then leads to the conception of truth as correspon-
   dence rather than aletheia.) As an enquiry into the nature
   of the objectivity of objects, Kant's transcendental method
   springs from an assumed subjectivity of reason in which
   Being conceals itself from itself as Being, to the utmost
   degree. (Cf. Kantbuch; Kants These über das Sein; Der Satz
   vom Grund; Nietzsche I and II.)

   Whether Heidegger's criticism of the subjectivism of the
   notion of the transcendental imagination holds in all cases,
   will be considered in further detail in Part II of this
   volume.

89   SZ 323.

obtained not merely by way of logical deduction, but which indicated a synthesizing "I bind together".90

But while Kant was able to give the "I think" a genuine phenomenal starting point, where he fell short was in his inability to exploit this starting point ontologically: nowhere does Kant show the kind of Being of this "binding" and "accompanying". "Kant has indeed avoided cutting the 'I' adrift from thinking; but he has done so without starting with the 'I think' itself in its full essential content as an 'I think something', and above all, without seeing what is ontologically 'presupposed' in taking the 'I think something' as a basic characteristic of the Self".91

But if this is so, where then do we turn to grasp the ontological meaning and unity of selfhood? If it is not to be found in the notion of a hypokeimenon, in the sense of an underlying substance, any more than in the notion of a subjectum, where then do we seek an understanding of the unity of the totality of Dasein? While we may not wish to see it in terms of some substantial permanence, there is, after all, some sense in which we would want to identify the unity of the ways and the possibilities of Da-sein in its Being. Indeed, as Heidegger allows, Dasein can exist "only in such a way that it is itself this Being

---

90   SZ 319.

91   SZ 321.

in its essential possibilities - that in each case, I am this entity"92; and he even adds that it is indeed this "I" which in some sense does seem to "'hold together' the totality of the structural whole". But the question still remains as to how, more specifically and in terms of its temporal roots, the self-sameness of the "I" is to be ontologically revealed.

"In principle", Heidegger reminds us, "we have already fixed upon a clue for this problem, for if the Self belongs to the essential [wesenhaften] attributes of Dasein, while Dasein's 'Essence' ['Essenz'] lies in existence, then 'I-hood' and Self-hood must be conceived existentially".93 In fact, selfhood is to be discerned existentially, precisely in the authenticity of Dasein's Being as care.

I have suggested previously that the meaning of individua-tion is in fact revealed in the transcending activity of a Da-sein which is essentially Being-in-the-world. It is precisely inasmuch as Being-in-the-world is an essential character of Dasein that its Being for the world is in essence "caring".

The self, according to Heidegger, is therefore to be under-stood in terms of care, and not vice versa; and therefore, the unity of the self must be sought by way of the items which are constitutive for care, that is, through existentiality (the

---

92   SZ 317.

93   SZ 318.

project of understanding), facticity (situatedness, thrownness, mood) and fallenness (the condition of being lost in the imperso- nal "one" or "they").94   Seeing as these items refer to the future, the past, and the present respectively, where else then can we seek the unity of selfhood than in the unity of care and being-in-the-world, which is temporality?

Indeed, we have noted above that to be a self is to be ahead-of-oneself as existentially in-the-world and caring of it. Dasein is ontically distinctive because while the desk or the pen are, they do not ex-ist, their self-identity is not an existing- beyond-themselves, and therefore, the unity of human existence can only be sought in the unique dynamic unity of world and self, in care, and in its essential root, temporality.

---

94   Cf. SZ 126-30; 134-40; 142-48; 175-80; and 328.

(ii)   Temporality as the Meaning of Care

We should remember that however we seek to define the self, there is, after all, a certain givenness of an individual situatedness, and it is this givenness of human facticity which Heidegger points to in the notion of "thrownness", which is reflective of the significance of the past. "Dasein is, as a Self, the entity that has been thrown. It has been released from its basis, not through itself but to itself, so as to be as this basis. Dasein is not itself the basis of its Being."95

Within the givenness of one's situation, however, one is also often absorbed in dealing with the concerns of the immediately present, with the here and now. In this case, caring for things around us becomes a caring for them insofar as they are instruments to some immediate purpose;   indeed, even Dasein itself can be regarded as an instrument, in which case it becomes the impersonal "One". When we ourselves exist as the impersonal "One", then we too function in the way in which one instrument may be seen to fit in with another: we fulfill a function which could be fulfilled by another equally well and so become part of a collectivity.

On the other hand, it could be said that we lose ourselves in this way inasmuch as everything is rendered common in this "care of averageness" and "levelling down" of all possibilities

---

95   SZ 284.

of Being. "Every kind of priority becomes glossed over as something that has long been well known. Everything gained by a struggle becomes just something to be manipulated. Every secret loses its force."96

While this mode of Being is "that of inauthenticity and failure to stand by One's self," it is an _existentiale_; "and as a primordial phenomenon, it belongs to Dasein's positive constitution."97

Although Heidegger himself says that this "special way of Being-alongside the things with which one concerns oneself.. is the Present"98; and if the significance of the past as a givenness is reflected in the thrownness of one's situation, it is important to remember that Heidegger has a unique conception of time in mind here. Clearly, the past is not merely dead and gone "nows" of yesterday, nor is it followed by a present which precedes the nows yet-to-come. Moreover, these items of care (facticity and fallenness) are not going to be pieced together by Heidegger to uncover a unity of temporality which has itself been pieced together out of the future, the past, and the present. In fact, it becomes evident that the future ecstasis itself plays a large part in the identification of that primordial time which is

---

96   SZ 127.

97   SZ 129.

98   SZ 337.

the condition for our everyday conception of time. Heidegger's
contention is that "the primary and authentic temporality is the
future"99, which is not to say that by the term "futural", we
merely "have in view a 'now' which has not yet become 'actual'
and which sometime will be for the first time. We have in view
the coming [Kunft] in which Dasein in its ownmost potentiality-
for-Being, comes toward itself".100

This means that the past is never past [vergangen] in the
sense of something finished behind me, but it is already having
been, in the sense of the "I am as having been".101 Indeed, it
is inasmuch as man is authentically futural that he is as having-
been. Anticipating one's possibilities means essentially to come
back understandingly to one's ownmost "been", to one's past, to
appropriate it as one's own in order to pro-ject new possibilities into the future. "The character of 'having been' arises, in
a certain way, from the future".102

Similarly, the present is no longer a mere moment within a
sequence of "nows"; rather, the present remains included in the
future and in the past in the mode of primordial temporality.

---

99   SZ 378.

100   SZ 325.

101   SZ 328.

102   SZ 373.

Unless we want to hypostatize duration within an understanding of time as a sequence of discreet instances, one is led to the condition of such an understanding, as revealed in an integral and primordial unity of the ecstases of time wherein "the character of 'having been' arises from the future, and in such a way that the future which 'has been' (or better, which 'is in the process of having been') releases from itself the Present".103 In short, one is led to the unity of a future which makes present in the process of having been - to the unity, therefore, of the phenomenon described by Heidegger as primordial temporality.

"Temporality is the primordial 'outside-of-itself' in and for itself... Temporality is not, prior to this, an entity which first emerges from itself; its essence is a process of temporalizing in the unity of the ecstases."104   Because it is not an entity at all, we conclude with Heidegger that primordial temporality is not, in the sense of being something present-at-hand or ready-to-hand, but rather, it temporalizes itself, making possible the multiplicity of man's modes of Being, but too, the unity of primordial temporality makes possible the unity of existence, facticity and falling, in this way constituting the totality of

---

103 SZ 326.

104 SZ 329.

the structure of care.105 The meaning of care is what makes care possible in its constitution, and thus the meaning of care and individuation is temporality.

It must be remembered that when Heidegger enquires about the meaning of care, he is asking what makes possible the structure of care as an articulated totality: indeed, he is not only understanding individuation and temporality in a unique way, but he is understanding the word "meaning" to signify the oftentimes hidden condition of the very possibility (the "upon-which") of the primary projection of the understanding of Being.106 Just as in any projection of entities, meaning is in fact the hidden "upon-which" of the projection, rather than a conceptual, cognitive representation of a transparent significance, so too the meaning of man's Being is not something other than and out-side of his essential constitution, but on the contrary, is the temporal, self-understanding Dasein itself.

That is why the meaning of individuation cannot be temporality understood in any reified sense of the word, nor can it be understood as something "outside" of me or "containing" me. On the contrary, once we see that meaning is an opening or a space in which things are related to one another, then to say that

---

105 "Zeitlichkeit ist der Grund der Möglichkeit dieser Struktu-ren der Sorge selbst." Cf. Heidegger, M. Logik: Die Frage nach der Wahrheit, p. 410.

106 SZ 324.

primordial time is the condition of the possibility (the meaning) of individuation suggests that it is that sheer oc-currence which is the condition, which "makes room", for self and world, for man and Being, to be appropriated to one another in the first place.

What begins to be evident here is that if temporality is not to be understood in any ontic sense in terms of entities, and if it is not to be seen to somehow "contain" Dasein, nor is it the cause of the unity of care; rather, the horizontal character of time suggests an openness and, at most, a directionality.107 The very concept of horizon indicates that an object or phenomenon shows itself as what it is, only within a certain context or perspective which is not of the character of an entity at all, so when we speak of temporality as ecstatic-horizontal, time is not a realm   within which man exists, but it is the dynamic oc-currence and transcendental horizon of the comprehension of Being, and that in which human transcendence is rooted.

That is why we can say that to understand primordial tempo-rality in this unique way, is in fact to place a lack at the core of man's Being. If temporality is not some-thing, but is the condition of the appearance of world and self, then as the other to all that is, it is no-thing. Nullity permeates the essence of care, and this means that inasmuch as man as "guilty", is called forth by the call of conscience, the call of care, to recognize

---

107 Cf. Joan Stambaugh, "Introduction" to On Time and Being.

this nullity, there is a possibility of an "understanding of oneself in one's ownmost potentiality-for-Being"; which means that "in understanding the call, Dasein is in thrall to [hörig] its ownmost possibility of existence. It has chosen itself".108

How exactly does one "choose oneself" authentically in this way? According to Heidegger, the call of conscience does not give any "practical" advice: it is a call heard and received by each one of us alone. Summoning Dasein to its ownmost potentiality-for-Being-itself, this "reticent self-projection upon one's ownmost Being-guilty in which one is ready for anxiety-we call 'resoluteness'";109   and it is in resoluteness, Heidegger tells us, that we arrive at the primordial truth of Dasein as authentic. "Dasein is authentically itself in the primordial individualization of the reticent resoluteness which exacts anxiety of itself."110

But there are two things which we must keep in mind regarding such "individualization of resoluteness".

The first is that resoluteness as authentic disclosedness, is nothing else than Being-in-the-world. In other words, as authentic Being-one's-Self, it "does not detach Dasein from its world, nor does it isolate it so that it becomes a free-floating

---

108 SZ 287.

109 SZ 297.

110 SZ 322.

'I'... Resoluteness brings the Self right into its current concernful Being-alongside what is ready-to-hand, and <u>pushes it into solicitous Being with Others</u>."111   I believe that this is extremely important, because it shows that Heidegger is not interpreting individuation in any ontic sense of the word, that is, the individuation of resoluteness does not refer to the particular as opposed to the universal, nor to the concrete individual as opposed to the abstract notion, for such categories can only be seen to apply to the entities encountered by man in-the-world. The fact that Heidegger speaks of resoluteness both in terms of "primordial individuation" and in terms of solicitous Being with Others only suggests a problem if one considers the notion of human Being-there in other than an ontological sense, that is, if the individuation of Dasein is seen to signify no more than the biological fact of the singleness, and in this sense, aloneness, of each human being - which is not a very revealing discovery.

What is revealing, however, about Heidegger's notion of individuation, and what any thought-ful phenomenological descrip-tion of man must uncover, is the ontological roots: if we are not talking about man in the concrete or abstract, or about man as a particular or as a universal, because that would be to consider

---

111 SZ 298. Emphasis mine. We shall see later the extent
     to which Being-with-Others is a fundamental characteristic
     of Being-in-the-world; it is an "existentiale".

man as no more than an analyzable physical entity-then what we must realize is that everything Heidegger has to say leads back to the question of the meaning of _Being_. Heidegger's notion of individuation does not point to just the particularity or any ontic phenomenon of isolation, nor is it a subjective rooting of all truth in man. What it does suggest is that existence and the notion of "mineness" penetrate one another, only to the extent that Dasein is in essence a relation to Being as a possibility which remains uniquely one's own; what it does suggest is the uniqueness of each individual human existence, in its anticipatory resoluteness in the face of a future and a transcendental horizon towards which it projects itself, in order to confer meaning in its world.

That the transcendence of Dasein implies individuation or that temporality is at the root of transcendence and individuation, does not suggest that the locus of truth is in the "particular" Dasein. But it can suggest that each human being is open to Being in a unique way, and that openness of human existence which is essentially Being-in-the-world, can find meaning within an authentic, resolute solicitous Being with Others, as long as such Being with Others is grounded in an authentic openness to Being itself. In subsequent chapters, I shall show how this is the case, and how, in fact, Heidegger's concept of individuation is the very condition of authentic solicitude.

The other point to keep in mind is that inasmuch as temporality must be seen to be at the very centre of man's Being, this suggests why finitude reveals not merely the condition of a <u>Zu-Ende-Sein</u> but a <u>Sein-zum-Ende</u>. For if primordial temporality implies more than an ontic reference to beings, but reveals instead the ontological roots of Dasein in the nothingness of Being, then the very finitude of human-being is not just a "fact" to be accepted in terms of an ultimate incident of my ceasing-to-be; that finitude, that nullity, must rather be seen to <u>permeate my very Being, and all my ways of Being</u>.

Only in this context can Heidegger's understanding of the phenomenon of Being-towards-death be at all comprehended in the fullness of its essential insight.

**

CHAPTER TWO

TEMPORALITY AS THE MEANING OF BEING-TOWARDS-DEATH

A.   Inauthentic Understanding of Death

"A couple of years ago, an up-to-date mortician in Atlanta offered a modern solution to the 'viewing' problem; he built a drive-in mortuary where the tilted body of the deceased could be viewed through a window. People could drive by, perhaps leave a card, and keep on going. They didn't have to get dressed up. And they didn't have to get involved in the uncomfortable business of personally sharing grief and offering compassion. It seems a logical innovation for a cool, cool land of fragmenting people. Another logical innovation - since so many people are dying far from their immediate families, who upon hearing the news rush to arrange the funeral - is that many funeral parlors now routinely offer to provide pallbearers."[1]

In "Die Zeit des Weltbildes", Heidegger offers an important suggestion which may help to explain why, to quote Fromm, "our own era simply denies death".

Heidegger remarks that the basic procedure of modern scientific research is seen to rest on an objectification of Being, where truth is transformed into the "certainty of representation". Mathematical science "is not exact because it makes exact

---

1   Packard, V. A Nation of Strangers, (NY: David McKay, 1972.) p. 198, cited in Watson, J.R. "Being...There, the Neighbourhood of Being", in Philosophy Today, Vol. 19, No. 2/4, Summer 1975, p. 118.

calculations; rather, it must make such calculations because its way of adhering to its sphere has the character of exactitude."2 This desire for "exactitude" characterizes not only mathematics, however, but the entire scientific/technological epoch which seeks the re-presentative certainty of calculative understanding.

> "Understanding as research holds the existent to ac-
> count on the question of how and how far it can be put
> at the disposal of available 'representations'.
> Research has the existent at its disposal if it can
> either calculate it in advance, in its future course,
> or calculate it afterwards as past.. Only what thus
> becomes an object is, is recognized as existent.
> Science as research occurs only when it is in this
> objectification that the being of the existent is
> sought."3

The essence of this sort of ob-jectification of the exis-tent takes place in a re-presentation which seeks to present that which exists, in such a way that the calculating person can be secure, that is "certain" of the existent. As man becomes a subject (subjectum as the translation of the Greek hupokeimenon, "that which gathers everything to itself to become its basis"), the entity assumes the position of ob-ject (Gegen-stand) and only as such does it "receive the seal of Being". Man therefore "posits himself as the setting in which the existent must from now on represent itself, present itself, that is, be a view or picture."4 To "'put oneself in the picture about something means

---

2   "Die Zeit des Weltbildes", in HW 73, e.t. 272.

3   HW 80, e.t. 277.

4   HW 85, e.t. 281.

to represent to oneself the existent itself with respect to its state and so presented to keep it constantly before one."5   In this way, man becomes the representative of the existent in the sense of the objective.6

The epoch itself then is an epoch which relies on <u>represen-tatio</u>, in a flight from Being to the certainty and exactness of adequation and correctness. Re-presenting involves relating the essent back to oneself; in fact, as the human being confers meaning upon the essent, utilizing it and projecting subjective values upon its ultimate purpose in an anthropocentric universe, the human existent becomes the normative realm for the being of the essent itself. The sphere of human powers becomes the place for measuring and mastering the existent as a whole.7 The world is there principally and primordially, in an epoch of re-presentation, as an ob-ject for the manipulation and control of man.

Such a re-presentative measuring is also evident, says Heidegger, in our modernday conceptions of death. Generally, we tend to act as if we were immortal, as if death belongs to others,

---

5   HW 82, e.t. 279.

6   HW 84, e.t. 281.

7   Cf. HW 83, e.t. 280, where Heidegger notes: "To re-present
       here means to bring what is present before one as something
       confronting oneself, to relate it to oneself, the person
       representing it, and to force it back into this relation
       to oneself as the normative area."

but does not affect me in any fundamental way. Life is there for us to control as best we can, and death, as an uncontrollable phenomenon, as a possibility which denies a substantial, absolute status to our being, is simply ignored, as it does not fit into the "Weltanschauung" of the day. If we do pay attention to the phenomenon of death at all, it either becomes controllable through scientific advances which allow us to prolong life at all costs; or else it becomes an everyday occurrence that we read about in newspapers and therefore does not touch us personally.

No one will deny, in superficial discussion, that death is "a reality". However, the "reality" of death more often than not fails to recognize the ontological roots of man's being as Being-towards-death; while evading Being-certain, yet publicly we acknowledge, in the face of the death of others, an empirical certainty of death: the "'dying' of Others is something that one experiences daily." Death becomes an "undeniable 'fact of experience'".8

> "In the publicness with which we are with one another in our everyday manner, death is 'known' as a mishap which is constantly occurring -as a 'case of death'. Someone or other 'dies', be he neighbour or stranger. People who are no acquaintances of ours are 'dying' daily and hourly. 'Death' is encountered as a well-known event occurring within-the-world. As such, it remains in the inconspicuousness characteristic of what is encountered in an everyday fashion."9

---

8   SZ 257.

9   SZ 253.

Significantly, the "'they' has already assured itself [gesichert] an interpretation for this event." But the "Sicherheit" of such an interpretation is the certainty of the representation of death by way of the death of other Daseins, a representation within an ultimately ambiguous and impersonal acceptance of the fact that "one dies".

> "In Dasein's public way of interpreting, it is said that 'one dies' because everyone else and oneself can talk himself into saying that 'in no case is it I myself', for this 'one' is the 'nobody'. 'Dying' is levelled off to an occurrence which reaches Dasein, to be sure, but belongs to nobody in particular."10

In a certainty of reifying, ob-jectifying and ultimately inauthentic re-presenting of the phenomenon, "death gets passed off as something 'actual'; its character as a possibility gets concealed"; its character as the possibility of the "measureless impossibility of existence" becomes concealed. Covering up the very real possibility that death -one's own death- is possible at any moment, "everyday Being-towards-death evades this indefiniteness [of its 'when'] by conferring definiteness upon it"11 -- a definiteness of representative certitude.

But not only is death understood inauthentically in a general acknowledgement that "everyone must die someday". Heidegger's analysis shows how we re-present and objectify the actual empirical experience of the death of the Other, and consequently,

---

10   SZ 253.

11   SZ 258.

are unable to authentically come to an understanding of the ontological meaning of Being-towards-death within such an objectification.

It may seem at first, that the best way to understand death as the ontological delimitation of Dasein's totality, is to observe the death of another Dasein; since Dasein is essentially Being-with-Others, it may seem that "in this way, a termination [Beendigung] of Dasein becomes 'Objectively' accessible."12

But such ob-jectivity, replies Heidegger, affords no more than a representative, reifying certainty of an empirical event, thus hiding the essence of an underlying structure of totality. The end of the living human being is seen as the beginning of that being as a present-at-hand entity.

Heidegger adds that theoretically, "even the corpse which is present-at-hand is still a possible object for the student of pathological anatomy, whose understanding tends to be oriented to the idea of life. This something which is just present-at-hand-and-no-more is 'more' than a lifeless material Thing. In it we encounter something unalive, which has lost its life."13

This is not to say, however, that we are always presented with no more than a "mere corporeal Thing". Indeed, Heidegger distinguishes between the dead person [dem Gestorbenen] and the

---

12   SZ 237.

13   SZ 238.

"deceased" [der 'Verstorbene'], who has been "torn away from those who have 'remained behind'; and is an object of 'concern' in the way of funeral rites, interment, and the cult of graves." The deceased is said to be "still more" than a mere item of equipment; Heidegger acknowledges that in their mourning, the "Hinterbliebenen" are with him in a mode of respectful solicitude, and so the "relationship-of-Being which one has toward the dead is not to be taken as a concernful Being-alongside something ready-to-hand." And Heidegger even allows that in Being-with the dead, "those who remain can still be with him".14

But can they be with him authentically?

Since Being-with implies Being with one another in the same world, such Being-with the dead in effect affords us no access at all, says Heidegger, to the loss-of-Being which the dying man suffers. "The authentic Being-come-to-an-end [Zuende-gekommensein] of the deceased is precisely the sort of thing which we do not experience."15 As an ontological possibility-of-Being in which Dasein's very Being is at issue, Heidegger has stressed that death "is in every case mine insofar as it 'is' at all". Luther had put it this way: "the summons of death comes to us all, and no-one can die for another. Everyone must fight his own battle with death by himself alone."

---

14   SZ 238.

15   SZ 239.

While it is true that it belongs to Being-with-one-another
in the world, that one Dasein can   at times be represented by
another (Heidegger uses the verb "vertreten" in this connection,
rather than "vorstellen"), one cannot of course be another and
consequently cannot authentically experience his coming-to-an-
end.16   At best, such representation suggests itself in the
everyday manner of our absorption with things in the "world" of
concern, and therefore carries no significant ontological import,
according to Heidegger.

Indeed, what becomes clear is that the ontic sense of death
-that is, death as the point of termination of "one's" life as a
final incident producing the condition of "no-longer-Being-in-
the-world" - is to be distinguished from the   existential structure of being-mortal, the way in which Dasein exists. It is only
in an inauthentic fleeing in the face of death that the "they-
self" interprets the phenomenon as no more than a "case" of
death, an everyday incident that   one may read about in the
papers, or sometimes experience among those who are close to
us. Death as an existentiale is not understood, and therefore
gets levelled down to the state of the inconspicuous.17

---

16   SZ 239.

17   Cf. Dave Godfrey's descriptions of our levelling down of
      the phenomenon of death - in Death Goes Better With Coca-
      Cola. "Death too, I think at times, is just another one
      of our match box toys." (69).

Not that such an inauthentic fleeing in the face of death is insignificant. It is only because Dasein possesses a primordial self-knowledge and awareness of its own existential fragility that it evades the question of its own death, preferring the false, tranquilizing assurance and empirical certainty of death as another ordinary, everyday fact of living.

Indeed, what inauthentic Dasein is not willing to own up to, is its inherently temporal, that is, finite essence, reflected in the truth (rather than the empirical certainty) of the structure of Being-towards-death. Time itself is pictured as no more than a series of now-points; in the true empiricist tradition, the really-real is seen to be the present; the future is not yet here; and the past's nows are dead and gone. Thomas Hobbes' description of the essence of time is a perfect example of the western conception of temporality, understood in terms of the present. He writes that:

"The present only has a being in nature; things past have a being in the memory only, but things to come have no being at all, the future being but a fiction of the mind..."18

If it is the present which is seen to be the primary ecstasis, then Dasein's main concern will be towards those matters most immediately confronting it, those details and trivialities

---

18   Hobbes, T. Leviathan, (New York: Macmillan Publishing Co., 1962.) p. 30.

of everyday concern. The consequence of such a time-perspective is that Dasein's very Being will be conceived only in terms of a given, static, here-and-now nature, and therefore its futural essence as a pro-jecting Being-toward-death, indeed the very phenomenon of death itself, will be ignored. Moreover, evading the unpleasantness of death, the overriding significance attributed to the present anyway, simply makes it easier for Dasein to escape the reality of death in the everyday distractions of trivialities in the present.

When the inconvenient case of death does present itself in the case of the death of another Dasein, it is levelled off and interpreted as the ceasing-to-exist of a "man who has been present-at-hand 'in time'".19 Time itself "goes on" just as before, in the name of a public time which belongs to everyone-"and that means to nobody"; while the temporal essence of man's individualizing, Being-towards-death remains veiled.

But not only is time conceived in terms of the present; it is conceived as a series of now-points, that is, it is seen linearly. Time itself is seen to be an infinite supply of now-points without beginning or end, which contains man. Yet, it is significant that even in this inauthentic conception of time, Dasein's authentic futurity is felt and reflected when one says that time "passes away". "When Dasein talks of time's passing

---

19   SZ 425.

away, it understands in the end more of time than it wants to admit; that is to say, the temporality in which world-time temporalizes itself has not been completely closed off, no matter how much it may get covered up... In the kind of talk which emphasizes time's passing away, the finite futurity of Dasein's temporality is publicly reflected."20

Thus, "he who flees in the fact of death is pursued by it even as he evades it... just as in turning away from it, he must see it nonetheless."21

B.   Temporality and Authentic Being-toward-Death

If we want to avoid the mere empirical certainty of representing the phenomenon of death to ourselves in view of the "case" of death of another Dasein, that is, if we want to allow death as that which shows itself, to be seen from itself in the very way in which it shows itself from itself in its truth, then where are we to start?

In Being and Time, Heidegger tells us that if we are to say that an assertion "is true", this signifies that it uncovers the entity as it is in itself. It "'lets ' the entity 'be seen' in its uncoveredness". This means that the "Being true (truth) of

---

20   SZ 425.

21   SZ 425.

the assertion must be understood as Being-uncovering."22 Thus truth is by no means structured as an agreement between knowing and the object in the sense of a likening of a subject-entity to an Object. Rather, "the most primordial phenomenon of truth is first shown by the existential-ontological foundations of uncovering."23 Being-true is Being-uncovering, or authentic disclosedness.24

But disclosedness itself is a kind of Being which is peculiar to human being. Only inasmuch as Dasein is, can there be anything like truth because "the kind of Being that is essential to truth is of the character of Dasein, all truth is relative to Dasein's Being."25

Why then, does Heidegger say that I cannot come to an understanding of the truth of death, by relating the case of the death of the other to myself, and thereby understanding my own Being-toward-death?

Heidegger does, in this connection, admit that "cases of death may be the factical occasion for Dasein's first paying

22   SZ 220.

23   SZ 220.

24   Cf. SZ 397.

25   SZ 226, 227.

attention to death at all";26 but he adds that as long as Dasein remains in the empirical certainty which we have mentioned above, the essence of death, in the way that it "is", remains concealed.

Thus, while "all truth is relative to Dasein's Being", it is wrong to say that the truth of the phenomenon of death is relative to Dasein as representatio: "to relate what is present to oneself, the person representing it, and to force it back into this relation to oneself as the normative area". But what is the difference between, on the one hand, such representational "forcing back into a relation to oneself as the normative area" - and saying, on the other hand, that "all truth is relative to Dasein's Being"?

The important thing to remember in answer to this question, is that for Heidegger, truth is not dependent upon a productive subjectivity, bringing the object into relation to itself in an authoritative, massgebend activity of evaluation.   Saying that truth is relative to Dasein's Being does not imply that Dasein is the normative area for all truth, but rather, that truth must be conceived as a fundamental existentiale.27 "Thus to presuppose 'truth' means to understand it as something for the sake of which Dasein is."28   Truth as disclosedness and uncovering belong

---

26   SZ 257.

27   Cf. SZ 297.

28   SZ 228.

essentially to Dasein's very Being as a Being-in-the-world. Only because "Dasein is as constituted by disclosedness (that is, by understanding) can anything like Being be understood."29 Truth is relative to Dasein's Being, not in the sense that man is to be seen as a calculative measuring stick of correctness, nor is truth to be seen as something incidental to man's Being-in-the-world; rather, as a discerning, open, futurally projecting understanding, Dasein uncovers truth as a living force in the dignity of art, in poetry, in language, as a condition of being human.

Being, and not entities, be they "subjective" or "objective", is something which "there is" only insofar as truth is. "And truth _is_ only insofar as and as long as Dasein is. Being and truth 'are' equiprimordially"30, which means, therefore, that to enquire into the _truth_ of death is to enquire into its ontological roots; it is to enquire into the Being of Dasein itself.

But it is not to enquire about _my_ Being by way of relating it to, or re-presenting it through, another Dasein's death. To understand death as "end", it is not sufficient that we see the "end" of another Dasein, and then bring that death into relation to ourselves as the "normative" areas, in order to realize our

29   SZ 230.

30   SZ 230.

own finitude. Heidegger warns against this significant and
common misunderstanding of the phenomenon of death. Death as end
is not just an end-point, empirically accessible by way of a
single, or even multiple Todesfälle. Rather, coming to an end
implies a mode of Being in which it is simply not possible that a
particular Dasein be represented by someone else. Nor can death
be re-presented in terms of a "stopping" of something which is no
longer present-at-hand; or in terms of a "ripening", or a
fulfilling, or a "finishedness" or even a disappearing, for if
Being-at-an-end were to be understood in any of these senses,
Dasein will have been treated as something present-at-hand or
even ready-to-hand. On the contrary, "the 'ending' which we have
in view when we speak of death does not signify Dasein's Being-
at-an-end [Zu-ende-Sein] but a Being-towards-the-end [Sein-zum-
Ende] of this entity. Death is a way to be which takes over
Dasein as soon as it is. 'As soon as man comes to life, he is at
once old enough to die'".31 Death as an "end-point" is of far
less concern to Heidegger than death as that way of Being in
which Dasein is towards its death as "end".

But this means that Heidegger's investigations are more than
merely theoretical considerations: while death as a way of Being
is an existentiale, is "in the widest sense a phenomenon of
life"- yet, "if we make a problem of 'life', and then just

---

31   SZ 245.

occasionally have regard for death too, our view is too short-sighted."32 Heidegger emphasizes that a phenomenological description of death becomes artificial and dogmatic if initially, one restricts oneself to a "theoretical" discussion and then tries to "round it out" by making it more "practical" in tacking on to it some kind of an ethic.33

Hardly a theoretical or abstract enterprise, the analysis of death in _Being and Time_ remains rooted in the phenomenon of Being-in-the-world, which means that "it Interprets that phenomenon merely in the way in which it enters into any particular Dasein as a possibility of its Being".34 Moreover, such a "this-worldly" ontological interpretation of death must take precedence over an ontical Other-worldly speculation. These two points regarding the "this-worldly" - that it points to the individual Dasein and the possibility of its very Being, and that it takes precedence over "life-after-death" theories or other-worldly speculation - are essentially related: Being-toward-death as an existentiale, reveals Dasein's own finitude, and reveals it to be an essentially temporal phenomenon; (any suggestion of the a-temporal only makes sense against the back-

---

32   SZ 316.

33   SZ 316.

34   SZ 248.

ground of the temporal.)   We have already considered in some detail how temporality itself is the meaning of individuation.

What does remain, however, is to outline Heidegger's preliminary sketch of this phenomenon of Being-toward-death as something which each of us must come to grips with on our own.

(i) Existentiell Attestation of Potentiality-for-Being-One's-Self

The Call of Conscience:

While man may strive to "be authentic", it remains true for Heidegger that in large part, my Selfhood is defined by the they-self. Absorbed in the tasks, rules and standards of "das Man", one is led to evade essential de-cisions, gradually losing oneself to the indefinite comfort of choices made by "nobody" specifically.

But this process _can_ be reversed, although such a "Sich-zurückholen" from the "they" means that one's "they-self" is therby modified _in an existentiell manner_, inasmuch as one makes a concrete choice for an authentic potentiality-for-Being; one chooses to bring oneself back from the lostness of the "they", to "find" oneself.

To be sure, Dasein never loses its potentiality-for-Being-its-Self, but nevertheless it needs to have this potentiality attested.35 Heidegger claims that this "potentiality" is "attes-

---

35   SZ 268.

ted" through that which, in Dasein's everyday interpretation of itself, is called "the voice of conscience" (<u>Stimme des Gewissens</u>).36

As expected, the phenomenon is hardly presented as a psychological, a biological or even a theological one, but is ontological in its basis, resting on existential foundations. As such, it is revealed as a <u>call</u>, (<u>Ruf</u>), an appeal, a summoning to Dasein's ownmost Being-guilty.

Strictly speaking, however, the call has no specific content; "the call 'says' <u>nothing</u> which might be talked about, gives no information about events".37   But the strange indefiniteness of both the caller and the impossibility of identifying more definitely what this caller is, are not just nothing; they are distinctive in a <u>positive</u> way, for the call reaches the they-self of concernful Being-with-Others, "passing over" the "they" and thereby pushing it into insignificance.38

But this means that it is the authentic Self which gets brought to itself by the call. "<u>In conscience, Dasein calls itself</u>".39 This is not to suggest that the call is something which Dasein willfully plans for or voluntarily performs. "'It'

---

36   SZ 268.

37   SZ 280.

38   SZ 275.

39   SZ 275.

calls, against our expectations and even against our will... The call comes <u>from</u> me and yet <u>from beyond me and over me.</u>" Not to be understood as some-thing present-at-hand, this means that the caller can be defined in a "worldly way" by <u>nothing at all</u>. This no-thingness, this gap or abyss between the "they-Self" and the authentic Self, calls as   an   alien   voice, revealing the "unheimlich", the "bare 'that-it-is' in the 'nothing' of the world." The caller is therefore Dasein in its uncanniness.40

As a basic kind of Being-in-the-world, uncanniness is co-vered up in an everyday fashion, but it is out of the depths of this overwhelming kind of Being that Dasein itself,   as con-science, calls as a threat to that very lostness in which it has forgotten itself as thrown individuation. Indeed, "what could be more alien to the 'they', lost in the manifold 'world' of its concern, than the Self which has been individualized down to itself in uncanniness and been thrown into the 'nothing'?"41 What could be more alien to the "they" than the "not", the Ab-grund, which is revealed as the wound of existential <u>guilt</u>?

From the depths of uncanniness, the call of conscience calls Dasein to the negativity of its guilt: "In the idea of 'Guilty!', there lies the character of the 'not'... Hence we define the formally existential idea of the 'Guilty!' as 'Being-the-basis

---

40   Cf. SZ 276-77.

41   SZ 277.

for a Being which has been defined by a 'not', that is to say, as 'Being-the-basis of a nullity.'"42   Such   Being-a-basis, however, means   "never   to   have   power   over one's ownmost Being from the ground up.   This 'not' belongs   to   the   existential   meaning of 'throwness'."43   While never a complete master of its own Being, nonetheless as guilty, Dasein has the responsibility of accepting its authenticity,   because through this negativity, guilt reveals to Dasein that it is not being or doing what it should!

In short, it is uncanniness which beings Dasein face to face with its   primordial nullity, calling Dasein   back from its lost-ness in the "they", to its throwness and   the null   basis of the individuation of authentic Selfhood.   As a "summons to Being-guilty," conscience is a calling-forth to that very potentiality-for-Being which,   as a   Dasein, I am already.   In such an appeal, the "they-self" is summoned to its   ownmost Being-guilty of the individual Self.

How do I, on an existentiell level, choose to understand such an appeal? Heidegger answers that   understanding the appeal means "wanting   to have   a conscience", which means that "wanting to have a conscience becomes the taking over of that essential

---

42   SZ 283.

43   SZ 284.

consciencelessness within which alone the existentiell possibility of being 'good' subsists."44

But wanting to have a conscience is revealed as no less than
a readiness for anxiety; and it is this "distinctive and authentic disclosedness, which is attested in Dasein itself by its
conscience - this reticent self-projection upon one's ownmost
Being-guilty, in which one is ready for anxiety" - which Heidegger names "resoluteness".45

Resoluteness:

The counterpart of calling, is hearing or listening, and it
is resoluteness (Entschlossenheit) which is the existential
structure of proper listening to the call of conscience. In the
affirmation of one's existential guilt, Dasein is summoned back
to authentic existence in a reticent readiness-for-anxiety, and
in a soundless summoning to the stillness of the true self, which
means, in an anticipatory resoluteness.

We all have experienced the guilt about which Heidegger
speaks, when we are summoned, not by a call outside of me, but by
a conscience deep within my being, apart from any external
authorities or witness. Clearly, though, such a summoning back
to the authentic Self is not an appeal directed toward the solip-

---

44   SZ 288.

45   SZ 296.

sistic Subject or Ego; Heidegger makes it clear that Dasein's whole Being-in-the-world, "that is to say, the world, Being-in, and the Self which, as an 'I am', this entity is", is disclosed with equal primordiality.46   It is especially clear that resoluteness is authentically nothing less than Being-in-the-world, because it is resoluteness which hears the call of conscience about Dasein's inauthentic existence, and therefore, it is resoluteness which thereby affirms the very structure of Being-with, bringing the Self "right into its current concernful Being-alongside what is ready-to-hand", and pushing it into solicitous Being with Others.

Moreover, resoluteness brings Dasein into its true "Situation". By virtue of its ontological essence, resoluteness, explains Heidegger, is always the resoluteness of some factical Dasein at a particular time, and so Dasein in fact discloses itself in resoluteness only through a definite resolution. Resoluteness, in short, is not a permanent condition; after all, "Dasein is already in irresoluteness [Unentschlossenheit] and soon, perhaps, will be in it again."47   But this only attests to the fact that when the call of conscience summons us to our potentiality-for-Being, "it does not hold before us some empty

---

46   SZ 297.

47   SZ 298.

ideal of existence, but <u>calls us forth into the Situation</u>".48
Understood existentially, "situation" is not the ontic framework
of opportunities accessible to the "they-Self", but it is the
ontological condition of such inauthentic activities; it <u>is</u>, as
the "there", disclosed in resoluteness, only to the extent that
Dasein affirms its unique four-dimensional spatiality."49

Advancing Resoluteness:

It is clear, then, that inasmuch as Dasein is ready to
accept its own existential guilt, it is open to the past through
the moment of thrownness or the facticity of its existence; and
that inasmuch as this moment is a summons into a present
"situation", it is the condition of the possibility for an understanding of the aspect of Dasein's fallenness, or Being-with.
But Heidegger is yet to show the relation of resoluteness, to the
moment of Being-ahead-of-itself to the future, and this he does
in Section 62 of <u>Being and Time</u>, where he considers "advancing
resoluteness as the way in which Dasein's potentiality-for-Being-
a-whole has Existentiell Authenticity".50

---

48   SZ 300.

49   Cf. SZ 299; 101-113; and 367-369.

50   "Advancing" is translated from the German <u>vorlaufen</u> which
      has a special connotation of "running ahead", not in any
      ontic sense but rather, my <u>Being</u> involves a <u>Being-ahead</u>
      of myself. Sometimes "anticipatory" may be used by transla-
      tors, interchangeably with "advancing". In this connection,
      cf. <u>Being and Time</u> translator's footnote on p. 306: "While

Here the "limit-situation" of Dasein's existential of totality, the extreme and all-embracing possibility of the impossibility of Dasein's very existence, is an extension of Dasein's guilt, right unto its end.

Resoluteness, therefore, attains to its own authenticity in Dasein's advancing toward death. "When the call of conscience is understood, lostness in the 'they' is revealed. Resoluteness brings Dasein back to its ownmost potentiality-for-Being-its-Self. When one has an understanding Being-towards-death... one's potentiality-for-Being becomes authentic."51

It is through advancing toward the future that resoluteness in fact harbours the existentiell modality which brings it to full authenticity. Calling Dasein forth to its constant Being-guilty, advancing resoluteness reveals the final and most fundamental ground of this guilt in the certainty of death, in the certainty of its own uncertainty, and the greatest indeterminacy, in the confirmation of one's total guilt and negativity. However, it is precisely this kind of understanding which, as authentic, disperses all "fugitive Self-concealments", and, within

---

    we have used 'anticipate' to translate 'vorgreifen', which occurs rather seldom, we shall also use it - less literally- to translate 'vorlaufen'."

51   SZ 307.

an attitude of a free acceptance of death, opens up the authentic power-to-be-whole.52

Significantly, however, this question of the potentiality for Being-a-whole is more than a mere methodological requirement of the Daseinanalytic. Heidegger is asking us to contemplate the pre-reflective, unmediated understanding which each one of us possesses at certain moments, as we discern, through the ontological depths of our conscience, a call toward the meaning of being-towards a future which is-not-yet, but which nevertheless is the stamp of human finitude. This question of the potentiality-for-Being-a-whole involves much more than mere theoretical speculation; it affects Dasein in his existential structure and indeed, as the most concrete and most significant question of all. It is precisely inasmuch as it is seen by Heidegger to reach into the ontic-existentiell realization of Dasein's concrete existence that he sees it to be decisive for the actual attainment of Dasein's authenticity. "Advancing 'is' not some kind of free-floating behaviour, but must be conceived as the possibility of the authenticity of that resoluteness which has been attested in an existentiell way."53

Advancing resoluteness therefore must be seen to _be_ authentic Being-towards-death. As resoluteness is Dasein's authentic

---

52   SZ 308-9.

53   SZ 309.

potentiality-for-Being-a-whole, so too death is the only existential of totality. It is only as resolute that Dasein can come to
an   understanding   of   death   as   essentially   non-relational,
unüberholbar, certain though indeterminate, and as   one's ownmost
individualizing possibility, not to be outstripped. Liberated
from the "they" within an affirmation of its own negativity,
Dasein now becomes open to what Heidegger calls an "impassioned
freedom towards death - a freedom which has been released from
the Illusions of the 'they', and which is factical, certain of
itself, and anxious."54 Being-towards-death no longer evades the
thought of death, but in advancing resoluteness, is freed for its
acceptance.55

   As liberated from the "they", however, death becomes not
only the most certain of life's potentialities, but also the most
personal; for "death does not just 'belong' to one's own Dasein
in an undifferentiated way; death lays claim to it as an
individual Dasein.   The non-relational character of death as
understood in anticipation, individualizes Dasein down to itself... It makes manifest that all Being-alongside the things

---

54   SZ 266.

55   We shall return to analyze further this theme of free accep-
      tance of death later in this volume, particularly in our
      discussion of terminally ill patients.

with which we concern ourselves, and all Being-with Others, will
fail us when our ownmost potentiality-for-Being is the issue."56

Permeating one's whole existence, then, "holding death for
true... demands Dasein itself in the full authenticity of its
existence", as the ground of such existence and the full force of
the meaning of life and death are brought to the fore.

(ii) Ontological   roots: the   temporal   structure   of Advancing
     Resoluteness

> "'...and don't all the philosophic theories do the same,
> when by ways of thought strange and unnatural to man, they
> lead him to a knowledge of what he knew long ago, and knows
> so surely that without it, he could not live?...'"

A central   character of Tolstoy's Anna Karenina poses this
question, but for us it is not irrelevant.   Divergent as the
world-views of Tolstoy and Heidegger may be, images seem to
converge here as Heidegger's own questioning of the meaning of
Being-towards-death is a questioning, not of the extrinsic
intelligibility, but of the ultimate interior ground, pre-ontolo-
gically understood by Dasein, of the condition of any existentiell realization - in other words, of its transcendental, unifying temporal roots.

Therefore, inasmuch as the "meaning of Dasein's Being is not
something free-floating which is other than and 'outside of'

---

56   SZ 263.

itself, but is the self-understanding Dasein itself" - to ask what makes possible the Being of Dasein, and therefore its factical existence, is to ask what makes authentic Being-a-whole possible with regard to the unity of its articulated, structural whole. This, in fact, is to enquire after the essentially temporal structure of concern.57

Authentic existence has been shown to consist of advancing resoluteness which, as the mode of authentic care, is possible only through temporality. Resoluteness, therefore, has a triple structure, corresponding to the moments of concern represented.

Resoluteness in the face of guilt in the moment of already-Being-in; the summons into a situation as the concretion of the moment of Being-with; and advancing toward death as the concrete expression of Being-ahead-of-itself, each correspond to (as grounded in) the temporal structure of having-been, presencing and the future.

The roots of the dimension of the past consist in Dasein's acceptance of its own existential guilt, and the negativity of its thrown facticity and already Being-in. In the thoughtful listening to the call of conscience, Dasein comes back to itself as the ground of its very negativity.

Representing the primordial phenomenon of the present in the form of a "summons into a situation", advancing resoluteness in

---

57   Cf. SZ 325 ff.

this case is a summons to the authentic acceptance of fallenness or Being-with; it is the structure through which Dasein is circumspectively concerned with what has presence environmentally. It is this existential-ontological presence structure which is the condition of the possibility for Dasein to existentielly and ontically give itself over to its situation; indeed, it is only a resolute dedication to a situation which will constitute the authentic understanding of the existential present of Being-there.

Finally, inasmuch as Dasein is essentially futural in its very Being, Dasein can "let itself come to itself" in its extreme potentiality-to-Be. In affirming its most fundamental futurity within an authentic understanding of its own Being-towards-death, Dasein in fact stands before itself in its most extreme possibility of Being. In allowing itself in its own extreme possibility to come to itself, Dasein opens itself to a realization of the approaching of the future into the present. The dimension of the future is thus revealed to be at the very heart of Dasein's existence, as fundamental to, and pervading of that existence in its totality.

Wolfgang Kroug reminds us that Heidegger does not of course understand death as a "possibility" to mean "death as something which is or is not possible", that is, as something which may or may not be. "Offenbar versteht Heidegger unter Möglichkeit des

Todes eine ganz andere Möglichkeit als die landläufige."58 It is
neither the category of "possibility", nor the empty, purely
logical conception which Heidegger has in mind. Moreover, "die
Möglichkeit [ist] nicht das Fehlen von etwas, sondern eine
Befindlichkeit". The "State-of-mind" which is Understanding is
therefore Dasein's understanding of itself in terms of possibilities: "es ist das Selbstverstehen". Heidegger explains that:

> "the character of understanding as projection is such
> that the understanding does not grasp thematically that
> upon which it projects, that is to say, possibilities.
> Grasping it in such a manner would take away from what
> is projected, its very character as a possibility, and
> would reduce it to the given contents which we have in
> mind; whereas projection, in throwing, throws before
> itself the possibility as possibility, and lets it be
> as such. As projecting, understanding is the kind of
> Being of Dasein in which it is its possibilities as
> possibilities."59

Therefore, understanding death as a possibility is in fact a
letting-be of the possibility of the very impossibility of
existence itself. The "case of death" is again not as much a
matter of concern as is the meaning of my own death as potentiality-for-Being.

---

58   Kroug, Wolfgang, "Das Sein zum Tode bei Heidegger", in
     Zeitschrift für Philosophische Forschung, 7, (1953), page
     392ff.

59   SZ 145.

To use Karl Lehmann's words, "Kurz gesagt: Existieren und Möglichkeit-haben ist dasselbe."60

Thus just as Heidegger explains that "by the term 'futural', we do not here have in view a 'now' which has not yet become 'actual' and which sometime will be for the first time; we have in view the coming [Kunft] in which Dasein, in its ownmost potentiality-for-Being comes toward itself"61 -- so too, in Being-towards-death, Dasein "does not have an end at which it must stop, but it exists finitely."62

At this point, it must be made clear that while temporality constitutes the primordial unity of ek-sistence, facticity and falling, these items of care are not just conveniently "pieced together" by Heidegger according to the three primary temporal ecstases. On the contrary, Dasein's very care-structure is essentially temporal. The three aspects of past, present and futurity are at the very root of its innermost ontological meaning; this has been shown in Chapter One of this work, in the discussion of the "Meaning of Individuation", but it is worth repeating and emphasizing here.

It is also important to mention that while temporality is the ontological meaning and ground of authentic Being-towards-

60   Lehmann, Karl, Der Tod bei Heidegger und Jaspers, p.51.

61   SZ 325.

62   SZ 329.

death, the ontic/existentiell realization of Being-towards-death
can also reveal the authenticity of man's own temporality. In
advancing resoluteness, Dasein can become increasingly aware of
its three-dimensional temporal structure, which structure is
itself revealed to be the condition of an existentiell realization of Being-towards-death. In other words, there is a reciprocity revealed between temporality and authentic Being-toward-
death, a reciprocity testifying to the hermeneutic "circularity"
of Dasein's very being.

C. Historicity and Being-towards-Death

That Dasein is essentially temporal is further shown through
its existential historicity which Heidegger understands to be
"just a more concrete working out of temporality".63 Factically,
every Dasein has its "history"; and this can be so, inasmuch as
its very Being is constituted by historicality.64

We say "every Dasein has its 'history'", but what does this
really mean?   If Dasein is primarily futural as authentically
Being-towards-death, can it not be said (asks Heidegger), that
the orientation of the Daseinanalytic has so far remained "one-
sided"? After all, nothing has been said about Dasein's relation

---

63   SZ 382.

64   SZ 383.

to his birth, and therefore, may we not say that Being-towards-the-beginning has remained unnoticed, as has the way in which Dasein "stretches along between" birth and death?

In answer to such objections, it must be remembered that in the same way that primordial time is other than a succession of now-points, one's history is more than a series of human experiences, filling up the time line between birth and death. Thus birth and death are more than two separate points in time, between which Dasein "has a history" of other present-at-hand incidences.

To say, then, that "every Dasein has its 'history'" cannot mean that its existence is a mere extension between two limiting points of birth and death but rather, in the Heideggerean onto-logy, it must mean that Dasein itself _is_ this very extension, ek-sisting forward toward the futurity of death, against the back-drop of its thrown facticity, suspended in the dynamic presence of its situation. Dasein is historical, only because it is essentially and ontologically temporal.65

Heidegger's references to the historicity of Dasein- while too often overlooked- are extremely revealing in relation to the meaning of Being-towards-death. Once one grasps the essence of the term "historicity", it becomes all the more difficult to understand the phenomenon of death as being in some sense, an

---

65   SZ 385-6.

indication of Dasein as an isolated and private subjectivity. Indeed, the very temporality of Dasein's existential structure receives a better grounding.

The capacity to create a self over time and to have a history as Dasein stretches itself out through time, is itself called Dasein's "happening", that is, Dasein is a happening inasmuch as temporality "happens" or comes to be meaningful in it. Significantly, the term "happening" or Geschehen is etymologically related not only to Geschichtlichkeit, but also to "destiny", Geschick. The suggestion of the sending (schicken) of the "happening" of man's own destiny reflects an important consideration: an individual's "history" from his birth to his death is more than the actions he wills and the experiences which he orders and plans. The historian may tell us that "fundamentally, history is the story of men's efforts to get along with one another. It is as simple as that"66; but Heidegger knows that these historical efforts of men to "get along with one another" are even more "fundamentally" related to Being's own destiny and dispensation, to the history of the self-bestowal of Being (Seinsgeschick) to man within a primordial grace.67

This essential relation between the historicity of Dasein and the history of Being reminds us once again that the individu-

---

66   Reither, Joseph, World History at a Glance, (New York:- Barnes and Noble Inc., 1957), p. v.

67   Cf. FD 24, e.t. 24.

al Dasein is not an isolated ego, and that we can no more speak of historical understanding in terms of the reflections of a subject on some objective occurrences and experiences "in time", than we can speak of Being-towards-death as the reflections of a subject on some objective state which will eventually occur. A recognition of Dasein as essentially temporal, whether by way of a recognition of its historicity or its finitude, leads to a commitment to come to terms with what is most unique and individual about one's way of Being, but also to a most fundamental recognition of one's situation in a historical - world. This is why Heidegger writes: "Once one has grasped the finitude of one's existence, it snatches one back from the endless multiplicity of possibilities which offer themselves as closest to one - those of comfortableness, shirking, and taking things lightly- and brings Dasein into the simplicity of its <u>fate</u> [<u>Schicksals</u>]"68 -- that is to say, authentic historicality.69

In our everyday use of the word, "fate" is understood to imply a certain "predetermination" of events which are beyond our control, and we may wish to say that this ordinary conception of the word is retained by Heidegger, in the sense that "fate" is seen to be tied to the facticity of the historical situatedness which the individual inherits; and again, there is the sending

---

68   SZ 384.

69   SZ 385.

grace (<u>shicken</u>) of Being, at the root of the structure of the word "<u>Schicksal</u>". Indeed, circumstances around us do change, because we do not have an absolute control over the situation.70

But "situation" in Heidegger's sense of the word, is more than merely the physical forces around us; it includes the way in which we come to our own <u>understanding</u> of our Being-in-the-world. To understand one's situation in a different way is, therefore, in fact to change one's situation; in this way, one is "free to choose one's fate".

Through a concern for the way he has been, and for the way that he will be, man is free for an essential de-cision and resolution to accept his authentic historicity, and "let himself come to himself".

Significantly, though, the freedom "to choose one's fate" is far from being unrelated to the "freedom towards death" about which Heidegger speaks.71 "Only an entity which... is free for its death and can let itself be thrown back upon its factical 'there' by shattering itself against death... can be in the <u>moment of vision</u> for 'its time'"; for "only authentic temporality which is at the same time finite, makes possible something like fate".72 The concern for one's fate in Being-towards-death is an

---

70   Cf. WW 16ff, e.t. 308ff.

71   SZ 266.

72   SZ 385.

authentic grasping of one's own death in view of a particular, concrete, worldly situation "in a moment of vision for what is world-historical in its current situation."73

Within a fateful commitment to the situation, Dasein is open to a resolute acceptance of the essential unity of past, present and future in man's Being; as the hidden ground of the historicity of Dasein, man is open to authentic Being-towards-death. "Only if death, guilt, conscience, freedom and finitude reside together equiprimordially in the Being of an entity as they do in care, can that entity exist in the mode of fate."74

If Dasein is to choose his fate, though, that is, if he is to understand the historical Situation in a certain way, and is resolved to live by the consequences of that understanding, then he need not wait, as Aristotle said, until the end of his life in order to be "happy", in order to be authentic to himself. He need not wait for the "case" of death to befall him, but in an understanding of his very essence as a Being-towards-death, Dasein is then free to choose his fate and to live by that decision in a way which is authentic to himself.

In this way, Dasein is open both to the "individual" authenticity of his own project, while at the same time, shouldering a responsibility to relate that project to his historical situa-

---

73   SZ 391.

74   SZ 385.

tedness, which means also to the community within which he finds
himself. The meeting of individuation in Being-towards-death on
the one hand, and a fateful commitment and a response to one's
historical situatedness on the other (both notions linked to the
inherently temporal essence of Dasein) therefore explain the "my
ownness" of self-possession, while equally emphasizing the
importance of concrete meanings. Historicity explains how my own
past and future are essentially interconnected with the past and
the future of other human beings.75

In Heidegger's words:

"Fateful Dasein, as Being-in-the-world, exists essentially in Being-with-Others, its historizing is a co-
historizing and is determinative for it as destiny
(Geshick). This is how we designate the historizing of
the community, of a people. Destiny is not something
that puts itself together out of individual fates, any
more than Being-with-one-another can be conceived as
the occurring together of several Subjects. Our fates
have already been guided in advance, in our Being with
one another in the same world, and in our resoluteness
for definite possibilities. Only in communicating and
in struggling does the power of destiny become free.76

---

75   Cf. in this connection, Couzens Hoy, David, "History, Histo-
     ricity and Historiography", in M. Murray, Heidegger and
     Modern Philosophy, p. 340.

76   SZ 384. In his "Humanismusbrief", Heidegger speaks of
     mankind in the sense of a "historical people", but we must
     keep in mind that he is not reverting in some way, from
     speaking of Dasein in terms of individuality initially
     to a collectivity. In other words, it is not an ontic
     differentiation between "man alone" to "many men" which
     concerns Heidegger, for he is going beyond the subject-
     object relationship between man and beings, to the more
     fundamental ground of both: that is, to man's primordial
     relation to Being itself.

Dasein's realization of its Being-towards-death and an authentic acceptance of its "fate" is no more a choice of an isolated ego than it is an indication of the ontic phenomenon of the "aloneness" of the individual. On the contrary, it is a de-cision of a concrete Being-in-the-world, temporal in its core, which is open to its facticity in "guilt", to respond to a Situation in which it finds itself, in order to thereby respond to its authentic possibility within its futurally-projecting activity in the presence of other similar projects of a community of individuals, participating in a common destiny.

**

CHAPTER THREE

DEATH, TIME AND APPROPRIATION

A.   The Development of Heidegger's Thought

"...death now occupies a new position: it is no longer
located merely in the internal structure of Dasein, but
in the   relation of Dasein to Being.   It is an
existential imparted to Dasein by Being itself, for
Being sets Dasein in position as the necessarily shattering breach through which its holding sway is to
appear. The acceptance of this situation is at one and
the same time Dasein's supreme service to Being and the
achievement of its own authenticity."

- James Demske, Being, Man and Death, p. 117.

Many   commentators   have   tried   to express the feeling that

there is a development, if not outright change in direction or

"turning" in Heidegger's thought.   A great   number of these

descriptions fail to do justice to the continuity of Heidegger's

thought.

A transition "from the element of the questioner (Dasein) to

the   element   of   that-which-is-questioned   (Being)1;   from the

"viewpoint of Dasein alone" to "the 'objective' moment of Being

itself"2; from "Heidegger I" to "Heidegger II"3 are dangerous

characterizations if they   falsely suggest that somewhere along

the line, Heidegger had a change of heart as to his primary

---

1   Demske, J., Being, Man and Death, p. 192.

2   Ibid, p. 183, 184.

3   Richardson, W.J. Heidegger: From Phenomenology to Thought.

purpose; for this does not square well with what Heidegger himself saw to be the essence of Thought: "To think is to confine
yourself to a single thought that one day stands still like a
star in the world's sky."4   Moreover, Heidegger's by-now famous
retort to the suggestion that there is a divergence in the development from his early writings, must certainly inspire caution:
"only by way of what Heidegger I has thought does one gain access
to what is to-be-thought by Heidegger II. But the thought of
Heidegger I becomes possible only if it is contained in Heidegger
II."5

Heidegger makes it quite clear that it is the search for the
meaning of Being which must be seen to inspire and unify the
"way" of his thought. This "way" is not a "reversal" from a
subject-oriented, existential treatise, to a mystical awe in the
face of a transcendent and impenetrable reality, but a "way"
which is "decisively ful-filled in the thinking of the reversal",
that is, it is precisely the Whole itself which is reversed,
rather than a position which is exchanged: "'The Whole': this
means the matter involved in 'Being and Time', 'Time and Being'.
The reversal is in play within the matter itself."6

---

4   Heidegger, M. <u>Aus der Erfahrung des Denkens</u>, e.t. 4.

5   Heidegger, M. "Preface" to Richardson, W.J., <u>op.cit.</u>, page
     xxii.

6   Heidegger, M. in <u>Ibid</u>, p. xviii.

Heinrich Ott suggests that the name "turning" is grounded in the fact that "the consideration no longer proceeds from Dasein but toward Dasein"7.   However one wishes to express it, one gropes for a way to mark a development; to mark a realization that the phenomenological method employed in the Daseinanalytics requires some revision in order to more meaningfully seek an answer to the question of Sein.

If there is a problem of how to express the development in Heidegger's thought "from Dasein toward Dasein", so too is there a corresponding difficulty in expressing the development in Heidegger's consideration of the question of death.   James Demske identifies three "stages":

The "First Stage" is an investigation where "Dasein occupies center stage."   This, Demske tells us, means two things: 1. Dasein is necessarily understood "from the viewpoint of Dasein alone" which means that "purely from the method of questioning employed, Dasein is reduced completely to its own resources and is closed up within itself."8 The autonomy of Dasein is all the more guaranteed by man's Being-towards-death, inasmuch as each man has only his own death to die.

But at the same time, point no. 2 tells us that this "self-understanding of Dasein points beyond itself to the question of

---

7   Ott, H. Denken und Sein: Der Weg Martin Heideggers und der Weg der Theologie, p. 33.

8   Demske, J. op.cit., p. 183.

Being". While Demske wishes at this point to show in what way Dasein is "not entirely closed within itself but open toward Being", nonetheless, he believes that it is not clear in this First Stage whether or not Being is "anything more than a projection of man, the mere objective correlate of the question Dasein necessarily poses."9

The "Middle Stage", however, does investigate the "'objective' moment of Being itself." In both Vom Wesen der Wahrheit and Einführung in die Metaphysik, Demske sees Dasein's existence to have a meaning "which goes beyond himself, namely his service of Being... His existence has nobility and meaning because of the master he serves. This new trait in Heidegger's image of man springs from the fact that Being has now won a position of supremacy over man, in other words, from the fact that a turning has taken place."10

In the "Final Stage", "Being is the determining factor... The authentically dwelling man sees himself being carried along by Being, spoken to by Being in all beings, and living under the claim of Being... Being is the unchallenged superior power which shows man the favour of needing and using him."11

---

9   Ibid, p. 184.

10   Ibid, p. 184-5.

11   Ibid, p. 185.

To my mind, this kind of characterization of Being as the "unchallenged superior power", as the "'objective' moment", and the "master" which "uses" man and which man must therefore serve, is a dangerous one, reflecting an all-too-common tendency to metaphysicize ontology, and therefore misunderstand the very essence of appropriation and the Ontological Difference. For Dasein to <u>belong</u> to Being in a reciprocal relation of "owning", he must be more than "carried along by Being", itself an "<u>unchallenged superior power</u>". Certainly, in the face of the "universal priority of Being",12 man is only the "expectant and respectful shepherd of Being", but the question of the meaning of such "priority" requires further elaboration and a more truthfully Heideggerean, non-metaphysical explanation.

In <u>Die Grundprobleme der Phänomenologie</u>, Heidegger tells us that "all ontological statements are... temporal statements [<u>temporale Sätze</u>]. Only because ontological statements are temporal statements can they and must they be <u>a priori</u> statements."13 However, if we wish to speak of the "priority" of Being itself, or of its "a priori" essence, even though "Apriori heisst...'das Frühere'", this will not necessarily mean that we know Being "earlier" than we do essents. "For first and foremost, we experience beings; we encounter [<u>erkennen</u>] Being only later or

---

12   <u>Ibid.</u>

13   GP 461.

perhaps not at all."14   Clearly, then, this "Zeitbestimmung 'früher'" is not simply to be interpreted "durch den vulgären Zeitbegriff"; on the contrary, it can only be clarified through the "Temporalität des Seinsverständnisses", for it is primordial time as the condition of possibility itself (der Ursprung von Möglichkeit selbst) which shows itself as "das Früheste schlechtin":

> "Früher als jedes mögliche Früher irgendwelcher Art ist
> die Zeit, weil sie die Grundbedingung für ein Früher
> überhaupt ist."15

While one may wish to speak, as Demske does, of a "universal priority of Being", it is a mistake which is all too easy to make, to conceive of such priority in a metaphysical sense. Those who wish to ignore statements such as those of the Grund-probleme der Phänomenologie volume above, and who wish to speak of Heidegger's development "from Dasein to Being", or to speak of a "turning" wherein Heidegger "abandoned the approach to the question of Being by way of the analysis of human being"16-- will be shown to have misunderstood the very essence of the ontological difference and the meaning of appropriation.

What will become clear, therefore, is that while Heidegger's primary concern from Sein und Zeit onwards was the question of

---

14   GP 461-2.

15   GP 463.

16   Zimmerman, Michael E. "The Foundering of Being and Time",
        in Philosophy Today, Vol. 19, No. 2/4, Summer 1975. p.101.

the meaning of Being,   which question is only developed in his
later writings, yet even in these later writings, Heidegger has
not relinquished a concern for the concrete in favour of an
abstract ontology,   but on the contrary, in his deepening
understanding of the mystery of Sein, yet Heidegger will never
lose sight of the lingering essence of "the thing". Indeed, he
will never lose sight of the lived-world of Dasein's existence
among essents too.

       We shall return to this consideration in further detail, in
the final chapter of this volume.

B.   The Later Heidegger on Time and Appropriation

       Transcendence, we have seen, is rooted in the ecstatic-
horizontal essence of time; and so it follows that if there is a
development in Heidegger's thought on the question of the meaning
of transcendence, so too will there be a development toward a
more fundamental questioning of the essence of time.

       Clearly, one reason for Heidegger's "crossing out" of the
word "Sein" was to avoid any remaining tendency to understand
Being metaphysically.17 Similarly concluding that such concepts
as "horizon" - and "transcendence"- originate in too metaphysical

_____

17   "'Being' must be only a provisional word.   Let us guard
      against hanging on too close to this word in our thought".
      (Heidegger, M. "Logos", in VA.)

an attempt to re-present Being in terms of essents, Heidegger will eventually abandon these concepts as well.

> "..we determine what is called horizon and transcendence by means of this going beyond and passing beyond which refer back to objects and our re-presenting of objects. Horizon and transcendence thus, are experienced and determined only relative to objects and our re-presenting them... In this way, what lets the horizon be what it is has not yet been encountered at all."18

It is important to remember that while "Sein" is crossed out, and the term "transcendence" is relinquished in the later works, these are hardly negative signs, but reveal the very positive tendency of Heidegger to recall the Un-thought truth of Being by going beyond the obvious to its ground - or more exactly, to that void-without-ground (Ab-grund) which is the element prior to all fundament. The very freedom of Dasein itself leads to the discovery of the source of the "abyss" of Dasein in the "not" between beings and Being - to the Ontological Difference as difference. Through an initial elucidation of the understanding of Being that is a part of Dasein's ontological constitution, Heidegger is then led to an originative thinking of Being as a gathering, sheltering presence.

The constancy of presence (Anwesenheit) for Heidegger, however, clearly must indicate more than the phenomenon of the present. It is only because the meaning of the infinitive "to be" was determined in terms of the present "is" that the essence

---

18   Heidegger, M. Gelassenheit, p. 38, e.t. 64.

of Being as <u>Anwesenheit</u> was forgotten within a metaphysical tradition oblivious to the greatness of its Presocratic beginnings.19 Significantly, "presence" for the Greeks was indicative of something older than the phenomenon of the present precisely because they did not conceive of being present and abiding in terms of "mere duration" but rather, they thought in terms of "unconcealedness, the rising from unconcealedness, the entry into unconcealedness, the coming and the going away, the duration, the gathering, the radiance, the rest [and] the hidden suddenness of possible absenting". Presence as the presence of what is present does not specifically or completely show itself in the presence of what is present; what is present does not "come toward us men as an object".20 On the contrary, as "Anwesenheit", Being signifies that within which, or in the light of which, anything can appear before us as an essent.21

But if presence involves a rising from unconcealment, so too does it occasion a unique responsibility of man to "start something on its way into arrival. It is in the sense of such a starting something on its way into arrival that being responsible is an occasioning or an inducing to go forward [<u>Ver-an-lassen</u>]."22

---

19   EM 145f; IM 160.

20   cf. WD 143ff, e.t. 235-8.

21   US 201, e.t. 94-95.

22   "Die Frage nach der Technik", VA 10, e.t. (Lovitt) 9.

Such "occasioning has to do with the presencing [Anwesen] of that which at any given time comes to appearance in bringing-forth... Bringing forth comes to pass only insofar as something concealed comes into unconcealment. This coming rests and moves freely within what we call revealing [das Entbergen].23

It is significant that the verb entbergen is formed from "bergen", which means to rescue, to save or shelter, to harbour, to conceal - and that "ent" connotes a coming "forth" or "out" to change or negate a former condition. The task of revealing is, therefore, an opening out from protective concealing24 and a harbouring forth in gathering.

As Heraclitus has noted, concealment (Verbergung) and dis-closure (Entbergung) "love" each other, as constituting a uni-ty.25   Truth itself is therefore not the eternally abiding in a metaphysical sense, but is the happening of the interplay of overtness and covertness, which means that the truth of Being itself is a happening of withdrawal and concealing, but a concea-ling to which emergence into light essentially belongs.

Remembering this, we can conclude that:

---

23   VA 11, e.t. 11.

24   Cf. translator's comments in The Question Concerning Techno-logy and Other Essays, (W. Lovitt), p. 11n.

25   Physis kryptesthai philei. (Cf. "Logos", in VA 271.)

1.   Being as presencing is not to be understood in terms of the
     present. "It would be a mistake, then, for us to take the
     view that Being of beings meant merely, for all time, the
     presence of what is present."26   On the contrary, the
     presencing of Being involves both the happening of _disclo-
     sure_ and the dispensation (_Geschick_) of truth, as well as an
     essential _withdrawal_ of the Source as "_Ab-grund_".
2.   However, inasmuch as the truth of Being does not imply an
     eternal metaphysical presence, but points to a revealing/
     concealing essence, Being cannot be a realm standing over
     against man, existing by itself and only sometimes reaching
     up to man. As needing man in his essence, Being must give
     up the appearance of being a separate, _Für-sich_ reality.
     Heidegger explicitly states that "No way of thought, not
     even the way of metaphysical thought, begins with man's
     essential nature and goes on from there to Being, nor in
     reverse from Being and then back to man. Rather, every way
     of thinking _takes its way_ already _within_ the total relation
     of Being and man's nature, or else it is not thinking at
     all."27
     Both these points are reflected and reiterated in Heideg-
     ger's writings on the Ontological Difference and the meaning of

---

26   WD 143, e.t. 235.

27   WD 73-4, e.t. 79f.

Appropriation.   Rather than enquire into the Difference (the relation of belonging-together) by way of the different (for example, "man" and "Being"), Heidegger decides that in order to penetrate the difference as difference, the traditional concept of "Being" must once and for all be left behind, in favour of primordial appropriative relation.

The final step behind representational thinking to an essential thinking of Being, explicitly requires a relinquishing of Being as the ground of beings, in favour of the giving which prevails in unconcealment, i.e. in favour of the It-gives, in favour of the "It gives Being" as the unconcealing of presencing.   But what is the meaning of the "It gives" and is Heidegger here perhaps only leading us on an unnecessarily ambiguous road?

In "On Time and Being", the question is asked: what prompts us to name time and Being together? From the beginning of western thought, Being has meant the same as presencing, which in turn speaks of the present. Current representations suggest that the present, together with the past and the future, forms the character of time, and so Being is determined as presence by time. "That this is so could in itself be sufficient to introduce a relentless disquiet into thinking. This disquiet increases as soon as we set out to think through in what respect there is such a determination of Being by time".28 It becomes apparent

---

28   ZD 1, e.t. 2.

that while Being is not a thing (thus nothing temporal), yet it is determined by time as presence; and while time is likewise not a thing (thus nothing which is), yet it remains constant in its passing away without being something temporal like the beings in time.29   While we say, therefore, that Being and Time determine each other reciprocally, they do so in such a way that neither can Being be addressed as something temporal, nor can time be addressed as a being. "As we give thought to all of this", reflects Heidegger, "we find ourselves adrift in contradictory statements".30

How is one to escape the contradictions? Heidegger answers: "by cautiously thinking over the matters named here." Both Being and time are seen to be "matters" of thinking, but the "matter at stake" is in fact the relation of both issues; it is that which holds both issues toward each other and endures their relation. So, in reflecting upon the matter "Being" (a matter, but not a being), and upon the matter of "Time" (again, a matter but nothing temporal), we no longer say "Being is", "Time is", but rather: there is Being, there is Time; or better, It gives Being (Es gibt Sein), It gives Time. What now remains is to clarify the It and its giving by looking ahead to the It which gives Being and Time. Heidegger proposes to first think Being in

---

29   ZD 2, e.t. 3.

30   ZD 3, e.t. 4.

order to think it itself into its own element; this element shows itself to be a <u>giving</u>, to which Being belongs: "as allowing-to-presence, it belongs to unconcealing; as the gift of unconcealing, it is retained in the giving."31 This giving of the "It gives Being" proves to be a sending32 and a destiny of presence in its epochal transmutations. The giving in "It gives Time" proves to be an extending, opening up of a four-dimensional realm, i.e. time, as the name for the opening up and mutual self-extending of future, past and present, is unified in the interplay of each toward each - which constitutes the fourth dimension: "But the dimension which we call the fourth in our count is, in the nature of the matter, the first, that is, the giving that determines all."33 Can Heidegger now determine this very "It" which gives, in terms of the giving which he has described?

He cannot, if doing so requires an answer which will represent the "It" and its giving in some present being. The "It", as giving, "is precisely <u>not there</u>",34 that is, what is named by

---

31   ZD 5, e.t. 6.

32   Sending is shown by Heidegger to be a "giving which gives only its gift, but in the giving, holds itself back and withdraws." (8)   It is because the <u>gift</u> (Being as ground) has been the primary concern through the history of metaphysics, that the <u>giving</u> of that gift (the It-gives Being) has been forgotten in what Heidegger has described to be a history of <u>Seinsvergessenheit</u>.

33   ZD 16, e.t. 15.

34   ZD 18, e.t. 18.

the "It" is a <u>presence of absence</u>, but a presence which Heidegger will call: <u>Ereignis</u>, the event of Appropriation. Thus the relation of Being and Time, the "matter at stake", is not merely a relation retroactively superimposed on Being and Time, but it is that which "first appropriates Being and time into their own in virtue of their relation, and does so by the appropriating that is concealed in destiny and in the gift of opening out."35

What is Appropriation? To be consistent, Heidegger cannot attempt to describe Appropriation in terms of whatness; he cannot introduce Appropriation as another interpretation of Being, even a refined interpretation, which would think Being in terms of beings, as <u>idea</u>, <u>energeia</u>, <u>actualitas</u>. Appropriation is not the universal <u>concept</u> under which Being and time are subsumed.

Appropriation, as we have said, rather involves a presence of absence; to giving as sending, there belongs a keeping back. The sending source withdraws what is most fully its own from "boundless unconcealment"; expropriation thus belongs to Appropriation as such, which is why we can never <u>place</u> Appropriation in front of us, and re-present it as something over and against us or as something all-embracing.

Remember that this cannot mean that man is thereby excluded from appropriation; on the contrary, "In Being as presence, there is manifest the concern which concerns us humans in such a way

---

35   ZD 20, e.t. 19.

that in perceiving and receiving it, we have attained the distinction of human being. Accepting the concern of presence, however, lies in standing within the realm of giving. In this way, four-dimensional true time has reached us. Because Being and time are there only in Appropriating, Appropriating has the peculiar property of bringing man into his own as the being who perceives Being by standing within true time. Thus Appropriated, man belongs to Appropriation."36

Some may feel that we are hereby led into an unnecessary mysticism, or worse, into an intentional ambiguity.37 But, since Heidegger is speaking of the mystery of Being (something which, by definition, outdistances the "solid achievements" [Bertrand Russell] of methodological systematization and classification), Heidegger says: "Logical classifications mean nothing here"; so when we ask what is the meaning of Appropriation, the only response can be: Appropriation appropriates. "Saying this, we say the Same in terms of the Same about the Same". This may sound bizarre within the boundaries of traditional logic, but, Heidegger challenges, what if we consider that "this Same is not even anything new, but the oldest of the old in Western thought: that ancient something which conceals itself in

---

36   ZD 23, e.t. 23.

37   Cf. C.W. Richey's not very informed article, entitled "On the Intentional Ambiguity of Heidegger's Metaphysics", in Journal of Philosophy, Vol. 55, (1958), p. 1144-8.

a-letheia? That which is said before all else by this first source of all the leitmotifs of thinking gives voice to a bond that binds all thinking, providing that thinking submits to the call of what must be thought...".38

This means, therefore, that the history of Being is not to be understood as a series of occurrences "in time", but rather must be seen as Being itself, and the "it gives" of true time which is the very Source of the belonging from which man and Being as presence both emerge.

As Otto Pöggeler reminds us,39 this means that the essence for example, of technology or poetry, is not the trans-temporal validity of an eternal, unchanging idea, but rather that "ge-schickt" historical essence which reveals itself within a strict-ly temporal commitment (Verbindlichkeit) when Dasein accepts the mittance of Being (Seinsgeschick) and as the location of the truth of Being, is "identical" with it. In this way, beings are understood in their Being and the difference between Being and beings is broken open, within the simultaneous arrival of beings in the unconcealment of Being itself. In such a happening of Identity, of mutual owning and adequacy, there is the play of belongingness and uniting together of earth and sky, divinities

---

38   ZD 25, e.t. 24.

39   "Being as Appropriation", in Philosophy Today, Vol. 19, No. 2/4, Summer 1975, p. 172.

and mortals, which is to say, a uniting of world and things into each other's favour through a "Lassen" of the Ereignis.

Beyond all representational thinking, time itself is now a temporalizing in the sense of a ripening, and a contemporaneous bringing-forth in a concordant unity and gathering of what has been, with the arrival of the inexhaustible yet-to-be, within the rich fullness of still presence.

The mittance of Being, therefore, grants the clearing in which beings become manifest within the "bursting open" of a historical world.

C.   Death in History, Poetry and Language

We have pointed out at some length above, how Being as presence, and even as understood in terms of Ereignis, the Onto-logical Difference and Appropriation, all reflect Heidegger's going-beyond to the no-thingness of a mysterious Source which withdraws even as it reveals itself, while reflecting as well the essential belonging of this Source and needing of man. Both of these elements are reflected in what Heidegger has to say in his later Thought, about the essence of history, poetry and language.

When Heidegger speaks of the strange sense of peace which comes through an understanding of death as the arrival at a "quieter sojourn in the early morning"40, this is far from being

---

40   US 69, e.t. 187.

unrelated to history, even though the notion of an essential stillness and abiding presence at first glance does not seem to square well with our common notion of history as a dynamic series of events. But Heidegger tells us that as primordial history, as primordial time, Being is the Holy; it is "older than the ages", the "most ancient time", embracing all times as the ever-abiding source and "advent of the beginning".41 As the holy, Being is the primordial root of all that is past, and the "primal spring" of everything to come. It is the "one and only [das Einstige] in a twofold sense. It is the oldest of all former things and the youngest of all things to come."42 However, as the "first before all and the last after all", as "älter denn die Zeiten, über die Götter"43, the abiding of the Holy is not "the empty lingering of something ready to hand but... the unforeseeable originality of an origin."44 It affords man a home in the nearness of the Source which appears as a "still light" in the "gentleness of a soft embrace".45

---

41   Heidegger, M. Erläuterungen zu Hölderlins Dichtung, here-
     after HD. Translations from Demske, J. Being, Man and
     Death.

42   HD 61.

43   HD 73.

44   HD 72-3.

45   HD 62.

Yet, the notion of a sense of "peace" in such abiding can be deceptive; even in the nighness of the singing poet, there can be danger46, and indeed, in the gaping, yawning abyss of Being as primordial history, there is a "violent concussion of chaos which offers no foothold, the terror of the immediate which baffles every approach".47 There is a majestas of the overwhelming and omnipresent, which is also, though, the "all-creative", and therefore that which awakens and vivifies everything48, that which bestows all dynamism and energy in an opening of the hori- zon for the historical appearance of beings. "In its advent, the holy... grounds another beginning of another history"49 and so there is a dispensation and a granting of Seinsgeschichte.

Historical Being, therefore, is the event within which each epoch of history arises in a primordial happening. Even in the forgetting of Being characteristic of metaphysics, there is testimony to the historical modes and epochal transmutations through which Being has revealed itself. It is because Heidegger sees the history of Being to be one of the ways to a more funda- mental questioning of the meaning of Being itself, that he enga-

---

46   Heidegger, M. Aus der Erfahrung des Denkens, e.t. 8.

47   HD 68. Cf. 61, and e.t. 250.

48   Cf. HD 51, 58-9, and e.t. 251.

49   HD 73, Cf. e.t. 289.

ges in his dialogues with metaphysicians and thinkers of the past.50

Indeed, the revealing/concealing essence of Being in a historical "sending" once again reminds us of the essential relation to man. The "forgetting" of the question of the meaning of Being in favour of a questioning of "what is a being?" is not inconsequential51 - and neither is the culmination of a metaphysical tradition in a subjectivistic, technological epoch. Within an atomic age which threatens total destruction of human-kind, Heidegger looks beyond the horror of the ontic possibili-ties to their ontological ground, to uncover what he sees to be a much greater horror: the danger of the destruction and death of man in his very essence.

With the Cartesian cogito ergo sum characterizing modern thought, all interpretations of reality are ultimately derived from a hermeneutic grounding within a subject who is now lord of all and who feels that as such, he can manipulate through technology, all beings in the world. "What is deadly is not the much-discussed atomic bomb as this particular death-dealing machine. What has long since been threatening man with death, and indeed, with the death of his own nature, is the uncondi-tional character of mere willing in the sense of purposeful self-

---

50   Cf. EM, WM, the Nietzsche, Hegel and Kant volumes, and
      sections of Sein und Zeit.

51   WM 8-11, e.t. 334-339.

assertion in everything."52   In the age of humanistic subjectivism, man believes himself to be the technological master of
the world; "the willing that is willed by this will is already
resolved to take unconditional command." Indeed, it is a willing
to dominate even other men which culminates in the violence of
two World Wars, and, forgetting that he is the guardian of Being,
man loses his nearness to Being which constitutes his true essence and lives within a glorification of technology and an
illusory belief in his unlimited power.

The result is that "the wholesome and sound withdraws. The
world becomes without healing, unholy...".53

The only deliverance can come from what turns out to be an
essentially poetic response: "To see this danger and point it
out, there must be mortals who reach sooner into the abyss"54 and
these mortals are the artists and the poets. In fact, it is in
the work of art as a "form of Being", rather than simple endeav-
our of an individual, that there emerges a concretion of the
special relation of Being to man within a certain age or time.
Art, as the setting-unto-work (Ins-Werk-Setzen) of the truth of
Being, is a genuinely poetic projection, and, as such, is the

---

52   HW 271, e.t. 116.

53   HW 271, e.t. 116.

54   HW 273, e.t. 117.

disclosure of that into which human being as historical, is already cast.55

With the thinker, the poet becomes the bearer of the history of Being.   While the thinker "speaks Being", the poet "names the sacred", re-calling Being in this very act of naming the Holy, in an effort to "bring Being to house".

It is Hölderlin - the "poet of poets" because he explicitly writes of what it is to create poetry - who concretizes the message of our age: "Full of merit, yet poetically dwells man on this earth".56 But Heidegger then adds: "Do we dwell poetically? Presumably, we dwell altogether unpoetically.   If that is so, does it give the lie to the poet's words; are they untrue? No. The truth of his utterance is confirmed in the most unearthly way. For dwelling can be unpoetic only because it is in essence poetic.   For a man to be blind, he must remain a being by nature endowed with sight.   A piece of wood can never go blind...".57

It is the poet, then, who is "the mortal", who dwells between man and gods, and who sees man's ultimate remoteness from

---

55   HW 64, e.t. 74.

56   VA 190, e.t. 216.

57   VA 203, e.t. 228.

the Holy, only to thereby resolutely prepare for the "homecoming" and return into the proximity of the source.58

The poet is the messenger conveying "greetings" of the holy to men. But there is a great deal of significance in Heidegger's naming of the poet as "the mortal", belonging to Being and yet remaining tied to beings. Expressing the truth of Being, yet the poets are "sons of the earth" and so we are reminded that finitude is the proper and indeed, the essential mode of being human. The calling of Being is not the call of an eternal essence, and so man is distinguished from the divinities, the "immortals", and distinguished as well from all other ready-at-hand entities because of his unique relation to Being. The Being-towards-death of ek-sisting man is revealed once again, but this time in terms of a state of being-mortal which consists of a receiving, a guarding and a concretizing of the arrival of Being among beings.

In fact, the relation of authenticity and Being-towards-death is repeated in the later Heidegger, but by way of a different language. In his work on Georg Trakl's poetry, "Language in the Poem",59 death appears as the destruction (Untergang) to which the "soul", which is a "stranger on the earth", is summoned, which is to say, death is the destruction of the human

---

58   HD. Quoted from english translation, "Remembrance of the Poet", in Existence and Being, p. 258.

59   US 35-82, e.t. 159 ff.

form which is not "translucent with blueness" (durchscheinen von der Blaue)60 or does not "stand in the wind of the holy".61 To cease to be a "stranger on the earth"62, man must take his proper place among beings, that is, he must leave behind his inauthentic form, to dwell in the nearness of Being, in the "blueness" which is the "colour of depth"63 and the domain of the holy.64 Death is here a looking-ahead into the blue of the "spiritual night"65, a "night" inasmuch as it is a rejection of the familiar and the commonplace in the authenticity of human dwelling.66

But, beyond this transitional stage, there is a "second death", which means more than mere annihilation because the departed person passes "into the 'golden showers' of early mor-

---

60   US 47, e.t. 168-9.

61   US 47, e.t. 168-9.

62   The authentic Greek definition of man names man to be "the strangest of all". Man is the "strangest of all, not only because he passes his life amid the strange... but because he departs from his customary, familiar limits, because he is the violent one who, tending toward the strange in the sense of the overpowering, surpasses the limit of the familiar (das Heimische)." EM 115, e.t. 127.

63   VA 201, e.t. 226.

64   Heidegger is not the only thinker to bring together the colour of blueness with the notion of spirituality. Cf. William Gass's fascinating book, entitled On Becoming Blue.

65   US 55, e.t. 174.

66   Cf. US 146 ff., e.t. 48ff.

ning"67 as Being opens like the breaking of a new day, and the
"stranger" arrives at the authentic "beginning of his pilgri-
mage"68 which is "unto death".69 All this is further testimony
to the existential/ontological realization by man that his is in
essence a journeying Being-towards-death, and that only inasmuch
as he comes to terms with this essence can he pass over to authenticity in a return to the "fatherland", in "the proximity of
the source".

Such an understanding of mortality in relation to the poet
is further justified in Heidegger's musings on the nature of language itself, the "primordial poetry in which a people speaks
Being".70   It is inasmuch as we are employed for the speaking of
language that we dwell as mortals.71 But language is not something that man may possess simply as a tool; on the contrary, it
must be language which possesses man.72   That which speaks is
Being, exteriorizing itself, expressing itself to man, and thereby rendering the language and the logic of man possible. "Only

---

67   US 71, e.t. 188-9. (Translation by Demske, J., op.cit.)

68   US 52, Cf. e.t. 172-3.

69   US 23, e.t. 200.

70   EM 155, e.t. 169.

71   US 266, e.t. 134.

72   HW 60, e.t. 73.

when the language of historical man is born of the Word [of Being]
does it ring true."73

The relation of death to language is clear when Heidegger
remarks that the "mortals are those who can experience death as
death. The animals cannot do this. But neither can the animal
speak."74 Both Being-toward-death and discourse are existen-
tials. Being-mortal consists of sheltering and concretizing the
advent of Being, and so too, language involves a saying which
gathers and collects its form from the unconcealment of what lies
there together.75

Human speech itself carries the mark of finitude, inasmuch
as it is a receptivity: man is thrown into language which is the
given context within which he encounters other beings. While
man, as immersed in language, certainly changes it and reshapes
it, yet "man first speaks when and only when he responds to language by listening to its appeal".76

---

73   WIM 106, e.t. 360.

74   US 215, e.t. 107. Heidegger says at least twice (VA 150,
      178, e.t. 150, 179) that mortals can die. This, of course,
      does not imply that we have a choice as to whether or not
      we shall face the empirical fact of death. Since we are
      in an ontological, rather than an ontic dimension, clearly
      this suggests that we have a choice as to whether or not
      we shall resolve to come to terms with the authenticity
      of our Being-towards-death.

75   Cf. Heidegger's "Logos" essay.

76   VA 190-1, e.t. 216.

Significantly, both Being-towards-death and being-a-speaker
have a common source, then, in man's understanding of Being. Inasmuch as he is a Being-towards-death, man is mortal and therefore, he is thrown into language, responding to Being by way of
the very language which he speaks. But also, in expressing Being
by way of a pre-ontological, articulable understanding of Sein,
man is able to know death as death: "We now call mortals mortals,
not because their early life comes to an end, but because they
are capable of death as death. Mortals are who they are, as
mortals, present in the shelter of Being."77

That the relation of death and language is rooted in the
essence of man, and indeed, therefore in Being itself, is clear
especially when Heidegger writes:

> "Mortals dwell in that they initiate their own nature-
> their being capable of death as death- into the use and
> practice of this capacity, so that there may be a good
> death. To initiate mortals into the nature of death in
> no way means to make death as empty Nothing, the goal.
> Nor does it mean to darken dwelling by blindly staring
> toward the end."78

What it does mean, however, is that man, as capable of death
as death, preserves the fourfold79 so that Being may come to
presence. Man as mortal is the possible locus of a breakthrough
to Being itself.

---

77   VA 178, e.t. 179.

78   VA 151, e.t. 151.

79   VA 150, e.t. 150.

"Death is what touches mortals in their nature, and so sets them on their way to the other side of life, and so into the whole of the pure draft. Death thus gathers into the whole of what is already posited, into the positum of the whole draft. As this gathering of positing, death is the laying-down, the Law, just as the mountain chain is the gathering of the mountains into the whole of its chain. There, where the Law touches us, there is the place within the widest orbit into which we can admit the converted unshieldedness positively into the whole of what is. Our unshieldedness, so converted, finally shelters us within the Open."80

In death, "the supreme concealedness of Being crystallizes"81 and crystallizes through man's mortality because man is the shattering breach through which Being breaks into history. In death, Dasein "shatters" against Being. Heidegger tells us that violence against the overriding power of Being must shatter against Being as emerging power82 and this means, in other words, that

"All violences shatters against one thing. That is death. It is an end beyond all consummation [Vollendung], a limit beyond all limits. Here, there is no breaking-out or breaking-up, no capture or subjugation. But this strange and alien [unheimlich] thing that banishes us once and for all from everything in which we are at home is no particular event that must be named among others because it, too, ultimately happens. It is not only when he comes to die, but always and essentially, that man is without issue in the face of death. Insofar as man is, he stands in the

---

80   HW 280, e.t. 126.

81   US 23, e.t. 200.

82   EM 124, e.t. 136.

issuelessness of death. Thus, his being-there is the happening of strangeness."83

Through the phenomenon of death, then, man is able to recognize that, as thrown, he is in the service (the shepherd) of Being as the overwhelming gift which "rules in its essence".84 But that "happening of strangeness" whereby Being "hurls man into this breaking-away", in fact, drives man beyond himself, "to venture forth toward Being, to accomplish Being, to stabilize it in the work, and so hold open the essent as a whole".85 The Law of Being does not derive, therefore, from the ontic activity of a transcendent, efficient cause, even though man's mortal, "shatterable" being is under the claim of Being. While death is "the shrine of non-Being", yet "no-thing is that which makes the revelation of what-is, as such, possible for our human existence."86 As "das höchste Ge-birg", death is a concealing which gathers together, and thereby determines man's understanding of Being, world, and thing.

---

83   EM 121, e.t. 133.

84   EM 124, e.t. 136.

85   EM 124, e.t. 137.

86   WIM 12, e.t. 340.

D.   Death and the Emergence of Being
      in the Essence of the Thing

Death reveals the frailty and perishability of the totality

of beings, and yet, in spite of this negativity, beings are, and

indeed, man simply does not direct his attention primarily to

death, but to the things around him, and to Being which shines

through them.   Heidegger himself has said that death is not a

blind staring toward the end, but rather, is an essential moment

in the dwelling of the mortal who stands in the illumination of

Being, in an affirmation of the meaning of existence, of the

world, and the things around him.

But how, more specifically, is Heidegger's understanding of

the essence of the Thing relevant to his discussion of death?   Or

perhaps initially we must ask, what does it mean for a thing to

be?

The essence of the thing cannot consist in its being a mere

object (Gegen-stand).   Using the example of a jug, Heidegger

suggests that:

> "the vessel's thingness does not lie at all in the
> material of which it consists, but in the void that
> holds... How does the jug's void hold?   It holds by
> taking what is poured in.   It holds by keeping and
> retaining what it took in.   The void holds in a two-
> fold manner: taking and keeping."87

---

87   VA 170, e.t. 171.

Because it does not imply a lack of relation, the presence of the thing is not simply a standing still in the sense of a becoming rigid, but is a gathering together of the quadrate:- earth and heaven, gods and mortals. The thing things, appropriating the fourfold into something that abides for awhile into this thing, or that thing.88 In bringing together the fourfold, the thing "things" the world, gathering earth and sky, divinities and mortals together in a unity unto itself.

Man himself cannot be thought, except in relation to world and to things. "We are", says Heidegger, "called by the thing as the thing. In the strict sense of the German term _bedingt_, we are the be-thinged, the conditioned ones. We have left behind us the presumption of all unconditionedness."89 In dwelling in the fourfold, and with things, man tends the quadrate by gathering its unity and its essence into things.

But what does all this have to do with death?

Heidegger speaks of things often in terms of the art work, but he also speaks of "built things", using the bridge as an example. In that context, he writes:

> "Always and ever differently, the bridge escorts the lingering and hastening ways of men to and fro, so that they may get to other banks and in the end, as mortals, to the other side."90

---

88   VA 196, e.t. 222.

89   VA 179, e.t. 181.

90   VA 153, e.t. 152.

At first glance, one may conclude that Heidegger may be abandoning his stand from Sein und Zeit, where he speaks of his phenomenological concerns as strictly "this-worldly". He writes that mortals are "always themselves on their way to the last bridge, actually striving to surmount all that is common and unsound in them in order to bring themselves before the haleness of the divinities."91

But despite the initial impression, Heidegger by no means is speaking of a life after death in his references to the "whole" life "on the other side". It is not insignificant that these statements appear in his discussion of the bridge as thing, because it is precisely man's authentic dwelling among things that is being referred to. As with the Trakl poem mentioned previously, what is important is not some supposed reference to a soul which undergoes a transition to a new type of life after death, but rather, the wholeness of a life "on the other side" is the phenomenon of authentic existence within the mirror-play and the worlding of a world in the center of which the thinging of the thing takes place.92

Indeed, as the thing itself is the gathering and staying of the fourfold in a bringing-near93, so too is the authentic coming

---

91   VA 153, e.t. 153.

92   VA 179, e.t. 180.

93   VA 176, e.t. 177.

to terms with death, a sparing of death in its true essence, "so that there will be a good death".94   We have noted above that death is the gathering into the whole, just as the mountain chain (das Gebirg) is the gathering of the mountains into the whole of its chain;95   and so Heidegger now will speak of death as the shrine of   Nothing, and the shelter of Being, "Gebirg des Seins".96

The prefix "Ge-", which points to collectivity, as well as the word "Berg" as the root of the verb "bergen" which signifies a saving, and a sheltering concealing, both support the implications of "Gebirg" (mountain-chain) as indicating a mountain security, and secret retreat of Being itself. While death as "Gebirg des Seins" suggests a place where Being   hides in security, yet this stronghold is a place both of concealing (Verbergen) and revealing (Entbergung) as well.   As the extreme possibility of Dasein, death is still seen to be "capable of the greatest lighting-up of Being and its truth... Death is the still unconsidered measure of the immeasurable, i.e. of the sublimest game in which man is involved on earth."97   Death ultimately leads man to recognize the inexhausible Mystery and

---

94   VA 151, e.t. 151.

95   HW 280, e.t. 126.

96   VA 177, e.t. 179.

97   Heidegger, M. Der Satz vom Grund, p. 186-7. As cited in Demske, J., op.cit., p. 167.

immeasurability of existence. As all beings disappear, <u>nothing</u> appears to be left in a shrine of darkest concealment, but this is yet a revealing of Being itself.

It is this revealing/concealing essence of the phenomenon of death, which is mirrored in the Thing.

We must remember that Heidegger has said that the vessel's thingness "does not lie at all in the material of which it consists, but in the void that holds."[98]   The essence of thingness does not consist of its being a <u>res</u>, or an actual object, but rather, it consists of its being a void, emergent from the nothingness of Being in order to gather and to "hold".

Similarly, coming to terms with death itself involves a realization that man is ultimately the shepherd of Being, and in his essence, the location of the truth of Being as No-thing, and yet, to stand in the illumination of Being, man is not called to an "other-worldliness" after death, and nor is he called by Heidegger to an "empty staring at the end"; on the contrary, he is called to a more authentic "sparing", caring and sheltering of the things-that-are.

**

---

98   VA 168, e.t. 169.

CHAPTER FOUR

A PROJECT BEYOND HEIDEGGER

More than any other modern thinker, Heidegger has faced the issue of death in its all-embracing mystery and revealed to his readers the deepest insights into the phenomenon of man's Being-towards-death. Describing how death is more than simply the fact of cessation of life, but on the contrary, is definitive of our very finitude and of the essence of being-human, Heidegger has shown how death individualizes Dasein, making us realize that each human is a unique and irreplaceable being, with his own history and horizon of understanding through the prism of a finite, perspectival gift of existence. In his descriptions of being-mortal, Heidegger has begun to reveal the ontological roots of the belonging-together of death and Being, through his uncovering of the essence of death as an existentiale, a way of being of man which belongs to man as soon as he is.

That Heidegger has revealed, most brilliantly and original-ly, the ontological roots of the phenomenon of death, remains indisputable.

But, has he done sufficient justice to the description of the meaning of the ontic possibilities revealed by the phenomenon of death?

In the final section of Chapter Three, we have described briefly, the Heideggerean description of death in terms of the emergence of Being in the essence of the Thing.

However, as shall become evident in the proceeding sections, there is much more to be said, not only about death as an ontic e-vent, but also about the inherent belonging of the ontological description with the ontic.

**

PART TWO:

DEATH AS AN ONTIC EVENT:

Coming to terms
with the phenomenon of death
as a determinate possibility

INTRODUCTION

> "Death is here and death is there,
> Death is busy everywhere,
> All around, within, beneath,
> Above is death - and we are death."
>
> - Shelley, _Death_

Heidegger's penetrating descriptions of man's Being-in-the-world as a Being-towards-death reveal the ontological roots of the finitude of human existence, reveal how "we are death", but my next question must be: what can be said about death as an _ontic event_, as a concrete happening which shatters our everydayness and recasts the ontological meaning of our existential horizons through the prism of a new definitive, determinate figuration of our finite existence?

Part II of this volume presents some preliminary considerations in answer to this question, both from the point of view of one's own imminent death as well as from the perspective of the death of a significant "Other" in one's life, someone whom one loves.

But perhaps initially, it will be best to take a moment to consider the etymological significance of this word "e-vent", as we inherit it from Heidegger.

What is meant by the English word "event" can be expressed in German in several ways, but Heidegger seems to rely primarily on two terms: one is _Begebenheit_; the other is _Ereignis_.

When Heidegger writes:

"Dying is not an event; it is a phenomenon to be understood existentially";1

or

"The call does not report events; it calls without uttering anything";2

he is using the word "Begebenheit" in a way which seems to convey more the aspect of a fortuitous episode or incident, rather than an essential happening.   Indeed, this is even more evident when we read of how in anticipatory resoluteness, "Dasein becomes free from the entertaining 'incidentals' with which busy curiosity keeps providing itself -- primarily from the events of the World."3

"Ereignis" seems to convey a similar meaning in some parts of Sein und Zeit.   Heidegger tells us that an event (Ereignis) can be understood in the sense of an impending event encountered environmentally: "for instance, a storm, the remodelling of the house or the arrival of a friend, may be impending; and these are entities which are respectively present-at-hand, ready-to-hand, and there-with-us."4

---

1   SZ 240.

2   SZ 277.

3   SZ 310.

4   SZ 250; cf. also 152.

Death can be encountered as merely "a well-known event occurring within-the-world. As such, it remains in the inconspicuousness characteristic of what is encountered in an everyday fashion."5

In passages like these, Ereignis is almost interchangeable with Begebenheit; indeed, at one point, echoing the Begebenheit reference above, Heidegger repeats that:

"...the call asserts nothing, gives no information about world-events [Ereignisse]".6

On the other hand, even here one does sense a greater – breadth to the Ereignis (translated as "world-event"), than is evident in the more fortuitous nature of the Begebenheit, and in fact, further on in Sein und Zeit, there is an important change felt in how Heidegger employs the word Ereignis. The change comes primarily in those sections which center on the problems of temporality and historicity. Speaking of the "double meaning" of the "past", Heidegger remarks that "the past belongs irretrievably to an earlier time; it belonged to the events of that time; and in spite of that, it can still be present-at-hand 'now'".7 On the following page, the kind of questions posed by Heidegger reflect this slightly different usage of the word "event"

5   SZ 253.

6   SZ 273.

7   SZ 378.

(Ereignis). Suggesting that man is to be seen as the "subject"

of events, Heidegger asks however:

> "How is the historizing character of such events to be
> defined?   Is historizing a sequence of processes, an
> ever-changing emergence and   disappearance of e-
> vents?... Does Dasein first become historical by get-
> ting intertwined with events and circumstances?   Or is
> the Being of Dasein constituted first of all by
> historizing, so that anything   like circumstances,
> events and vicissitudes is ontologically possible only
> because Dasein is historical in its being?"8

Even more significant, though, is the   mention of "event"

("Ereignis") in terms of · a "historical happening" and in the

context of Heidegger's exposition of "the   ontological enigma of

the movement of historizing in general". He explains that:

> "...when, for instance, a ring gets 'handed over' to
> someone and 'worn', this is a kind of Being in which it
> does not simply suffer changes of location.   The
> movement of historizing in which something 'happens to
> something' is not to be grasped in terms of motion as
> change of location. This holds for all world-histo-
> rical 'processes' and events, and even, in a certain
> manner, for 'natural catastrophes'."9

Such an understanding of "event" begins to foreshadow the

later Heidegger's understanding of the term, where the "history

of Being" in its revealing/concealing truth is seen to be the

pure happening of the primordial disclosure as the Ereignis.

Such "history of Being" (i.e. Being in the sense of Ereignis)

begins with its epoche, its keeping itself to itself; the various

epochs of this history are the epochs of man's progressive fal-

---

8   SZ 379.

9   SZ 389. Emphasis mine.

ling out of his relationship to Being, which need not be negative but are both a positive manifestation of <u>man's relatedness</u> to Being, as well as a promise of a revelation of Being in its truth.

Therefore, as <u>Ereignis</u>, "event" is the truth of Being as the happening of the revealing/concealing illumination - and thus, as the belonging-together of man and Being. Meaning both advent (<u>ad-venire</u>: to come to, to arrive) as well as the event in the sense of <u>e-venire</u>, to come out, the E-vent as oc-currence is a disclosure of truth in the coming together of man and Being. "The Event", explains Heidegger, "delivers man and Being into their essential togetherness."10   Thus, while Thought thinks Being, "Being is not a product of thinking. On the contrary, essential thinking is an event (<u>Ereignis</u>) of Being"11, which means that <u>Ereignis</u> is not something that can ever "present" itself as an <u>object</u> to thought, or be re-presented within a certain <u>concept</u> of subject, object or substance. This is not to say that the leap out of metaphysical thinking away from the separateness of man and Being, is a leap into a vague, mystical, intuitive kind of cognitive experience, but on the contrary, in surrendering meta-physical concepts, the leap of thought becomes

---

10   ID 31. As cited in Versényi, L. <u>Heidegger, Being and Truth</u>, p. 156.

11   WM 103, e.t. 356.

a co-rrespondence to the   Ereignis, in a letting-be of truth in
its revealing/concealing mystery.

The big mistake, at this point, is to come to another kind
of metaphysical conclusion, that the Ereignis in the later Heidegger is no more than a domain "behind" Sein, which domain
renders the Being-man relation intelligible. This, I think, is a
common mistake, reflected in both the interpretations of the
metaphysician as well as the mystic. (The metaphysician too
easily conceives of the Ereignis in terms of a supreme "beyond",
and the mystic may similarly conceive of a domain "beyond" the
empirical world and inaccessible to it.)

But the fact that Heidegger is neither a metaphysician nor a
mystic in this last sense, simply goes to show that the Ereignis
is not an abstract domain or ground "behind" Sein"; it is an e-
vent. Etymologically related to the verb eräugnen: to appear
before the eyes, Ereignis is the lighting-up event whereby Dasein
can be present to its own authentic being.

This is important to remember. Rather than speak of Ereignis in terms of any sort of domain suspended in itself, we must
understand it within the context of the event of man and Being
reaching one another in their essence and therefore - belongingness. To realize this relationship of mutual owning - eignen- in
which man and Being belong (are ge-eignet) to one another, is to
meditate on the Ereignis.

Otherwise, the difference between Being and beings, the "between" itself, would be simply another metaphysical domain reflecting the separateness, rather than the essential belonging, of man and Being in the appropriative event. Inasmuch as the difference is more than a metaphysical domain, reflecting instead a belongingness, "overwhelming and arrival appear in each other in reciprocal reflection. Speaking in terms of the difference, this means: perdurance is a circling, the circling of Being and beings around each other."12   The leap beyond metaphysical thought is, therefore, something other than a simple forward leap into another abstract or even simply "mystical" domain, which, for originality's sake, we will now label "<u>Ereignis</u>" rather than "Being" or "God"; on the contrary, the event, as something other than a mere abstraction, allows of a unique concreteness (in an ontological, rather than an empirical sense) because it is a "circling" e-vent, rather than a mere conditioning ground or domain.

As shall become evident, the ontic e-vent is not just a particular incident, then, nor is it revelatory of a domain of "Being" beyond it; rather, as we intend to use the word, an e-vent is a happening, an oc-currence, an arrival (<u>ad-venire</u>) and a breaking-out, (<u>e-venire</u>), rooted in temporality -- which reveals, brings to light (<u>er-äugnen</u>) and yet conceals the mutual owning

---

12   ID 137-8; e.t. 69.

(eignen), the belongingness of man and Being- that is, the Ontological Difference itself.

**

CHAPTER ONE

REFLECTING ON ONE'S OWN DEATH:

A.   The Intelligibility of the   Phenomenon of My Death as a
     Determinate Event

     "All his life, he had recognized the fact that that
     famous syllogism seemed to apply perfectly to Caius,
     but it was in no sense applicable to himself. Caius,
     that is the man, man in general, and to this conclu-
     sion, there could be no objection.   However, he was
     certainly not Caius, nor by any means, man in general
     ... Caius is mortal, and it is quite in order that
     Caius should die, but I, Vanya, Ivan Ilyich, with all
     my thoughts and feelings - that is something entirely
     different."

                (Leo Tolstoy, Death of Ivan Ilyich).

Heidegger has told us that in order to be authentic to

ourselves, we must come to terms with the full existential signi-

ficance of our being-towards-death.   But, in a practical sense,

to what extent is this possible? Indeed, if it is possible, how

do we go about the task of realizing the full weight of the

ontological meaning of our finitude, in more than a merely

abstract, speculative way?

     Certainly the idea of the inevitability of one's own death

is intelligible. Our reason tells us that everything existing in

time has a beginning and an end; since I exist in time, I con-

clude that I too must some day die.   But this logical certainty

remains impersonal, and avoids Being-certain of the full existential weight of the phenomenon of death.1 As Max Scheler has so succinctly put it, "Mr. N. will die, because the Duke of Wellington and others died. We have 'taken note' of this in the form 'all men are mortal'. Are we to take it that death is an induction?"2

The task of comprehending the phenomenon of death in other than this very general, abstract way is, for some thinkers, impossible. Sigmund Freud concluded that in the final analysis, while we may accept the inevitability of death in principle, still "no-one really believes in his own death".3 Echoing these literary and psychoanalytical judgments, the phenomenologist Merleau-Ponty proposes that it is not possible for us to comprehend our death any more than it is possible for us to comprehend our birth, for otherwise, we would each have to be pre-existent to, or outliving ourselves in order to be able to experience these events; in such case, therefore, we would not be genuinely thinking of our birth or our death.4 Accordingly, I can apprehend myself "only as 'already born' and 'still alive' - I can apprehend my birth and death only as prepersonal horizons: I know

---

1   Cf. Heidegger, Martin, Sein und Zeit, p. 258, e.t. 302.

2   Scheler, Max, "Tod und Fortleben", in Schriften aus dem Nachlass, Vol. I, Berne, 1957, page 30.

3   Freud, Sigmund, "Thoughts on War and Death", in The Complete Psychological Works of Sigmund Freud, Vol. 14, London, 1957. p. 289.

4   Cf. Merleau-Ponty, M. Phenomenology of Perception, p. 216.

that people are born and die, but I cannot know my own birth and death."5   In the words of a character preparing to go before a firing squad in Sartre's short-story The Wall: "I see my corpse; that's not hard but I'm the one who sees it, with my eyes. I've got to think... think that I won't see anything anymore and the world will go on for others. We aren't made to think that, Pablo."6

While I can logically argue, then, to a conclusion of the inevitability of my own death, many authors believe that I cannot come to any fundamental awareness of my own death in order to accept it as a personal possibility.

There is a sense in which the foregoing conclusions have merit: the empirical certainty that others around me die is not really sufficient evidence to reveal to me the ontological necessity of my own mortality.   Moreover, echoing Epicurus, Merleau-Ponty is right that in an empirical sense of the word, we cannot "know" our death until we actually experience it.

However, it is important to recall that as phenomenologists, we are neither concerned with death as a general or abstract proposition about humanity, nor are we concerned with the event of death as it is seen to be an empirical matter of fact, or

---

5   Ibid, p.216.

6   Sartre, Jean-Paul, "The Wall", as quoted on p. 290 in Walter Kaufmann's Existentialism from Dostoevsky to Sartre, (The New American Library, Inc.: New York and Scarborough, Ontario. 1975). Emphasis mine.

"now-point" in time which I have yet to experience in order that it be meaningful for me. In the search for authenticity, it is not enough to think of oneself as a present-at-hand or ready-to-hand entity which must eventually die. "Being-certain in relation to death... does not belong at all to the graded order of the kinds of evidence we can have about the present-at-hand."7 A human being's own birth as his death are not just to be compared to the start and finish of an ob-jective state of being-alive; but this means then, that if I am to "know" death (Merleau-Ponty), it is not necessary that I know my death (or my birth for that matter) as an ob-jective moment in time.

In order that death as an ontic event have the deep and totally encompassing meaning which it does have to the terminally ill patient, for example, who is told that he has six months to live, as opposed to the metaphysician who speculates on gene-ralities, the phenomenologist will be seeking to describe not a quasi-rational formula, nor an empiricist's equally unimaginative suppositions. On the contrary, the phenomenologist will be seeking to describe the ontological significance which is revealed by an original, pre-reflective comprehension of the prospective ontic e-vent of death.

But the next question of course is: where do we begin to describe the personal significance and the various levels of

_____

7   Cf. Heidegger, M. Sein und Zeit, p. 265, e.t. 309.

meaning which this ontic event may have for each one of us? Is it a question of "knowing" this event of death (to use Merleau-Ponty's word), or of "believing" in it (Freud), or is it something else altogether? How do we begin to uncover the explicit and implicit ontological meanings revealed by the ontic phenomenon of death?

Heidegger has said that it is precisely when we flee death that we in fact unthematically acknowledge it to be ontologically meaningful to us. He has described extensively how we allow death to remain in the inconspicuousness of arbitrary, everyday explanations which help to conceal its true meaning.

But Heidegger has not described what is revealed about death when it acquires through special circumstances, a determinate meaning. He warns us that the "closest closeness which one may have in Being towards death as a possibility, is as far as possible from anything actual".8   But what we will describe in this section is not "the way one comports oneself when one 'thinks about death', pondering over when and how this possibility may perhaps be actualized".9

On the contrary, our task is to begin to uncover the ontological significance of death as it is revealed when we come face to face with our own mortality, through a determinate, ontic

---

8   SZ, 262, e.t. 306-7.

9   SZ 261, e.t. 305.

event whereby our very existence, and all that is meaningful to
us in our world, is at stake.

B.   A Pre-reflective Awareness of a Determinate Possibility: A Phenomenology of Imagination

If the ontic event of death is to be meaningful in other
than an empiricist or a rationalist sense - in short, if it is to
be ontologically meaningful - we must describe in more detail the
conditions of a pre-reflective, ontological awareness of the
phenomenon of my own death, when it is realized as a determinate
possibility.

Even though I have not yet experienced my own death, in what
sense, and under what circumstances, can the concrete possibility
of my death reveal to me, in the most fundamental and far-reaching
way, my own mortality?

The level at which each one of us is, to my mind, ontologically aware of our own death as a real possibility is on the
phenomenological level of the imagination.

But let us distinguish at this point a phenomenology of
imagination from an explanation of "imagination" as it may be
commonly understood.

First, a phenomenology of the imagination will not involve a
speculative imagining on an abstract level of intellectual game-
playing.

Second, a phenomenology of the imagination will not preclude the possibility of a genuine comprehension of an event which has not been previously experienced.

Let us deal with these two points, one at a time.

The Merriam Webster dictionary tells us that "imagine" means: to form a mental picture of; to picture to oneself; to fancy."   Thus, we may wish to engage in thought-games where we "imagine" what an alien creature from another planet may look like, or we "imagine" what our new house will look like when completed; or indeed, we "imagine" what it may be like to be dead or even terminally ill.   In these and similar cases, we "form a mental picture" of an idea, we re-present the idea of something before us, in order to define it by conceptualizing it into a manageable and ob-jective form.   When we imagine something by forming a "picture", then, as Heidegger explains, the human subjectivity becomes the authoritative ground and the sole arbiter of "objective" meaning. The primary purpose of the "picture" is that it exists to be seen-by-me; it is something which stands over and against me, in relation to me, and since it is only on account of me and my perception of the phenomenon that it is rendered meaningful, I, the subject, become the ground of the being of the image; I become the sole normative realm of this re-presentation (Vor-stellung).10   The process of "imagining" then, in this sense of the word, involves a setting-forth in front of oneself, a fanciful view (Bild) of some aspect of the world, and it is always a process under my own control. I may imagine an alien visitor's characteristics however I may wish, I may imagine life after death in whatever way I may wish, because ultimately, I am manipulating the images at my own will and discretion.

A second common interpretation posits that everything that we imagine can be traced back to specific experiences which ground each and every image. Thus, if I visualize a unicorn, I am able to do so only because I am able to combine in my imagi-nation my previous perception of a horse, for example, adding to it my vision of a single horn, resulting in the willfull con-struction of my fanciful image. In other words, such a theory postulates that I cannot imagine something whose individual, discreet elements are wholly absent from my past experience.

There is a sense in which it is true that I cannot imagine my death (or "life after death") without pro-jecting my under-standing of the world as I have experienced, or better still, -lived it to date. However, a phenomenology of the imagination, as it relates to death, will not involve simply a projection of

---

10   Cf. Heidegger, Martin, "Die Zeit des Weltbildes", page 82ff, in Holzwege, e.t. 129ff.

individual, discreet experiences; nor will it involve a formation of a "mental picture" of the state of being dead.

Gaston Bachelard provides us with particularly significant clues in this regard. In his Poetics of Space, he suggests that in order to "pave the way for a phenomenology of what is hidden, one preliminary remark will suffice: an empty drawer is unimaginable. It can only be thought of. And for us, who must describe what we imagine before what we know, what we dream before what we verify, all wardrobes are full."11

It is at the level of what we are before what we may verify by way of a "mental picture" or by way of previous experiences, that we possess an implicit understanding of our own mortality. Just as Bachelard points out how there is a spontaneous awareness of the meaning of the wardrobe, which always leads us to presume that the wardrobe is full, so too, it is our contention that on the phenomenological level of the imagination, we are aware of the existential significance of our mortality, even if we cannot rationally comprehend all of the implications of the ontic event of our death, or even if, technically speaking, we have yet to "experience" it.

Before we take this analogy of the wardrobe too far, however, let us consider some possible objections.

---

11   Bachelard, Gaston, The Poetics of Space, p. xxxiii-xxxiv.

One may wish to protest that this moment of imagining a wardrobe to be full, is a <u>learned</u> response to one's having opened so many wardrobes that one rationally must conclude that the purpose of a wardrobe is in fact, to contain something. Each individual ontic event of opening a wardrobe is, in other words, grounded in our past experience. Inasmuch as this is just a learned stimulus-response situation, then, we can go on from there to infer an analogy that the only meaning of the phenomenon of death for a terminally ill patient is the meaning which he <u>learns</u> from having seen other people die, or from "building a mental picture" of (re-presenting) the ultimate experience of his own death and dying process.

In response to this objection, we must point out that the phenomenologist is describing something other than socially-adapted behaviour. The particular, ontic event of opening a wardrobe, and expecting it to be full, is futurally grounded in a primordial meaning revealed in an <u>ontological anticipation</u>. To show how this is the case, let us take an image other than a wardrobe, which may have, after all some cultural connotations, and consider the more fundamental image of a door.

According to Bachelard, "man is half-open being".12 This is a truly exceptional phrase, fully capturing the meaningful pro-jection of the finite, human understanding. Thus when Bache-

---

12   Bachelard, Gaston, <u>Ibid</u>, p. 222.

lard continues to describe the door as "an entire cosmos of the Half-open", that image of the door is no longer a socially-acquired "picture" but rather, a lived image of the essence of Being human.

Projected in the concrete image of a door are moments of arrival and departing; of an open welcome to the world, and on the other hand, of a padlocked security from elements of that world; of temptation and desire; of respect and of return. These are not "pictures" which we superimpose on a concrete reality, but on the contrary, they are descriptions of moments which are revealed, and made meaningful through a determinate form.

We may ask ourselves, why is it that when we imagine the stairway to the cellar or the basement, always in this image, we ourselves are heading <u>down</u> the stairs; or when we envision the stair to the attic, always we see ourselves heading <u>up</u>? It is too simplistic to say that these images are the result of learned social behaviour.   Rather, they reveal a spontaneous awareness on our part, of directionality and meaning inherent in the staircase of our imagination.

Similarly, and even more primordially, in that wrenching moment when a patient becomes aware that his illness is terminal, the process of "imagining" his death involves much more than a superimposition of mental pictures; rather, one's whole way of being undergoes a fundamental transformation inasmuch as that whole way of being is now in question.

Before we take into consideration the special awareness of the terminally ill patient however, let us look instead at examples of a pre-reflective awareness of our vulnerability and mortality, as it appears to our imagination on a more "mundane" level.

Consider that I am driving along a very busy highway at the end of a long weekend, when all are tired from their long drives and anxious to get home. The traffic is stop-and-go, but eventually, it picks up and we are back to cruising at 100 kilometers per hour.

Suddenly, without warning, the driver in the car ahead of me hits his brakes.

My immediate response is to react to avoid mishap or catastrophe. Without hesitation, I lift my foot from the accelerator to move it towards the brake; but quite extraordinarily, the time that this small task takes to complete seems unbearable. As in a dream when one is trying to escape a danger, trying to run as quickly as one can while moving one's legs seems so impossibly slow, so too in these moments in the car, innumerable thoughts pass through one's mind in a time span which has the character of moving in a strange, slow motion. I know that I must hit that brake, I know that I must hit it quickly, it looks as if I will not make it, I will hit the car in front of me, the speed of my own vehicle cannot be controlled in time, and yet I try, I cannot give up trying to move my foot as quickly and efficiently as possible to slow my car down. All my concentration, my whole being is directed ahead of me, to my desperate _need_ to avoid catastrophe which is suddenly overtaking my world. I know nothing else now but my need to avoid the car in front of me, and finally, I press my brake down to the floor, I veer to the left into the shallow ditch at the side of the road, and I am safe.

Nevertheless, I am in shock. My limbs seem to be floating away from my body, the sense of alarm magnifies for a few moments as the impact of the incident continues to overwhelm me. I am shaking, I feel _suspended_ in a state of shock. Indeed, as my being-in-the-world, my existence has been threatened, I am in a state which feels almost like being in a state of "suspended animation": for a moment, the world is not a place wherein I orient myself, but on the contrary, I am _alone_ in my trembling sensation of standing on a threshold of existence which has not been under my control, but which has in a very real sense controlled me.

It takes more than a few minutes before I am back in control. Recovering from this incident, I feel relief at the knowledge that I am unhurt, as I feel anger at the driver responsible for this threatening moment. I feel that now I can orient myself in-the-world to the extent that I can begin to plan how to get back onto the road again, to continue my journey home.

Afterwards, I can rationalize the event, and I convince myself that my life was not really threatened, that only my car might have been badly damaged, and in fact, the episode will be seen to have been quite trivial as the daily flow of life continues on.

However, it remains quite unimportant for phenomenology whether or not one's life was <u>in fact</u> at stake. The critical nature of the moment of the accident was such that I imagined my personal survival to be in some sense in question. Indeed, the episode is fascinating for us, for a number of reasons.

It is significant that without ever stopping to contemplate the wider implications of the danger ahead of me, my immediate and spontaneous need (<u>Not</u>) was to do everything I could to avoid danger, to survive. This need to survive is not a need such as we describe in philosophy classes when we speculate about whether members of our society have a moral right to commit suicide freely; rather, it is the need which is felt by the suicidal person who has made a "rational" and deliberate decision that suicide is the only solution to his problems, but who, at the last moment, either cannot carry through his actions, or who performs them unsuccessfully. The ontic moments such as the one described above where I am about to be involved in a terrifying car accident, reveal a pre-reflective <u>need to Be</u>, need to survive, which defines my essence as an ek-sisting being-in-the-world.

On the other hand, this "need to survive" means also that I
possess an unthematic awareness of the fact that I may not
survive: in other words, while I may be taking this for granted,
nevertheless I am quite aware that I am not permanent. In short,
I am not atemporal, for my being is defined by time, which means
that I am in essence finite, and furthermore, vulnerable to
threats imposed on my existence by the outside world.   Were I
not pre-reflectively aware of the ever-present danger of death,
the ontological need to preserve life would not be there.

The disclosure of my vulnerability and finitude are by no
means made explicit to me at any particular moment, but they do
achieve a more concrete meaning through a determinate e-vent such
as the car accident described above. I do not ever calculatively
consider this moment when it happens, to explicitly realize that
death is nearer to me than it was a few moments ago, but
nevertheless, I am receptive, on the level of a transcendental
imaginative awareness, to the fact that I am losing control at
this moment over the course of my life.   Ahead of me is a
life-threatening danger in the form of an ontic event which did
not threaten me previously: I do not engage in fanciful imaginings
of "what it is like to be dead", but rather, recognizing the
implications of this e-vent, I immediately seek to avoid them,

actively engaging my whole being to the task of seeking a way of survival.13

Moroever, this encounter with the possibility of annihilation has left me in shock, in a state of what we have likened to a state of "suspended animation".   The shock abates shortly, after we realize that we are out of danger. Nevertheless, the shock experienced in the car accident provides a clue to understanding the somewhat similar, but much more far-reaching moment of shock experienced by a terminally ill patient when he is told that he has only a short time to live. We shall come back to this point later.

For now, let us explore some implications regarding the transcendental imagination, as it relates to two particularly significant moments described above: The sensation of time moving slower as in a dream, and the moment of shock, being

---

13   Cf. the writings of psychoanalyst, Gregory Zilboorg, who writes of how "such constant expenditure of psychological energy on the business of preserving life would be impossible if the fear of death were not as constant.   The very term 'self-preservation' implies an effort against some force of disintegration; the affective aspect of this is fear, fear of death... If this fear were as constantly conscious, we should be unable to function normally. It must be properly repressed to keep us living with any modicum of comfort. We know very well that to repress means more than to put away and to forget that which was put away and the place where we put it. It means also to maintain a constant psychological effort to keep the lid on, and inwardly never relax our watchfulness." (Zilboorg, G. "Fear of Death", _Psychoanalytical Quarterly_, 1943, 12; As cited in Becker, Ernest, _The Denial of Death_, pp. 16-17.)

suspended "in time", both point to the temporal roots of the transcendental imaginative activity.

If it is true that our most immediate "need to survive" reflects an indeterminate awareness on our part of our _imperma-nance_, then this phenomenon too, points to the temporal ground of an image which is not a rational, willful construction, but which appears through an immediate, receptive/spontaneous apprehension of our finitude.

Moreover, the temporal ground of the imaginative activity is confirmed when I experience the effect of "slow motion", or at least a "different movement" of time during strikingly critical moments in our lives. How is this confirmed, and why does time appear to "slow down"?

In his _Kantbuch_, Heidegger offers the following: the receptive character of pure intuition, itself rooted in the pure imagination, is commonly understood (by those inspired by empirical methods) as the act of receiving something given or actually present. The intuition of time, then, would mean no more than an intuition of a particular, discreet now-point or a series of now-points. However, Heidegger points out how in fact this cannot be the case, for if it were, the imagination could intuit an actual _now_ without the now-sequence and the _horizon_ which it forms, which is impossible:

"Strictly speaking, the simple act of receiving
something actually present could not even intuit a
single now, since each now has an essentially contin-
uous extension in a just passing and just coming
[Soeben und Sogleich]. The receptive act of pure intuition must in itself give the aspect of the now in such
a way that it looks ahead to the just coming and back
to the just passing."14

Heidegger then concludes that "we now discover, and in a more
concrete way, why it is that pure intuition, which is the subject
of the transcendental aesthetic, cannot be the reception of
'something present'".15   Rather, it points to the receptivity of
a transcendental notion of temporality which acts as the condition of the possibility of the revelation of any particular "now-
point". This has been shown already in some detail in Chapter
One of this volume.

However, our question to Heidegger is this: while it is
true that the imagination reveals the essential continuity of
"primordial time" as the horizon for a now-point in the present,
is it right to infer from this that primordial time is the "fundament", while so-called "now-points" are to be understood only
as inauthentic manifestations of the "actual present"? IS IT NOT
IN FACT THE CASE THAT A CRITICAL "NOW-POINT" IN THE FORM OF A
GATHERING-TOGETHER OF BEING, THAT IS, IN THE FORM OF A GENUINE
ONTIC E-VENT, REVEALS AND GATHERS RATHER THAN OBSTRUCTS THE TRUE
ESSENCE OF "PRIMORDIAL TIME"?

---

14   Heidegger, M. Kant and the Problem of Metaphysics, page 179.

15   Ibid.

This is precisely our contention. At a critical ontic moment (such as the car accident), our immediate apprehension of the fundamental significance of that moment forces the horizon of "just passing" and "just coming" [Soeben und Sogleich] to congeal around this e-vent. So time slows down for us, as all our futures and all our pasts gather around a moment which is a genuine existentiell "moment of truth"!

Even after the car accident, when I am in a mild state of "shock", recovering at the side of the road, when I feel "suspended", and my limbs are light - even then, my future and my past, beyond the concentrated limits of the present ontic event which I have just lived through, seem to bear little significance to me. The overwhelming power of the event not only disorients me in terms of my regular daily pattern of incidents, but it so concentrates all my pasts and all my futures into this present moment, that nothing else matters, all other daily occurrences lose their significance in the face of the overriding presence of this happening. My being is concentrated in this e-vent; in fact, it becomes so central that the meaning of all pasts and futures converges around the reality of this particular moment. It is almost as if I have no other significant pasts or futures, to the extent that I feel "suspended" in a world totally defined by the meaning and implications of this one discreet, and perhaps life-threatening event. It is not that I will this to be the case, but rather, it is something which overtakes me as only then

I seek to gradually recover from the impact of this happening, re-inserting it into a more regular and perhaps "well-balanced" temporal flow whereby it becomes no more than one interesting event among many others.

What critical moments like these reveal about the meaning of temporality must not be underestimated. It is true, as Heidegger has shown, that primordial temporality grounds the Being of the Da-sein as the condition of the possibility of any understanding of the world; but what our description above is showing is that there are not only two alternatives of understanding time either in an ontological sense of "primordial time", or on the other hand, in an inauthentic ontic sense of actual now-points. Rather, primordial temporality, as the condition of understanding, is seen to be "molded", so to speak, by specific, genuine ontic e-vents, which reveal Being through a concrete congealing in a full temporal presence.

Moreover, if this is indeed the case, then when a patient realizes that he is terminally ill, this moment of realization is much more than a now-point in time, and his death, now a determinate possibility, becomes much more than an imaginary "picture" of what it is going to be like to be dead. Such an e-vent, whereby one's entire existence comes into question, whereby the possibility of no-longer-being-at-all overtakes my whole way of understanding of the world, re-orients my pasts and my futures toward the full presence of a fundamental ontic revelation: I, as a historical being-in-the-world, will have no further history at all, beyond a determinate point which awaits me in the near future. As we shall see, time itself is re-defined in this instance. Primordial time is re-defined through the prism of an ontic e-vent.

C. My Own Death as a Determinate Possibility: Reflections on Terminal Illness

(i) My Own Death, against the backdrop of Being-there.

In order to more concretely explore how primordial time may be re-defined through the prism of an ontic e-vent, let us consider the case of a patient who is told one day, that he has a terminal illness. For the sake of argument, let us consider that he has from two to five years or more to live; in that case, the impending threat of death is not immediate (as with the example of the car accident), nor is it short-term, as it may be with the prisoner who is awaiting execution within a matter of days. Each of these moments of awareness of death is similar to one another, although the immediacy of the auto crisis concentrates certain reactions, and the prisoner awaiting execution has complicated emotional responses of anger and perhaps even violence, due to his special predicament.16

But first, let us recall some of our attitudes, which cha-racterize our everyday modes of being-in-the-world. In a sense, it is quite normal to deny the reality of death: here we are, secure in our past, presumably healthy at present, always pro-jecting ourselves toward a futural horizon of possibilities which appear, quite often, to be endless. We are told repeatedly, that the future is what we make it to be, it is our's to shape at will, if only we have enough faith and courage to work hard to realize our plans and our dreams.   On an even more fundamental level, though, we know from Heidegger that as Da-sein, as Being-there, we are defined ontologically as futural beings, as beings who are more than present-at-hand or ready-to-hand entities, but who are temporal ek-sistents, forging a future from out of the past, through the present, in an essential, existential participation in-the-world.17 Inasmuch as we are, we are as

---

16   Cf. Robert Johnson, Condemned to Die: Life under Sentence of Death, (NY: Elsevier North Holland Inc., 1981). On page 8 we read: "The adaptations of condemned prisoners are simi-lar to those employed by terminal patients and others exposed to life-threatening situations"; however, the book itself details many special examples of anger, fear, vulne-rability, and resentment arising out of the direct punitive implications of the prisoner's paying for an actual crime committed against society.

17   For a more extensive discussion of this point, see esp. Part One of this volume, Chapters One and Two.

temporal; indeed, inasmuch as we are, we are defined by the most primordial ecstasis: the future.

When it is said that each one of us "lives as though we were immortal", it is said scoldingly, and yet, it is normal and quite to be expected that we do live as though we would live forever. After all, for as long as we remember, we have existed; the fact of non-existence often comes as a very alien thought, and, as we have discussed above and as people like Freud have pointed out, it sometimes appears to be quite incomprehensible. I have "no time" to think of death: after all, I have reports to complete, deadlines to meet, people and places to see, and these pro-jects need, in the most fundamental ontological sense of the word, to be addressed in order that my life have meaning for me.

To be sure, most of us are aware that some day, in our very old age, we will be unable to work as hard, be as strong, live as actively as we do today. But then, we hope that poor health will not come for a very, very long time; we believe that we will be capable of living the same way as today, until some indeterminate time in the future when perhaps, we will be forced to slow down. Because of the indeterminacy of the future, we commonly tend to feel that for now, we can do nothing about such unpleasant possibilities, and therefore, there is little point in brooding about them. Instead, it is only normal to have faith in our good health, in our capabilities and in our much more immediate concerns which shape our lives from day to day.

It is against the backdrop of this unquestioning acceptance of life as a continual, neverending process - and indeed, more importantly, it is against the backdrop of the fundamental, existential constitution of a Being-there which is defined in terms of its futural pro-jections - that I ask the reader to enter into the situation of a person who one day is advised by a physician, that his future is limited, that the indeterminate, neverending temporal process which he has always known as his life, his existence, now has a determinate end in view.

It seems to me to be too easy to speculate how brave we might be in the face of such news -- but can we know for sure?

The point at which one realizes that one has a terminal illness need not come when a physician simply puts the truth in so many words. There are numerous accounts available in the literature on death and dying, of different ways of coming to the full realization of the truth of the illness.   Doctors and psychologists seem to be in agreement that those who suffer most in coming to terms with their illness, are those who are advised in a very sudden, cruel, and unfeeling fashion of the seriousness of their health problem.   These same experts agree that most patients eventually are well aware of the seriousness of their illness, whether or not they are explicitly so advised.

Consider the patient who presumably has already undergone a series of medical tests to determine the seriousness of a problem which was the initial cause of the visit to the physician.   The most difficult part of this wait for the results of the tests, is "not knowing": the patient has recognized a mysterious lump on her body, and does not yet know whether it is malignant or benign.

What are some of the implications of this "wait"?

First of all, the now determinate possibility of death is suddenly before me. It is not only fear of specifics such as the pain associated with illness, the threat of loneliness, the discomfort of more medical tests, the horror of spending more and more time in inhumane hospital environments, the all-embracing worry over family members who must share my difficult existence, which now stand as very real possibilities of my future. Terrifying though these specific fears are, there is also an unnamed horror accompanying these fears. My entire being-in-the-world is now threatened as never before, as I peer over the threshold of a new existence, modified by its being pierced through and through with the now determinate possibility of my non-existence too.

It is interesting to note how "outwardly", one may try to fit in to the ordinary, day-to-day progression of events which continue as before. There are different levels at which one moves in order to re-orient oneself in a world which "outwardly" has not changed much, although "inwardly", has undergone a fundamental transformation.

On the one hand, one may "objectify" one's condition, to try to see it as others see it. One has a certain amount of "time left" to live; one can expect certain treatments and health conditions; one can expect specific reactions from friends and relatives, and in expectation of these reactions, one will choose a certain mode of behaviour in order to accommodate and cope with these expectations.

These are all "things" which must be considered by the dying patient. Needless to say, they are hardly inconsequential; while on first reading of Heidegger, such "things" may appear to be incidental considerations, even on an inauthentic, "erring" level, nevertheless they form a part of the terminal patient's genuine ontic need18 to order one's plans and to operate on a realistic social basis from day to day.

But on another pre-reflective level, a torrent of emotions and sensibilities are modifying one's way of being-in-the-world within the determinate amount of time which now defines the future.

Let us consider these sensibilities in more detail, in order to further consider the implications of the meaning of death as an ontic event, and as revelatory of the ontological difference.

---

18 George Ghanotakis and Thomas Langan of the University of Toronto have pointed to the significance within the Heideggerean ontic terminology, of the notion of "genuine". As ontologically speaking, Dasein can be authentic or inauthentic, different ontic realities allow for a genuine (echt) or ingenuine (unecht) awareness. We shall return to this consideration in the final chapters of this book.

(ii) Some Patterns of a Terminal Illness:

The shock which may come either through the implicit, pre-reflective awareness of one's terminal illness or through an explicit announcement of the seriousness of the health problem, is unique. In previous sections, I touched on the notion of shock in the near-car accident, and described it as a sense of suspended animation. Let us look at this more closely.

There is a huge difference between the shock which I describe here, and other similar states of surprise, stupefaction, or even fear.

The moment of shock experienced in the realization of one's imminent death is not posed by a particular threat of one thing or another; it is grounded in an all-embracing nullity which rises up from the core of my being, to overtake all possibilities in my world. The all-pervasiveness of its presence leaves me suspended in a vacuum, panic-stricken, as the regular guideposts of my life disappear. "My mind has been going 200 miles an hour", a terminal patient reports. "When you are close to knowing you are going to die, even a glass of water is very meaningful. I always want to remember how it felt. I am trying to understand why we die. Trying to get used to the idea and accept it."[19] As the significance of my future reaches back into the fullness of this moment of awareness, as my past surges up to be

---

19   Report from the August 12, 1985 issue of _Time_ magazine, p. 44

gathered in the intensity of the present, I am alone in the horror of my eventual no-longer-being-I.

The sense of being suspended in a vaccuum through the heaviness of despair of the moment, is quite real: all my futures and all pasts seem to congeal and then drain through a vacuum whereby all my familiar points of spatio-temporal orientation disappear. I truly am suspended in an unfamiliar, "unheimlich" abyss as my total way of being-in-the-world is brought to issue.

On the other hand, almost immediately in parallel with the shock comes disbelief and denial, a refusal to admit the moment of death into one's life. Elisabeth Kübler-Ross identifies five stages through which a terminally ill patient normally passes:

1. Denial and Isolation

2. Anger

3. Bargaining

4. Depression

5. Acceptance.

While many critics infer from Kübler-Ross's writings that every terminally ill patient must necessarily progress through each one of these stages in a unidirectional movement, this is not her point. Rather, she and her colleagues have identified these basic emotions as common to many patients, and her descriptions of these stages assist the reader in understanding and empathizing with both the patient's special needs, and the more compassionate attitudes which might be projected by the doctor and those "significant others" who interact with the terminally ill person.

Rather than progress unidirectionally through these stages, the terminally ill patient hovers between them, moving from one situation to another, from one need to another, gradually attempting to come to terms with the implications of his illness.

The important point to me seems to be that from the moment the terminal patient comes to an awareness of the determinate nature of his death, his life alters: the peculiar demands of the ontic e-vent which now changes the colour of his life forces a total re-orientation within a temporal life-span which is now delimited. ONE'S PERCEPTION OF TIME NOW CHANGES FUNDAMENTALLY. Again, one vascillates between authentic and inauthentic perceptions and awareness, but the new ontic moment changes everything.

Shock as more than a mental state:

The moment of shock, the sense of "suspended animation" within a void, is a state of being "in-between" the "ever-more" and the "never-more"; one hangs suspended alone in a state of being "in-between" one's previous perception of life as stretching into a never-ending future, and a realization of the full meaning of one's finitude. In a sense, time "stops", that is, it is fully concentrated in the moment of truth wherein one's life as one knows it, is completely and totally to be re-oriented around a determinate e-vent which, while not empirically here, fully captures my imagination and my total way of being-in-the-world.

Not everyone experiences such shock; but for those who do experience the anguish of realizing the full implications of their illness, the meaning of their lives, past and future, must change irrevocably.

Take the recent case of the U.S. Senator who is told he has 8 years to live. He realizes that he has missed being with his 7 and 11 year-old daughters when they were young, and decides to leave his work in order to spend time at home with his 2-year old daughter for as long as he can. Re-assessing his past, he realizes that he has allowed significant moments to pass him by; re-assessing his future, he determines not to allow such moments to escape him in the "time he has left".

This reaction is understandable. It is also a reaction which one will not normally have, unless one faces the now-deter-minate possibility of one's end. The full weight of one's fini-tude shatters against the everyday routines which up to now, have provided a sense of security, a sense of normality. As one patient put it, "When I heard [the truth], I went all to pieces... Emotionally... I always thought that I couldn't have anything like that...".20

This sense of "shock" is not merely a "mental" state; to confine the phenomenon to a psychological explanation, is to lose sight of the full existential weight of the moment. Heidegger and Sartre talk about the state of Angst as anguish before myself, as opposed to fear about something present-at-hand or ready-to-hand. The "shock" which overwhelms one in the realization of his imminent death, seems to me to be one of the most concrete manifestations of man's anxious encounter with the nothingness of his existence. It is a state of being suspended in the "between", in a void, to the extent that all my traditional orientational signposts disappear for the moment, as I seek to take in the full meaning of the e-ventful possibility of my no-longer-being-I. The lightness of limbs described previously in the "shock" of the near auto-accident, is a physical manifestation of an existential awareness that the "old rules of life", are suspended, they no longer apply, as my whole way of Being-in-the-world, especially in terms of a presupposed never-ending future, is brought into question.

How does "time stop" in such moments of shock? On the one hand, the regular progression of everyday occurrences becomes completely irrelevant, the outside world becomes remote and quite

---

20   Report from Kübler-Ross, Elisabeth, On Death and Dying, p. 186.

inconsequential;21 on the other hand, the mind races within itself (remember the patient who confessed that his mind was going "200 miles an hour"), trying to comprehend the full weight of truth, trying to understand, yet also denying the absurdity of the possibility that one day soon, I and my world as I know it will no longer be. Suspended in the "between", this moment of shock is quite unique in its temporal manifestation. One feels as if he is thrown beyond control, into a new realm of meaning and import. It is something which, much as one tries, cannot be analyzed at all: it is not question of analysis. In that sense, it is much more than a "mental state": Time and the Self are entirely modified "in between" the world which was, prior to this moment, and the world which is now delimited, finite, and concretely defined.

Denial and Isolation:

The shock described above, does not remain for long, without moments of sheer denial. Kübler-Ross reports that "among the over two hundred dying patients we have interviewed, most reacted

---

21   Something similar is felt also in the process of mourning the loss of the Other to whom one is related in authentic solicitude. C.S. Lewis describes how "...it feels like being mildly drunk, or concussed. There is a sort of invisible blanket between the world and me. I find it hard to take in what anyone says. Or perhaps, hard to want to take it in. It is so uninteresting...". (From A Grief Observed, p.7). We shall return to the description of mourning the death of another in forthcoming chapters.

to the awareness of a terminal illness at first with the statement, 'No, not me, it cannot be true'".22

The phase of denial is not one which, it seems, a patient
ever leaves completely behind. Again, it is not a question of a
"mental" state which interests us, because the denial has
ontological, rather than psychological roots.

One must realize that the terminal patient is presented with
a fact: knowing quite specifically how much longer he has to
live, he is aware concretely now that his existence is finite.

Let us consider the implications of this for a moment; it is
not as simplistic as, at first, it sounds. We are telling the
terminal patient that there will be no future for him in, say,
five years. There is something quite unreal about this; one
reasons: "as long as I have understood anything in the world, I
have existed. My being is defined by temporality. You are telling me that I will have no future, you are asking me to
understand this fact, but that is impossible, for as long as I
have understood anything in the world, there has always been a
future. If there is no future, then there is no time, there is

_____

22   Kübler-Ross, Elisabeth, On Death and Dying, p. 38. Kübler-
      Ross describes extensively, the amazing lengths to which
      patients went to deny their illness to themselves, and to
      others -- including "shopping around" from doctor to doctor,
      seeking reassurance that their illness was, in fact, not
      terminal.

no self, my essence is destroyed, there is no meaning -how can
something meaningless be underderstood?"

Heidegger refers to death as the "strange and alien [un-
heimlich] thing that banishes us once and for all from everything
in which we are at home..."23 The stage of denial is not just a
stubborn refusal on man's part to accept a simple "fact of life."
Dasein is as being-there; Dasein ek-sists within   a futural
horizon of possibilities which define his essence. Now this
"strange and alien" reality of one's end, as an ontic e-vent, is
revealed, and the fundamental absurdity of death as it now enters
the imagination, is impossible to grasp.

Certainly, death defines us in our finitude, and, in the
abstract, we know that such finitude defines us in our essence.
Nevertheless, on the other hand, there is a very strong sense in
which Simone de Beauvoir is quite right when she says that "our
death is inside us, but not like the stone in the fruit, like the
meaning of our life; inside us, but a stranger to us, an enemy, a
thing of fear".24

Inasmuch as I am, I am. This is not a mere tautology. It
points to the origin of being-human, of Da-sein, and of the truth
of my existential roots in the ecstases of past, present and
future. It is offensive, and even perverse to suggest to me that

---

23   EM 121, e.t. 133.

24   Simone de Beauvoir, The Force of Circumstance, cited in
      Elaine Marks' Simone de Beauvoir: Encounters with Death, p. 8!

this "strange and alien" thing called "death" will end everthing for me, in my world, in such a way that I will no longer be. It is incomprehensible, from this perspective, and totally unacceptable to the terminal patient, who therefore must choose to provisionally deny the reality of the e-vent, in order to re-orient himself in what amounts to no less than a new and funda-mentally different way of being-in-the-world.

There are many different levels of denial. On a basic level, one is not simply choosing to refuse to come to terms, intellectually, with the fact of death. The psychologist will love to point out how a patient may be denying the extent of his illness "outwardly", although "inwardly", he is aware of the seriousness of his ill health, and this is supposed to be particularly discerning on the psychologist's part. But the sort of denial which we are trying to come to terms with, on the ontological level, is part of an encounter with what Marcel will have called the "mysterious" (as opposed to "problematic") aspect of death, and that mystery, as it overtakes my whole way of being-in-the-world, can only appear, at this moment, quite simply, as no less than the most outrageous offense.

We have said that the denial operates on many different levels: one anxiously faces the absurdity, the outrage of one's death, and, in another moment of Being-with, one may decide that those who are closest to one, must not suffer the emptiness and the unheimlich irruption and assault of the full weight of this ontic, e-ventful possibility which now presents itself. Therefore, one moves to protect those whom one loves, by "denying" one's death on a more intentional level. As Betty Leal, a Hospice volunteer in Windsor, Canada, reports:

> "There's no doubt that a patient will tell much more to one of us than to their own family. A lady told me one night, 'I'm not going to make it. My family thinks I will, or at least, they're pretending. I wish they could just accept that I'm going to die and we could drop all the pretense.' I suggested that she tell her family exactly that, but she said 'oh no, I couldn't hurt them like that'".25

The ontic fact that one isolates oneself from those whom one loves in order to protect them, often serves to reflect the ontological truth of the individuation of each Dasein who must face his own death on his own. One is reminded of the Eskimo society, where it is accepted that the old and the sick must isolate themselves, and prepare for their deaths alone. On the other hand, this is also the moment for a genuine sharing of one's grief, with those who are close. As a nurse from the same Hospice reflects, "You'll see families stiffen themselves up to go into a patient's room. They think the worst thing they can do is cry. They ask us, 'What if I break down?' Usually, of course, that's exactly what they should do, exactly what the patient needs."26

---

25   As reported in The Globe and Mail (Toronto, Canada), September 15, 1984, page 10, story by Bryan Johnson, entitled "Helping the Dying to Live".

26   Ibid.

Another story was related to me by a health care consultant, Margaret Church, who worked with dying children and their families in the Sick Children's Hospital in Toronto. A five year old boy, dying of a brain tumour, drew a picture which consisted of an array of open-ended circles, and a straight line at the bottom of the page. Asked to "guess what the picture was of", the health care consultant pondered for awhile. Concluding that his brain surgery was perhaps being symbolized by the open-ended circles, she eventually answered: "Could it be a picture of you?" The boy was immensely pleased, and responded positively.

As the conversation evolved, however, the meaning on the page became even more significant. "If I had so many eyes as you have drawn on the page", Miss Church continued, "I could see around the corner of the room, down the hall, across the street, and all the way to your home to your mother, your father, your brothers and sisters." She paused. "You seem really sad today. Would you like to talk about it?" The five-year old was brought to a privileged admission. "I wish my mom and dad wouldn't cry every time they come to see me because I won't be here very long. I'm dying, you know". He continued: "I wish they could just be happy for the time we have left."

Children can be most perceptive: this child had been in a state of reverse isolation; his immune system was so destroyed by the medications, that anyone entering his room had been required to wear a protective mask. Perhaps this is why his parents' sad eyes were so much more meaningful to him than they otherwise might have been. In any case, the picture revealed how this child required a genuine, open relationship which, no doubt, he had previously had with parents and friends, but which had suffered some grave disruption in the course of the family's having had to cope with the reality of his illness.

According to Margaret Church, the amount of energy required by both the terminal patient and those to whom he relates, to mask true feelings is enormous; and indeed, once true feelings are carefully revealed, a final time of relaxation and peacefulness may be possible. We shall return to the significance of solicitude in the next chapters, particularly as it relates to the death of the Other; and while it is not within the scope of this volume to analyze the relation of Being-with in its many nuances, suffice it to say that the significant-other in one's life plays a very large part in the process of coping psychologically with the meaning of one's terminal illness. Whether one is protecting the Other from the difficulties encountered through the phenomenon of death; or whether one is concerned with how they will survive him with the least possible grief and damage to their lives, the phenomenon of Being-with grounds many a moment in the process of dealing with the ontic, e-ventual possibility of one's own death. As Marcuse points out, men can only die without anxiety "if they know that what they love is protected from misery and oblivion."27 In the next chapter, we shall consider how one copes with the death of the Other to whom one is related in authentic solicitude; it is worth noting that at times, the dying patient has to cope with the solicitous relation in his own way, perhaps being all the more strong in his search to remain honest and open with those whom he loves.

There are many psychological realities which find expression in sentiments such as denial, anger or fear of the unknown; these are described at length and in vivid detail by authors like Kübler-Ross, Edwin Shneidman and others. It seems to me, however, that these sentiments are each rooted in a more fundamental, ontological need to be. This need itself is grounded in the unity apperceived in the horizontal and exstatic figure of temporality, particularly as pro-jected toward the future. Needless to say, this "need to be" is not a mere "mental state", which can be "seen from different angles", and thus surpassed. It is part of the very constitution of Da-sein, Being-there, (rather than no-where, which is the vision of many vis-a-vis their own deaths). To that extent, it grounds sentiments such as anger and fear, which express themselves outwardly against the world, against others, against the horror of possibilities unknown.

---

27   Marcuse, H. Eros and Civilization, (New York: Random House, 1962.) p. 216.

On the Road to "Acceptance"

Kübler-Ross identifies two kinds of depression which set in for the terminally ill patient. The first is what she calls a "reactive depression"; the second is a "preparatory depression".

Whether the psychologists are correct to identify depression as repressed anger, it does seem that the first sort of "reactive" depression is related to the loss of control over one's life and the sense that the changes taking place to one's body leading one toward death, are leading to a loss of a great many things in life, from moments with loved ones, to one's health, to the ability to carry on one's work as before, and so on. Apparently, a useful approach to dealing with this first type of "reactive" depression is an encouraging attitude to "look at the bright side of life, at all the colourful, positive things around them... It will help a mother to know that the children.. continue to laugh and joke..., that they function in spite of mother's absence."28

With the second type of "preparatory" depression, such encouragement and reassurances to look at the "sunny side of life" are not as significant or useful. According to Kübler-Ross, if the patient is allowed to express his sorrow, and share his thoughts with someone who is not constantly telling him not to be sad, then this sort of depression may be the start along

---

28   Kübler-Ross, Elisabeth, On Death and Dying, p. 87.

the road to what Kübler-Ross and many others have referred to as a stage of "Acceptance".

With the state of depression, I believe that the terminal patient becomes less angry with his state, less denying its absurd intrusion into his life, and more (particularly in the "preparatory" phase) aware that this intrusion is, in some sense, beyond his control, and he has no choice but to submit to it. This, of course, is depressing, both in a "reactionary" as well as "preparatory" phase. Nevertheless, it is a start to a way of thinking which begins to accept that I am indeed thrown into this life, I cannot simply will my state-of-being to be different, because the grace of existence is a gift, something which I neither created myself, nor can ultimately and completely control.

Another moment in this phase of such awareness that I am not totally in charge but am beholden to something beyond my subjectivity, comes in the stage identified by Kübler-Ross and her followers, as a stage of "Bargaining". "If God has decided to take us from this earth and he did not respond to my angry pleas, he may be more favourable if I ask nicely".29   The termi-nally ill patient subconsciously believes that perhaps he may be "rewarded for good behaviour", like the child who finds it impossible to get what he wants through temper tantrums, and then appeals to the parent's conscience by promising to be good and in

---

29   Ibid, p. 82.

fact performing helpful tasks, in the hope that the parent's decision will thereby be reversed in his favour. Whether it is someone (for example, in the person of God), or something ("fate"?) with whom or with which one endeavours to bargain, the same sense that one is beholden to a force greater than one's own ego, encourages the pre-reflective awareness of the facticity of one's existence, encourages the awareness that we are obliged to submit to certain givens of our existential Situation, which are beyond our willful control.

The number of patients who actually acquire a peaceful Acceptance of death are very few. Martha Heath, a nurse at the Windsor Hospice in Canada, reports that "Not all patients or families reach acceptance. Not by any stretch of the imagination. Denial, anger... a lot of that lingers right to the end. The percentage of those who don't accept it is probably higher than those who do. Probably, its quite a bit higher..."30

But what is really meant by this word "Acceptance"? The Chief Psychiatrist at a major hospital for terminal cancer patients in Toronto, told me that in his view, no-one ever truly "accepts" one's own death; it would be abnormal to do so, in his view. Indeed, his contention was that Kübler-Ross and others were misleading the public in encouraging a belief in the notion of "acceptance" at all; at best, he suggested, one was able, in

---

30   Quoted by Bryan Johnson, "Helping the Dying to Live", The Globe and Mail, 15 September, 1984, p. 10.

the final   analysis,   only   to <u>submit</u> to death, but never "accept"
it.

At first, I took this   psychiatrist's   view   at   face value,
believing that   he must   be right, but now I think otherwise.   To
understand why, let us look at what is involved in this notion of
"acceptance".

There is   a very   big difference in meaning between "submission" and   "acceptance".   "Submission"   suggests   surrender, and
giving up,   resignation, and   it has a passive, defeatist ring to
it.   "I   submit to   your authority"   signifies that   I am backing
down for   the time   being, I   am subjecting myself to your authority, although if I really had a choice, I would do otherwise.

I am sure that, in fact, many do   "submit" to   death in this
way.   Particularly when physical strength wanes, one biologically
speaking, almost has no choice but to "give up", but   this is not
what   Kübler-Ross   means   by   "acceptance",   and it is not what I
believe to   be the   core of   the meaning   of authentic acceptance
either.   Nor   can such   "submission" in the face of death be seen
as identical to, or a proper   substitute for   the authentic sense
of acceptance   which becomes much more of a moral and ontological
(as opposed to biological) challenge.

"Accepting", as opposed to   "submitting" to   death, may also
imply   compliance,   a   non-resistance   and   subservience to one's
fate, but "acceptance" also means much more.

To digress for a moment, consider the nature of "duty" or "obligation" to an authority. If I feel that I must complete a task, that I am obligated to do so, and the nature of my obligation is such that I feel _forced_ to do so, I resent that obligation. I may complete the task begrudgingly, but never as well as when I recognize my duty and _freely accept it_ as something which must be done, since no-one else can do it for me, and which is therefore made _mine_, so that I must complete it in the best possible way that is within my own capability. I feel encouraged, I feel motivated to complete my duty as best as I can, not because I feel forced or _pushed_ to do so, but because I feel motivated and _pulled_ to strive to achieve my moral purpose. In this case, it may appear that I am "submitting" to my duty, but in actual fact, more than submitting to it, I am actively engaging myself in my task, freely accepting it as through it, my existence becomes all the more meaningful to me.

Similarly, "accepting" death means more than submitting to it, giving up. It is not a passive moment, to which I subject myself. While I may yield to death, while I may be humble in the face of the grace of my existence which now must be taken from me, there is nevertheless a challenge in the notion of "acceptance" which suggests a free and active participation in the necessity (_Not_) of the ontic fact of death. How is this so?

We remember the hero, Socrates, who went so far as to _welcome_ death as a release of the soul from the body, as a means to achieving pure and unfettered contemplation of eternal forms. Here, we must be careful too. To welcome death: does that lead to an argument for suicide? By no means! On the contrary, such "welcoming" acceptance does not imply ever, a willful manipulation of death. "Freedom" here does not mean the same as "license" to do whatever one wishes. Rather, the challenge to actively accept one's death is a challenge to stand before the e-vent of no-longer-being, to find meaning in this e-vent, to step outside of one's egotistic, manipulative subjectivity and come to peace with the grace of Being itself.

Nietzsche speaks of "free death". I used to find this very strange, but it is not so strange at all. He writes of the hateful death, the "grinning death, which creeps up like a thief-and yet comes as the master."31 The death to which I submit, brings no peace.

But the death which comes at the right time? Nietzsche writes: "My death, I praise to you, the free death which comes to me because I want it... Free to die and free in death, able to say a holy No when the time for Yes has passed: thus he knows how to die and to live."32

I am not suggesting an exclusively Nietzschean interpretation of "acceptance", but his writings do serve to elicit the

31   Cited in Kaufmann, Walter, Existentialism: From Dostoevsky to Sartre, p. 108.

32   Ibid, p. 108-9.

sense of learning, in his words, "to practice the difficult art
of leaving at the right time".

There are many practical factors which will serve to allow
me to come to peace with my death, to accept it, to "leave at the
right time". Kübler-Ross describes these at some length,
suggesting that sometimes, a patient may wish to complete a
project at work, a final operetta, a report, a special task. He
may wish to ensure that those whom he leaves behind are well
taken care of; he may wish to find religious peace through a
minister; he may wish to be assured that he is not dying in vain,
that his being has some continuity through his work, his children,
his friends. Perhaps one may never really ever be _finished_ with
these things completely, but if one is able to achieve a sense
that people and things which are important to him will carry on
sufficiently well without him, that will bring a great sense of
repose and a peace of soul, preparatory to this final phase of
"acceptance". Once again, to quote Nietzsche, "Verily,
Zarathustra had a goal; he threw his ball: now you, my friends,
are the heirs of my goal; to you I throw my golden ball. More
than anything, I like to see you, my friends, throwing the golden
ball. And so I still linger a little on the earth; forgive me
for that. -Thus spoke Zarathustra."33

-----

33   _Ibid_, p. 109.

Kübler-Ross cautions that this phase of acceptance must not be mistaken for a happy stage; it must also not be misconstrued as a stage which can be <u>willed</u>, which can be forced in any way. The peace which may come when one puts oneself in the hands of God, or fate, or best, in the shelter of Being itself, can never be a product of wilfull, subjectivistic manipulation.   As the "final rest before the long journey",34 acceptance has its origin in the depths of meaning revealed by a grace of Being which ultimately protects, gathering the Fourfold, the earth, the sky, the divinities, and the mortals, in an in-finite relation wherein truth is   illuminated, and a serenity is achieved in the fulfillment of one's own, individual finite essence.

(iii)   Some Implications regarding the analysis:

Denial, anger, isolation and some forms of "reactive" dep-ression seem to me to be rooted in Da-sein's need to ek-sist, and in his reaction to the truth of the now determinate possibility of no-longer-being-at-all.

As we have seen, the roots of denial are found in the funda-mental, existential pro-ject of man, which pro-ject is essenti-ally directed toward a future which is-not-yet. The fact which death presents to my imagination, that some day soon, I will have no future, goes against the essence of being-human as a being-

---

34   A patient's remark, quoted by Elisabeth Kübler-Ross, <u>op.-</u>
<u>cit.</u>, p. 113.

there, and in this sense, it is not unusual that Dasein will deny (not just inauthentically) the "unüberholbarkeit" of his death.

Similarly, anger, isolation, fear and some sorts of depression are essential human reactions to the affront of death, as it projects an end to my future as I have always known and expected it to be.

In all of these cases, death is an outrage, an affront to my being-in-the-world, it is an indignity and an injury to my Self, and to the temporal structure of my ek-sistence as I have understood it up until now.

It is an affront upon the Da of my Self as a Da-sein; it is an affront upon the transcendental individuation which is my essence, and which I am now to try and understand is not-to-be after a certain determinate point in time; it is an affront to the temporal horizons which have defined my way of being-in-the-world until now.

This one side of death as an offense, as an absurd intrusion into my regular patterns and ways of being-in-the-world, finding expression in these emotions of denial, anger and so on, can be distinguished from the ground of the second series of emotions, such as preparatory depression, bargaining and final acceptance. In the case of these latter sensibilities, the limits of my individuation, the affront upon me as a Self, fade in the light of a releasement, and a final peace to be found in the shelter of Being itself.

In other words, as one vascillates between the first group of emotions (denial, anger, isolation, fear, and perhaps reactive depression) and the second group of emotions (preparatory depression, bargaining, and acceptance), what we see at play is the need of human individuation in the first place, rooted in temporal ecstases of past, present and future, rooted in my world among things; and in the second place, the grace of Being as it is illuminated within the ontic moment. In short, what one sees is the Ontological Difference at play within the ontic e-vent itself.

Heidegger has told us that the Difference is a "dimension", not in the sense of a "precinct already present independently in which this or that comes to settle", but rather, as "the dimension, insofar as it measures out, apportions, world and thing, each to its own."35   On the basis of our analysis of terminal illness, it is wrong to conclude that the ontological grounds the ontic in the sense of an abstract dimension which "meaures out" ontic values, however. On the contrary, while It-gives Being, It-gives Time, while Being hides itself, yet it "whiles" in a determinate way [Jeweiligkeit], and moreover, the determinate e-vent "makes room" and opens the way for an always unique and privileged moment of ontological revelation.

---

35   US 25, e.t. 203.

Indeed, if the essence of primordial Time is to be more than a mere abstraction, then it makes sense to speak of a circling of the ontological and the ontic. In our case, the ontic e-vent of death concentrates all my pasts, my present and my future into new horizons of meaning. Time itself, as revealed to the transcendental imagination, changes in significance. The primordiality of Time against the backdrop of a concentrated ontic e-vent, may change the essence of the revelation of primordial Time itself.

In short, the emotions described by the psychologist are hardly incidental; from the stages of denial, anger, fear, isolation, to depression, bargaining and final acceptance (if that stage is reached), these emotions but reflect the struggle of man to come to terms with Being: they reveal the Ontological Difference as it is manifested within the prism of an ontic event.

In the following sections, we shall see how temporality defines the relation of authentic solicitude, and how that temporal essence defines further another kind of ontic e-vent: the death of the Other to whom I am related in authentic solicitude.

**

CHAPTER TWO

THE DEATH OF THE OTHER

A. Solicitude: condition of the possibility of an ontological
    awareness of the ontic e-vent of the death of the Other

(i) A Heideggerean perspective:

What, if anything, can Heidegger teach us about the possibi-

lity of true understanding, love, and authentic solicitude?

Several commentators have claimed that there is simply no

real place for authentic solicitude in the Heideggerean enter-

prise.   L. Binswanger, F.H. Heineman, P. Fürstenau, Karl Löwith

and L. Versenyi1 have each expressed varying degrees of uneasi-

ness with Heidegger's treatment of the practical aspects of

inter-personal relations, and even a devotee like Otto Pöggeler

has remarked how "it is, of course, beyond doubt that Heidegger's

enquiry into social being (Gemeinschaft) is among the most unsa-

tisfying aspects of his work."2

Other critics have been more harsh in their expressions of

dissatisfaction. In his review of the English translation of

---

1   Cf. L. Binswanger, Grundformen und Erkenntnis menschlichen
     Daseins, 2te. Aufl., (Zurich, 1953); F.H. Heineman, Exis-
     tentialism and the Modern Predicament, (New York 1953);
     P. Fürstenau, Heidegger: das Gefüge seines Denkens (Frank-
     furt-am-Main, 1958); K. Löwith, Heidegger: Denker in dürfti-
     ger Zeit, (Frankfurt-am-Main, 1953); and L. Versenyi, Hei-
     degger, Being and Truth, (New Haven, 1965).

2   Pöggeler, Otto, Der Denkweg Martin Heideggers (Pfüllingen,
     1963), p. 307, n.32.

<u>Sein und Zet</u>, William Hordern suggests3 that it is only as the ominous "they" that other persons enter Heidegger's analysis; that authentic Dasein so fills the center of its world that it leaves no room for love; and that consequently, there is no room for any true concern for other men, nor any conception of true community. Therefore, we should not be surprised, he concludes, that Heidegger was as attracted as he was to Nazism and dictatorship, when his own description of authentic Dasein was of a being so "curved in on himself".

A similar statement is put forth by Renèe Weber, who writes of how Heidegger "exiles his entity 'Dasein' to an inhuman, egoistic vacuum, where it is condemned forever to turn it upon itself".4 Like Hordern, Weber expresses a concern as to whether it is "merely ironical that the only time Heidegger sought social and political application of his own system to the daily world where men live, love, and fear death was when he gave it as part of the philosophical foundation to National Socialism?"5

W.B. Macomber is another who remarks how "unfortunate" it is that "Heidegger tends to portray all communal or social exis-tence, all being in the presence of Others... as characterized by

---

3   in <u>Christian Century</u>, December 5, 1962.

4   Weber, R., "A Critique of Heidegger's Concept of Solici-tude", in <u>New Scholasticism</u>, Vol. 42, Fall 1968, p. 559.

5   <u>Ibid</u>, p. 560.

impersonal One... Unless the individual decides, no-one decides;"6 Macomber allows that this "deficiency" stems from the inadequate analysis of Dasein's initial encounter with others, although he then seems to want to explain away this deficiency as "probably" representing "the intrusion of Heidegger's existential commitment into his phenomenological analysis".7

Jean-Paul Sartre expresses similar doubts about the possibility of discovering in Heidegger any sound basis for an understanding of authentic solicitude, when he suggests the empirical image of a crew as best symbolizing Heidegger's intuition:

> "The original relation of the Other and my conscious-
> ness is not the YOU and ME; it is the WE. Heidegger's
> being-with is not the clear and distinct position of an
> individual confronting another individual... It is the
> mute existence in common of one member of the crew with
> his fellows, that existence which the rhythm of the
> oars or the regular movements of the coxswain will
> render sensible to the rowers and which WILL BE MADE
> MANIFEST to them by the common goal to be attained."8

In reply to many of these critics, one must first emphasize that it is only a misunderstanding of Heidegger which supports a conception of Da-sein as being "curved in on himself" or even "turned upon itself". "'Jemeinigkeit' means that Dasein is not to be understood as an example of 'Vorhandensein'. It does not mean that Dasein can only relate to its own 'self'. Like

---

6   Macomber, W.B. Anatomy of Disillusion, p. 89.

7   Cf. Ibid.

8   Sartre, Jean-Paul, Being and Nothingness, p. 332.

'Vorrang', 'Jemeinigkeit' is a justification for Heidegger's methodology".9 Dasein is <u>essentially</u> a Being-in-the-world; the significance of this statement has already been explained in the discussion of the meaning of transcendence in the first section of this book. Moreover, another thing must be made clear, and that is the critics' common mistake in concluding that other persons are <u>only</u> described by Heidegger in terms of the impersonal "they".10 Heidegger explicitly allows that in addition to "das Man" over against whom the "I" stands out, there are those from whom, for the most part, one does <u>not</u> distinguish oneself -- those among whom one <u>is</u> too. He tells us that:

> "Being with Others belongs to the Being of Dasein, which is an issue for Dasein in its very Being. Thus as Being-with, Dasein 'is' essentially for the sake of Others. This must be understood as an existential statement as to its essence".11

It is worth quoting Heidegger in some length, in order to make this point quite clear. He openly states that:

---

9   Goldstein, J. "Buber's Misunderstanding of Heidegger", in <u>Philosophy Today</u>, Vol. 22, No. 2/4, Summer 1978, page 162.

10   F.G. Sturm has a rather pointed reply to Hordern in his article: "Authenticity and Other Persons", in <u>Christian Century</u>, Vol. 80 (1963), p. 340-42.

11   SZ 123.

"...because Dasein's Being is Being-with, ITS UNDER-
STANDING OF BEING ALREADY IMPLIES THE UNDERSTANDING OF
OTHERS. This understanding, like any understanding, is
not an acquaintance derived from knowledge about them,
but a primordially existential kind of Being, which,
more than anything else, makes such knowledge and
acquaintance possible. KNOWING ONESELF (Sichkennen) IS
GROUNDED IN BEING-WITH, WHICH UNDERSTANDS
PRIMORDIALLY".12

Later, Heidegger adds: "Not only is Being towards Others an

autonomous, irreducible relationship of Being: this relationship,

as Being-with, is one which, with Dasein's Being, already

is... Being-with is an existential constituent of Being-in-the-

world... So far as Dasein is at all, it has Being-with-one-ano-

ther as its kind of Being."13

Further on, this idea is reiterated in the context of Being-

there as Understanding: "The kind of Being which Dasein has, as

potentiality for Being, lies existentially in understanding..

Dasein is in every case what it can be, and in the way in which

it is its possibility. The Being-possible which is essential for

Dasein, pertains to the ways of its solicitude for others and of

its concern with the 'world'."14   The world, Dasein-with and

existence are "equiprimordially disclosed."15

---

12   SZ 123.   Emphasis mine.

13   SZ 125.

14   SZ 143.

15   SZ 137.

Finally, Heidegger makes it quite clear that authentic existence is possible only in terms of a genuinely solicitous relationship with the Other, rather than a "lostness" in the "they". He stipulates that "in resoluteness, we have now arrived at that truth of Dasein which is most primordial because it is authentic"; and then he adds:

> "Resoluteness, as authentic Being-one's-Self, does not detach Dasein from its world, nor does it isolate it so that it becomes a free-floating 'I'. And how should it, when resoluteness as authentic disclosedness is authentically nothing else than Being-in-the-world? Resoluteness brings the Self right into its current concernful Being-alongside which is ready-to-hand, and pushes it into solicitous Being with Others...
>
> When Dasein is resolute, it can become the 'conscience' of Others. Only by authentically Being-their-Selves in resoluteness can people authentically be with one another -- not by ambiguous and jealous stipulations and talkative fraternizing in the 'they' and in what 'they' want to undertake."16

And in another volume, Heidegger stipulates that insofar as Dasein is essentially in-the-world, and therefore "Miteinandersein", solicitude is a fundamental kind of Being of Dasein, as "besorgend-fürsorgende Sorge".17

That Heidegger does in fact speak of the Others in terms other than the inauthentic "they" and that he does so explicitly in terms of the possibility of a truly authentic relationship of solicitude does not mean, however, that there are no problems

---

16   SZ 298.

17   Heidegger, M. Logik: Die Frage nach der Wahrheit, p. 225.

when one speaks of solicitude in the context of Heidegger's analysis. In reading his discussion of the authentic vs. inauthentic modes of Being, one sometimes can have the impression that there is some sort of polarity established between the access to Being revealed in the mode of authentic Being-one's-Self on the one hand, and the "levelling down" (Einebnung) of all possibilities of Being by "das Man"; one senses this sort of polarity, for example, when Heidegger writes: "The Self of everyday Dasein is the they-self, which we distinguish from the authentic Self, that is, from the Self which has been taken hold of in its own way (eigens ergriffenen)".18

There are other problems as well. How is one to reconcile the non-relational character of Being-towards-death, and indeed the recognition that care as the very being of Dasein can never be delegated to another -- with the possibility of authentic solicitude which is said to "leap forth and liberate", as the resolute Dasein becomes the "'conscience' of Others"?19 Heidegger himself suggests that "all Being-with-Others will fail us when our ownmost potentiality-for-Being is an issue"20; while he explicitly denies that this statement destroys his concept of solicitude, one does feel justified in asking whether we are not

---

18   SZ 129.

19   SZ 298.

20   SZ 263.

hereby reduced to being attentive to others only in incidental ways, rather than in truly fundamental ones.21

If one is to evaluate honestly Heidegger's concept of solicitude, one must be prepared to deal honestly with this last question. That one can speak in terms of a truly _fundamental_ solicitous relationship, and still be consistent with Heidegger's own analysis and indeed only thereby further advance it, is something which we intend to show later in this chapter; in advance of this discussion, however, it is necessary to extract and place in the foreground what Heidegger himself has had to say regarding the possibility and the meaning of authentic solicitude.

(ii) Heidegger on Solicitude:

The problem touched on above, of reconciling the "own-ness" of authentic Being-one's-Self (as witnessed in statements such as: "The primary item in care is the 'ahead-of-itself'; and this means that in every case Dasein exists _for the sake of itself_"22) with the possibility of a solicitous giving of the other's "care" back to him authentically as such for the first time23 -- is a problem of reconciling the own-ness of a transcendental and

---

21   This is R. Weber's contention in _op.cit_.

22   SZ 236 - Emphasis mine.

23   Cf. SZ 122.

futurally projecting Dasein with the possibility of a genuine and productive Ich-Du relationship: it is a problem of which Heidegger is not unaware, although in reconciling these two factors, he is not about to relinquish his phenomenological and ontological concerns. In fact, he will contend that the two positions are not mutually exclusive but, on the contrary, are mutually supportive, that is, while Being-with is a part of one's existential constitution, authentic Being-with is possible only if one is authentically Being-one's-Self. In other words, if I am not aware, I cannot be aware of the Other in any ontologically relevant sense (or even in any genuine ontic sense). As Heidegger states in his Grundprobleme der Phänomenologie volume, "Nur weil ich ein existierendes Selbst bin, bin ich ein mögliches Du für einen Anderen als Selbst."24

Heidegger is not saying that I must first be-alone, as a condition of authentic Being-with, for Heidegger is not talking about the existentiell phenomenon of solicitude or aloneness, nor is he talking about the ontic encounter with "Others of my kind".

On the contrary, he will write that "Being-alone is a deficient mode of Being-with".25

Therefore, the ontological "primordiality" of the Dasein only allows for an ontological understanding of the fact of

---

24   GP 422.

25   SZ 120.

Being-with.   Heidegger   is   speaking   of more than a mere _formal_ primordiality of Dasein, and   therefore, the   significance of the statement is   more far-reaching   than that   of a mere abstraction which would   isolate   a   non-relational   Dasein   from   a concrete social context.   In fact,   any asserted   "primordiality" of "the Dasein" with respect to our discussion   of solicitude   only makes it possible   (and phenomenologically plausible)   for Being-with to be seen in its proper ontological context.

In _Sein und Zeit_, Heidegger explains how "one   must not fail to notice   that we   use the   term 'Dasein-with' to designate that Being for   which the   Others who   are (die   seienden Anderen) are freed   within-the-world.   This   Dasein-with   of   the   Others   is disclosed within-the-world for a Dasein.. only because   Dasein in itself is essentially Being-with.   The phenomenological assertion that   'Dasein   is   essentially   Being-with'   has   an existential-ontological   meaning.   It   does   not seek to establish ontically that factically I am not present-at-hand   alone, and   that Others of my   kind occur.   If this were what is meant by the proposition that Dasein's Being-in-the-world   is   essentially   constituted by Being-with, then Being-with would not be an existential attribute which Dasein, of its own accord,   has coming   to it   from its own kind of Being."26

---

26   SZ 120.

The critics who suggest that Dasein is seen by Heidegger to
be an isolated Self definable apart from its so-called "social
context", are making the mistake of viewing Dasein as an abstract
Subject, whose solicitous relations with another must then necessarily remain on an incidental, rather than fundamental level.
According to Renée Weber, Heidegger seems to imply that the only
true gift one man can bestow on another is to "convince him to
turn away from human beings in order to silently commune with
Being"27; this, of course, would reduce relations among humans to
a secondary or incidental importance.

What Weber forgets, however, is that Dasein is and remains
his relation to Being, whether or not he ontically decides to
"turn away from human beings"; indeed, because "Dasein... is
ontological"28 and is seen by Heidegger in its ontological significance to be in-the-world, the possibility of Dasein as a Being-
in-the-world achieving an authentically solicitous relation with
another, and the possibility that such a relation would be
fundamental in its ontological significance-- is only enhanced.
In other words, Dasein does not suddenly become ontological in a
privileged "commune with Being" which is at the expense of Being-
with-others; rather, as already defined as Da-sein and the

---

27   Weber, R. op.cit., p. 551.

28   SZ 12.

"location of the truth of Being"29, the possibility of an

authentically solicitous relation, rather than an incidental one,

is all the more conceivable. Heidegger himself emphasizes the

fact that it is only insofar as man is seen in his ontological

significance to be a Being-in-the-world, that we can speak of any

meaningful Ich-du relation:

> "Only insofar as the 'Subject' is determined through
> Being-in-the-world, can it become, as this Self, a You
> (ein Du) for another... The fundamental condition for
> the possibility of the Self to become a possible You in
> Being-with-Others, is grounded herein: that the Dasein
> as the Self which it is, is in such a manner that it
> exists as Being-in-the-world. For then You means: You,
> who are with me in a World... Self and World belong
> together in the unity of the fundamental state of
> Dasein, of Being-in-the-World. This is the condition
> of the possibility of an Understanding of the other
> Dasein."30

While in characterizing the encounter with others, one is

still oriented by that Dasein which is in every case one's own,

yet "by 'Others', we do not mean everyone else but me - those

over against whom the 'I' stands out. They are rather those from

whom, for the most part, one does not distinguish oneself - those

among whom one is too. This Being-there-too [Auch-da-sein] with

them does not have the ontological character of a Being-present-

at-hand-along-'with' them within a world. This 'with' is

---

29   Heidegger, M. "Einleitung zu: 'Was ist Metaphysik'", in WM,
      e.t. cited from "Way Back into the Ground of Metaphysics",
      p. 221.

30   GP 422-423.

something of the character of Dasein; the 'too' means a sameness of Being as circumspectively concernful Being-in-the-world."31

Being-with certainly also entails the possibility of an inauthentic mode of existence with regard to the "they-self"; but, as should be clear by now, authentic solicitude is hardly incompatible with the notion of Being-one's-self. Indeed, the possibility of authentic solicitude is there in Heidegger's analysis, although it is not explicitly explored in particular depth or detail.

What little Heidegger does say about such a possibility, however, is contained primarily in Sein und Zeit, where we learn first, that there are two kinds of solicitude: one negative and the other positive.

Negative solicitude is based on the recognition of a funda-mental ontological difference between Being-towards-entities which are ready-to-hand, and a Being-towards Dasein in a relation of Being-with. "Those entities towards which Dasein as Being-with comports itself do not have the kind of Being which belongs to equipment ready-to-hand; they are themselves Dasein. These entities are not objects of concern, but rather of solicitude".32

As a result, our neglect of things is different from our neglect of persons, because as persons who are essentially Being-

31   SZ 118.

32   SZ 121.

there, we cannot "be together" in the same way in which things are together; and thus our neglect of things is, ontologically speaking, very different from our neglect of the other Dasein.33 In fact, the very neglect of another Dasein constitutes an interaction with him, however inapparent. "Being for, against, or without one another, passing one another by, not 'mattering' to one another - these are possible ways of solicitude. And it is precisely these last-named deficient and Indifferent modes that characterize everyday, average Being-with-one-another."34 Failing to notice a person is qualitatively different from failing to notice a physical entity or piece of ready-to-hand equipment; failing to notice a person thus constitutes solicitude, though in its negative mode.35

But there are positive modes of solicitude as well, and in this connection, Heidegger discusses "two extreme possibilities". The first concerns a "leaping-in" for the Other, the

---

33   SZ 121.

34   SZ 121.

35   Critics like Weber all too lightly pass over this negative
      mode as being a mere statement of a "restraint from action
      with others"; and having done so, proceed to seek a better
      understanding of solicitude through only the so-called
      "positive" modes. The result of their investigation into
      Heidegger's fundamental ontology inevitably then appears
      "glaring and disturbing". (R. Weber, op.cit., p. 558.) In
      the following section, we shall show how the ontological
      import of the apparent "restraint from action with others"
      in negative solicitude is not separate from the positive
      mode, but helps to define it.

second a "leaping-ahead" of the Other in his potentiality-for-Being.

The first kind of solicitude, Heidegger explains, "takes over for the Other that with which he is to concern himself. The Other is thus thrown out of his own position; he steps back so that afterwards, when the matter has been attended to, he can either take it over as something finished and at his disposal, or disburden himself of it completely."36

Such "leaping-in" for the Other involves other human beings somewhat indirectly, however, for it "pertains for the most part to our concern with the ready-to-hand". For example, it may express itself in a benevolent concern in providing food, clothing, or nursing care for the Other. Heidegger suggests that in this kind of solicitude, the Other "can [and I underscore the word 'can'] become One who is dominated and dependent, even if this domination is a tacit one and remains hidden from him."37 I think that it is important to stop here for a moment, and consider the meaning of the word, and the possible forms of "domination".

Particularly since Heidegger himself does mention "welfare work" [Fürsorge] in this section, it may seem that this first form of solicitude is an inherently problematic notion, and indeed that we may be hard pressed to explain this initial kind

36   SZ 122.

37   SZ 122.

of Fürsorge as a solicitous relation at all: if I leap-in for the Other only to dominate him, while I may appear to be going through the motions of expressing a concern for the Other, perhaps I am only, in fact, going through these motions for the sake of my own peace of mind, in which case, I am not only not showing a form of positive solicitude but am, on the contrary, being inauthentic in my expression. Welfare work of volunteer work or charitable contributions are often motivated by precisely such inauthentic concerns; indeed, when the western world has sought to "help" developing countries in the name of genuine concern, their "dominance" has often expressed itself in an imposition of their own standards and beliefs, which is obviously undiscerning of the actual concerns of the "Others".

Thus, the first positive mode of solicitude may be construed to be actually much less a solicitous concern than an inauthentic imposition and domination of the Other, motivated by some degree of self-interest. Indeed, distinguishing between the first mode of solicitude, and an inauthentic expression of false concern for the Other, may at times be quite difficult.

This being said, however, we must not forget first, that Heidegger suggests that in such leaping-in for the Other, it is possible that the Other can become one who is dominated (that is, he need not); and second, we must keep in mind that there are various degrees and meanings of domination. In fact, my suggestion is that the line between leaping-in for another, and leaping-ahead of the Other to free him in his potentiality-for-Being, is not a sharp line which separates two alternate possibilities. In other words, some degree of "domination" of the Other may well be the condition for the "leaping-ahead" of the Other and may free him to be himself; and consequently, such initial "domination" may indeed be an expression of the first of the two positive and authentic modes of solicitude about which Heidegger speaks.

An example should make this clear. When a parent provides ready-to-hand equipment such as food, clothing and/or nursing care for his child, there may be a sense in which we can say that the parent is "dominating" the child inasmuch as the child comes to be dependent upon the parent for the provision of such equipment. However, it could be (and in many cases is) simply false to suggest that the parents' provision of food and clothing and especially nursing care is motivated by a mere desire for a peace of mind, rather than a truly positive   and solicitous concern for the Other (the child) in his uniqueness.

Indeed, such "domination" of the parent and dependence of the child (or we could use any comparable example of authentic concern for the "welfare" of the Other) may in itself not only be an expression of genuine concern, but may be an important step along the way, and even a condition for the second form of positive solicitude which Heidegger refers to - a form which "does not so much leap in for the Other as leap ahead [ihm vorausspringt] in his existentiell potentiality-for-Being, not in order to take away his 'care' but rather to give it back to him authentically as such for the first time. This kind of solicitude pertains essentially to authentic care, that is, to the existence of the Other, not to a 'what' with which he is concerned; it helps the Other to become transparent to himself in his care and to become free for it."38

Here indeed is an explicit Heideggerean reference to solicitude as pertaining to authentic care; here we have the beginnings of a truly authentic relationship. But here too is where Heidegger stops short: explaining that everyday Being-with-another maintains itself between these two forms of positive solicitude and thereby manifests "numerous mixed forms", he adds simply that "to describe these and classify them would take us beyond the limits of this investigation".39

It is therefore left up to us to take the clues which Heidegger offers, and attempt to "go-beyond" Sein und Zeit, toward a more complete and concrete understanding of the relationship of authentic solicitude.

---

38   SZ 122.

39   SZ 122.

(iii)   The Relationship of Authentic Solicitude:
           Beyond Sein und Zeit

The "Negative" Conditions for "Positive" Solicitude

We have mentioned above, the qualitative difference between
our failure to notice persons as opposed to the failure to notice
an entity such as a house or a tree. Wherein does this difference lie, and what constitutes it?   When I am walking along a
crowded street, why is it that my failure to explicitly notice
other persons is more significant, ontologically speaking, than
my failure to take notice of the particular windows, or sidewalk,
or even the buildings around me?

The   answer   lies   in   what   we   shall show to be a concrete
ontological awareness that we are not independent of one another,
and therefore, that we are in essence solicitous beings.

That we say: "we are not independent of one another" does
not mean to suggest that "we are dependent" on all those around
us. This is an important point, for we do not mean to suggest
that we have an explicit awareness of any direct dependence on
other persons, as opposed to buildings or sidewalk. I may not
depend on people in the crowd for any explicit purpose or
intention, but my situatedness is such that I am not independent
of them nonetheless. "They are those from whom, for the most
part, one does not distinguish oneself", as Heidegger has said.40
Equally important, my being "not independent" of them is dif-

---

40   SZ 118.

ferent from my being not independent of my physical environment,
because the potential influence and meaning that a person or
persons may have on me is quite different from the influence of
entities.   True, things around me affect me indirectly and without my conscious awareness of their effect at all times, but such
physical entitites belong to a general context of meanings and a
referential unity (<u>Bewandtnisganzheit</u>) within which I, as an
intentional being, situate them.

On the other hand, when we say that we are "not independent"
of one another, this very "not" implies a potential influence
beyond my control or expectations, of the intentional projections
of another Da-sein, of another "freedom", in Sartre's words.
This "not" implies, in other words, possibility, and a potentiality of communication and discourse between persons.

This possibility of discourse between persons, arising by
virtue of the fact that we are in a unique sense not independent
of one another, reveals a commonality and community of all
Daseins.   Not that the human community instituted by language is
to reveal a resemblance of genus or common cause, but rather,
being-human implies being-with and a <u>logos</u> of communication and
meaning. We influence one another in this unique way, in the
"not" of being "not independent of one another", because the very
"'with' [of 'Dasein-with'] is something of the character of
Dasein; the 'too' [of 'Being-there-too' with others] means a
sameness of Being as circumspectively concernful Being-in-the-

world."41 Such a sameness of Being means that we are involved in mankind, but this "mankind" is no mere abstraction, any more than the fact of our being not independent of one another indicates some abstract realm of potentiality. It is only man the uninfluenced who could be "man" in the abstract, but what we are rather indicating here is a very concrete ontological awareness of a community and a fraternity which, though evident in a negative form of solicitude and in the "not", nonetheless points to the possibility of discourse (be it authentic or in-authentic).42

Such community or "fraternity", however, must be understood as prior to the Sartrean conflict as the original meaning of being-for-others43, and prior too, to a benevolence towards others exercised on behalf of an ideal of community and brother-hood44; for it is the ontological condition, expressed in the "not", and indicative of the concrete sharing among Da-seins, of the fate of Being itself.

---

41   SZ 118.

42   This is why Language, rather than man, speaks. "Language brings what is, as something that is, into the Open for the first time. Where there is no language, as in the being of stone, plant, and animal, there is also no openness of what is, and consequently, no openness either of that which is not and of the empty." (Heidegger, M, in HW 61, e.t. 73.)

43   Cf. Sartre, Jean-Paul, Being and Nothingness, p. 475.

44   "'Empathy' does not first constitute Being-with; only on the basis of 'Being-with' does 'empathy' become possible." (SZ 125.)

"Destiny is not something that puts itself together out
of individual fates, any more than Being-with-one-
another can be conceived as the occurring together of
several Subjects. Our fates have already been guided
in advance, in our Being with one another in the same
world, and in our resoluteness for definite
possibilities. Only in communicating and in struggling
does the power of destiny become free."45

Positive Solicitude: Authentic "leaping-ahead"

If it is Being itself which provides the clue for the negative "fraternity" among Daseins, we shall see that it provides an
equally important clue when we come to the point of exploring the
positive content of the solicitous relation.

Among the many reasons that Heidegger "crosses out" the word
"Being" in his later thought, one of the more important is that
he wants to ensure that "Being" is not conceived metaphysically
as a being, as a domain beyond entities, or as a reality which is
separable and independent from entities. Indeed, Heidegger wants
to ensure that man is seen to be in his very essence, remembrance
of Being and intrinsically part of Being. The "crossing out"
mark then, cannot signify a mere cancellation but rather points
to the positive understanding of the significance of the
Ereignis, the Ereignis which is not the conception of a Being
beyond Being, because it is not to be represented as some-thing
which only occasionally reaches up to man. Man is never to be
seen as excluded from Being. On the contrary, the Ereignis

---

45   SZ 384.

points to an essential belonging-together, a "oneness", of mortals, with the earth, the sky and the gods in their gathering in the _Geviert_. "This simple oneness of the four", writes Heidegger, "we call the _fourfold_".46

That dwelling in the fourfold is more than a mystical participation in some vague unity and that it indeed involves a concrete action and interaction in-the-world, is perhaps made more clear when Heidegger speaks of dwelling as a "staying with - things". He reminds us that "staying with things is the only way in which the fourfold stay within the fourfold is accomplished at any time in simple unity. Dwelling preserves the fourfold, by bringing the presencing of the fourfold into things."47 Indeed, Heidegger continues, it is not an exaggeration to say that:

> "We are in the strict sense of the term, the be-thinged [_die Be-Dingten_ - that is, conditioned by our relationship with things.] We have left behind the arrogance of being in any way unconditioned."48

What we wish to show in this section, is that just as "things themselves secure the fourfold only when they themselves _as_ things are let be in their presencing"49, significant ontic moments in an authentically solicitous relation between persons,

---

46   "Bauen, Wohnen, Denken", VA 150, e.t. 150.

47   VA 151, e.t. 151.

48   "Das Ding", in VA 179, e.t. 181.

49   "Bauen, Wohnen, Denken", in VA 151, e.t. 151.

between an "Ich" and a "Du", may "secure the fourfold" in a particularly meaningful way as well.

But let us go back for a moment, to clarify the meaning of the "fourfold".

Heidegger tells us that the earth is "the serving bearer, blossoming and fruiting, spreading out in rock and water, rising up into plant and animal."50 It is that out of which everything emerges, serving and supporting, as a sustaining principle. "Earth is that which comes forth and shelters. Earth, self-dependent, is effortless and untiring. Upon the earth and in it, historical man grounds his dwelling in the world."51 Using the example of a stone's heaviness, Heidegger describes how we may wish to analyze that heaviness scientifically: if we attempt to break open the rock, the secret of its weight is not yet revealed. If we place the stone on a balance, we achieve no more than to bring its heaviness into the domain of a calculated weight; "this perhaps very precise determination of the stone remains a number, but the weight's burden has escaped us."52 No matter how we analyze the stone, its weight as weight remains undisclosed. Similarly, "colour shines and wants only to shine.

---

50   "Bauen, Wohnen, Denken", in VA 150, e.t. 149.

51   "Der Ursprung des Kunstwerkes", in HW 35, e.t. 46-7.

52   "Der Ursprung des Kunstwerkes", in HW 35, e.t. 46-7.

When we analyze it in rational terms, by measuring its wave-lengths, it is gone." In essence, then,

> "earth shatters every attempt to penetrate into it. It causes every merely calculating importunity upon it to turn into a destruction... The earth appears openly cleared as itself only when it is perceived and preserved as that which is by nature undisclosable, that which shrinks from every disclosure and constantly keeps itself closed up... The earth is essentially self-secluding. To set forth the earth means to bring it into the Open as self-secluding."53

Earth is the hidden in all unhiddenness, the closure within which all disclosure is rooted and preserved.

But this description is more than mere rhetoric on Heidegger's part. It is also more than a vague ontological comprehension of the impenetrable "mystery of existence". The essence of the "earth" is revealed in the very relation of one Dasein to another; for example, it is manifested in the Otherness of the Other, which is not simply to imply a conflict, but serves as a reminder of the fact that each and every Dasein (as earth-ling!) is irreplaceably unique, and therefore unknowable at each and every moment by any other Dasein. "Thus, in each of the self-secluding things, there is the same not-knowing-of-one-another."54 The earth, as essentially self-secluding, is the symbol of the hidden in the unhiddenness of another personality and the ground of his uniqueness.

---

53   "Der Ursprung des Kunstwerkes", in HW 35, e.t. 47.

54   "Der Ursprung des Kuntswerkes", in HW 36, e.t. 47.

The necessary correlate of earth is found in the notion of the sky or heaven, which is the pure principle of light and the horizon of openness, where that which emerges into unhiddenness shines forth as what it is. "The sky is the vaulting path of the sun, the course of the changing moon, the wandering glitter of the stars... the drifting clouds and the blue depth of the ether."55

The openness of the sky as the pure principle of light is the condition of understanding and communication in the e-ventful moments of solicitude. In the happening of love or true friendship, genuine sharing, perhaps even in the absence of spoken words, signifies a purity of being-together in an honest, and unmediated revelation of one's most intimate sentiments and thoughts.

The divinities are the "beckoning messengers of the god-head. Out of the holy sway of the godhead, the god appears in his presence or withdraws into his concealment."56

When we read in Heidegger's writings, of the poets invoking the dimension of the Holy57, and particularly when we remember how Hölderlin's poetry was for Heidegger a fundamental re-thin-

---

55   "Bauen, Wohnen, Denken", in VA 150, e.t. 149.

56   "Bauen, Wohnen, Denken", in VA 150, e.t. 150.

57   "The writing of poetry is the fundamental naming of the gods." - HD, from "Hölderlin and the Essence of Poetry", in Existence and Being, p. 287.

king about God in terms of the arrival of the Divine as an event to be prepared for by a deeper insight into the very meaning of truth and Being58, we can perhaps agree with Schulz59 that if the poet is seen to be the mediator, the Holy has been determined by Heidegger as the Unmediated.   We can only begin to overcome the godlessness of the epoch when we come to realize with Hölderlin, that the Holy is the primordial truth (<u>aletheia</u>) beyond gods and mortals, and the medium for the manifestation of the Divinity. Though it may be revealed through the mediation of a god, or find expression in the word of the poet, the Holy is in itself pure immediacy.

But if the immediacy of the divine is manifested in the word of the poet, so too is it manifest in the rare and privileged moment of contemporaneous immediacy of solicitude.   Contemporaenity here means that the single, unique Other as a "single thing that presents itself to us achieves in its presentation full presentness, however remote its origin might be. Thus, contemporaneity is not a mode of givenness in consciousness but a

---

58   "To prepare joyously the fitting proximity to the Near for the greeting heralds, who bring greeting from the still-reserved discovery - that is what determines the vocation of the homecoming poet. The holy does indeed appear. But the god remains far off. The time of the reserved discovery is the age when the god is lacking... Nevertheless, because the discovery in being reserved is at the same time near, the failing god sends greeting in the Near of the heavenly." From HD, "Remembrance of the Poet", in <u>Existence and Being</u>, p. 264.

59   W. Schulz, <u>Der Gott der Neuzeitlichen Metaphysik</u>, p. 54-58.

task for consciousness and an achievement that is required of it. It consists in holding on to the thing in such a way that it becomes contemporaneous, but this means that all mediation is dissolved in total presentness"60 and in the immediacy of the Holy.

The fourth region of the fourfold encompasses mortals. "The mortals are human beings. They are called mortals because they can die. To die means to be capable of death as death. Only man dies, and indeed continually, as long as he remains on earth, under the sky, before the divinities."61 Inasmuch as mortals are capable of dying, and accepting death as the "shrine of Nothingness" and as a part of life; and since Nothingness is Being experienced as the sheer other to what-is, mortals by definition embody the relationship to Being as Being-- which is why we can experience the "joy we feel in the presence of the Being -- not merely the person -- of someone we love."62

---

60   Gadamer, Hans-Georg, Truth and Method, p. 112-113. Gadamer tells us that this notion of contemporaneity comes original-ly from Kierkegaard who gave it a particularly theological emphasis, in the sense of being present as a sharing in the redemptive action itself. For Kierkegaard, it was a formulation of the believer's task of so totally combining one's own presence and the redeeming act of Christ that the latter is experienced as something present, not as something past.

61   "Bauen, Wohnen, Denken", in VA 150, e.t. 150.

62   Heidegger, M. WIM in WM 8, e.t. 334.

Heidegger tells us that each region of the fourfold belongs to the other, constituting an indissoluble and "simple oneness". The fourfold in its unity is the happening of a mutual owning and acknowledging of each region by the other, so that each is at the same time expropriated into the freedom of its own nature. Heidegger calls this play of reflection in owning-expropriating fourfoldness, the mirror-game (Spiegel-Spiel). The mirror-game of the world, which is to say the play of the fourfold in its unity, is that which constitutes the round dance of the occur- rence of owning (Ereignen).

In "Hölderlin's Erde und Himmel",63 and following Hölder- lin's usage, Heidegger speaks of the interrelationship of the four regions of the fourfold as "the in-finite relation", "in- finite", because in their relation, each region is freed from its onesidedness and "finitude". The centre or mediating core of this relation, its very "intimacy" (Innigkeit), is the Ereignis, or what Heidegger here calls the Geschick, which holds the four together in their intimacy and constitutes the heart of the in- finite relation. Mortals themselves are in the fourfold by dwelling. "Mortals dwell in the way they preserve the fourfold in its essential being, its presencing."64

---

63   Hölderlin-Jahrbuch, 1958-1960, p. 25, 31.

64   "Bauen Wohnen Denken", in VA 151, e.t. 150.

In the e-vents of dwelling with the Other, where the e-vent is the occurrence of owning in the intimacy of the in-finite relation of the fourfold, authentic solicitous relations appear, building up histories of vulnerable, but unique human relations.

(iv) The In-finitude of Authentic Solicitude:

> "All union of the sexes is a sign of death;
> and we could not know love were we to live
> indefinitely."
>
> -   Anatole France

The fact that there could be no love without finitude rings strange to western ears. Despite its more bizarre imagery, Aristophanes' Myth65 would probably be more readily accepted at the end of a metaphysical era.

But the belonging of any kind of solicitude to finitude itself is, to my mind, extremely significant if we are to remain true to the thrust of Heidegger's phenomenological Thought.

---

65   In Plato's Symposium, Aristophanes reports the mythical tale of how the original human was a self-sufficient creature, containing both sexes within itself. Angering Zeus through its arrogance, the creature was punished by being split in half: into man and woman. From that time onward, humans were condemned to searching the world for their "other halves", moved by the quest of love.

The monistic interpretation of love is, to my mind, best symbolized by this myth which portrays love as a driving force of incomplete beings, yearning to become whole through union with one ideal partner.

Indeed, unless we are to begin with a recognition of Heidegger's notion of individuation as outlined in Part I of this volume, there can be no authentic understanding of solicitude.

But we must be careful here. Understanding the primordiality of individuation does not require an acceptance of the fact that the Other is merely an intentional creation of my own. This would be the case, perhaps, if individuation were understood in an ontic sense, which would imply an inevitable solipsism. On the contrary, because Heidegger's ontological understanding of individuation is of Dasein as a Being-in-the-world, what emerges is that, if finitude belongs to solicitude, individuation is the very condition for the bridging of distance.

Contrary to the monism of the Aristophanes myth, we can say that the notion of authentic solicitude explicitly calls for an understanding of the individuality of another person distinct in character from oneself, and an endorsement of his being the unique individual that he is. This sharing of freedom, independence and individuality is essential to the meaning of authentic solicitude. The romantic idealist may wish to speculate on the ideal identity of the persons, but unless there is a mutual respect of one another's unique individuality, there is no possibility of authentic solicitude.

In Scheler's words, "If the difference of the persons were an illusion, and if the consciousness of this which accompanies love in its increasing reverence and delicacy of approach to the absolute intimacy of the other's self - if this consciousness of personal diversity, greatest when love is deepest, were likewise an illusion, then love itself would indeed be illusion too."66

It is only within a fundamental recognition of the finitude of individuation that solicitude is properly grounded. This is why the relation of solicitude can never be simply "infinite", and yet may still be seen to be in-finite, if one recognizes a two-fold meaning to this latter term:

First, one may interpret the "in-finite" essence of the relation of solicitude to be "within" finitude, as rooted in it. If primal finitude includes, as we have said before, a primary relation of receptivity, then perhaps one of the prime conditions of authentic solicitude is an openness and receptivity in the form of original respect for the Other. Only within such receptivity and openness toward the Other in his uniqueness, can there be genuine surprise or exposure to the unassumable. Not that such openness is ever complete in the sense of an achieved comprehension, for the receptivity of finitude as a "principle of narrowness" or indeed, as including the notion of a closing within the openness, is also perspectival, which means that I can never fully, once and for all, grasp the Other to fully understand and know him. My proximity is never close enough, but that

---

66   Scheler, Max, The Nature of Sympathy, quoted from the article entitled "Love as Perfection of Differences", in Norton, D. and Kille, M., Philosophies of Love, p. 73-75.

is why there is an ever-more to the Other in the relation of solicitude.

Secondly, however, in my in-finite relation to the unique Other, I know much more than an entity: I am in relation to a Dasein as a no-thingness. This means, of course, that the notion of being in-finite as rooted "within" finitude, can by no means signify that the Other is merely a finite thing, as a delimited ob-ject in my world. On the contrary, the in-finite suggests a non-finitude, which is grounded in the no-thingness of the Da-sein. In a relation of authentic solicitude, one does not relate to the Other as a circumscribed set of objective characteristics (this is why computer-dating matches rarely work!); one does not know parts in such a relation, one does not love someone because his hair is brown or his eyes are blue, but rather, one enters into an ontological relation. There is no-thing particular which one loves; the privileged relation between myself and the Other makes room for the revelation of Being itself.

This, perhaps, is at the core of Aristophanes' admission to Plato, that "there are people who pass their whole lives together, yet would not explain what they desire of one another!"[67] This also may be at the core of the moments of silent communication "between" human beings, in the absence of words. There is a

---

67   Plato, Symposium, 192c.

summons here, for me from the Other, a call which needs to be answered.   This call, from out of the space of the no-thing, cannot be reduced to a specific request, to an instant of time, but in a very true sense, plunges me into an ontological relation which remains essentially mysterious.

While the in-finite solicitous relation, then, is "within" finitude, the element of the "non" suggests that the <u>authentic</u> relation is more than the accumulation of the specific histories of the two Daseins.   My understanding of the Other is more than only my own, one-way intentional projection of him.   To use Joan Stambaugh's words in her reference to temporality, "the relation is more fundamental than what is related". It is not a question of "things", of "whats" that are related; authentic solicitude plunges me into a relation, ontologically grounded, whereby my being is opened to possibilities and horizons of the Other, never before encountered by myself alone.

Through the relation of authentic solicitude as an enlarge-ment of our own lives, we can even at times enter into the expe-rience of others, without ever having had that particular quality of experience before. At certain special ontic moments, because of the special ontological grounding of the relation, we can genuinely reach into and enter the other person's individual situation, "give [care] back to him authentically as such for the first time", to quote Heidegger.68 Normally, as good empiricists in the Humean tradition, we would conclude upon analysis that there can be no true fellow feeling if my understanding of the situation of the Other were to imply more than a mere remembering of a similar situation or a feeling that I had once possessed or share. But, ontologically speaking, the relation of authentic solicitude must reveal something more than this, and I think that this is shown most clearly by Max Scheler, to whom Heidegger was reportedly very close, both personally as well as according to their philosophies.69

Scheler disagrees with the theory that "fellow-feeling must necessarily be confined to processes and incidents in other peoples' experiences such as we have already met with ourselves. This conclusion is as little in accord with the facts as the

---

68   SZ 122.

69   Cf. Elisabeth Hirsch, "Remembrance of Martin Heidegger in Marburg", in Philosophy Today, Vol. 23, No. 2/4, Summer 1979, p. 160-169. Aside from sharing a criticism of the Neo-Kantian school, and agreeing on the need for a differentiation between the task of philosophy and the sciences, more significantly, Hirsch suggests that "Heidegger's concept of Dasein being-in-the-world and with other human beings corresponds in Scheler's philosophy to the notion of a person, that is the whole concrete man as a feeling, acting, loving and thinking being in relation to his world and to other people." In Sein und Zeit, (47), Scheler is quoted in support of Heidegger's own view that a person's actions are not the object of the science of psychology, but must be seen in the context of the whole person's Being. At Scheler's death, Heidegger gave a short talk remembering his colleague before he began the lecture course. Hirsch reports that the final words were simply: Ein Licht ist ausgegangen.

corresponding view, that we can only understand what we have actually been through ourselves." Continuing this line of argument, Scheler explains how:

> "we can have a lively and immediate participation in joy or sorrow, can share with others their appreciation of value, and can even enter into another person's commiseration for a third party, without ever having sampled that particular quality of experience before. A person who has never felt mortal terror can still understand and envisage it, just as he can also share in it. It is a futile evasion to argue that for this, we must at least have had real experience of the 'elements' of the state or value in question, such as those comprised in fear or in some sort of 'death-like feeling' in the present case. For what sort of 'elements' are these? How far must we descend in search of those mental principles which the atomistic psychology believes to be consistuent of experience? And on what principle or rule are these 'elements' to be compounded, if we do not already have some idea of what the end-product is to be, namely mortal terror? Are we to go on shuffling these elements in imagination, until they happen to fit the case?"70

Scheler goes on to talk about the Buddha's conversion. Having grown up in a home of luxury and splendour, the Buddha was led by only a few instances of poverty and sickness "to discern and respond to all the pain and misery of the world, so that his whole life thereafter took an entirely different course." A similar example is offered in Tolstoy's "Master and Servant", which shows how the master's heart is opened in his first experience of pure sympathy when he encounters his servant perishing of cold.71

---

70   Scheler, M., cited in Norton, D. and Kille, M., op.cit., p. 36

71   Scheler, Max, cited in Norton, D., and Kille, M., Ibid.

If such an understanding of the Other person72 is possible, then it follows that even "Jesus' despair in Gethsemane can be understood and shared, regardless of our historical, racial and even human limitations. And for every candid heart which steeps itself in that desolation it operates, not as a reminder or revival of personal sufferings, great or small, but as the revelation of a new and greater suffering hitherto undreamed of."73

The important point in all of this is that the ontological roots of solicitude in a relation of no-thingness suggest that I can come to an understanding of elements ofthe potentiality-for-Being of the Other, without actually having had a similar set of experiences in my own past; moreover, if solicitude makes me authentically aware of the potentiality-for-Being of the Other, is it not reasonable to conclude that it can also open the way to

---

72   The notion of self as "person" encompasses, in this volume, the notion of the original, ontological transcendence of a Being-in-the-world. Heidegger refers to Scheler to suggest what comes closest to his own definition of "person". He writes: "We have chosen Scheler's Interpretation as an example, not only because it is accessible in print, but because he emphasizes personal Being explicitly as such, and tries to determine its character by defining the specific Being of acts as contrasted with anything 'psychical'. For Scheler, the person is never to be thought of as a Thing or a substance; the person is rather the unity of living-through [Er-lebens]...Psychical being has nothing to do with personal Being...The critical question [of the meaning of 'person'] must face the Being of the whole man..."(SZ 47-8.)

73   Scheler, M., in Norton, D. and Kille, M., op.cit., p. 365.

an authentic understanding of death, by way of the death of the
Other?

**

B.   The E-vent of the Death of the Other

(i)   Understanding of the potentiality-for-being of Others:

> "As the non-relational possibility, death
> individualizes, but only in such a manner
> that, as the possibility which is not to be
> outstripped, it makes Dasein, as Being-with,
> have some understanding of the potentiality-
> for-Being of Others."74

To unpack this statement is to respond to a challenge, presented above by Heidegger himself, to understand the phenomenon of death, the most personal of life's potentialities, through Being-with other persons and through "some understanding of the potentiality-for-Being of Others".

The statement is a rather unique one in the context of Heidegger's general contention75 that the dying of Others is not something which we experience in any genuine sense, and that, at best, we can only be somehow "alongside"; on the other hand, precisely because it suggests something new, the statement cannot be passed off lightly.

---

74   "Als unbezügliche Möglichkeit vereinzelt der Tod aber nur, um als unüberholbare das Dasein als Mitsein verstehend zu machen für das Seinkönnen der Anderen." Martin Heidegger, Sein und Zeit, p. 264.

75   SZ II.1.

Using Heidegger's remark as a springboard, this part of the chapter will explore the possibility of coming to a fundamental understanding of death by way of the death of the Other.

This does not mean, however, that we will be bringing into dispute any of Heidegger's comments in Being and Time, regarding the ontological meaning of one's own Being-towards-death.

Nor does it mean that we will at all consider ways in which "the deceased has Dasein-with or is still-a-Dasein"76 in any "other-worldly" sense.

Finally, while Heidegger will concede that "cases of death may be the factical occasion for Dasein's first paying attention to death at all..."77, our intention is not to explore the ontic implications of a "case of death" (Todesfall).

Rather, this section is a response to Heidegger's comments generally concentrated in Division II, Chapter I of Sein und Zeit, where he states that in our "Being-with the dead, the authentic Being-come-to-an-end [Zuendgekommensein] of the deceased is precisely the sort of thing which we do not experience", because in the deceased, what we encounter "is something unalive, which has lost its life."78

---

76   SZ 239.

77   SZ 257.

78   SZ 238-9.

It is a response to Heidegger's general contention that in these circumstances, "the end of the entity qua Dasein is the beginning of the same entity qua something present- at -hand."79

It will be shown that while these comments do apply in most cases, the death of the Other can under no circumstances, be reduced to the status of the beginning or the end of a present-at-hand entity, if the death of the Other is the death of a Dasein to whom I am related in authentic solicitude.

Consequently, the Death of this Other is not a mere case of death, therefore no incidental occurrence, because the rela-tionship of solicitude is not an incidental occurrence. As solicitude is an existentiale, the death of the Other to whom I am related in authentic solicitude is not a re-presentable case of death from which one "recovers"80.   It is not a "case of death": it is A Death, a genuine ontic e-vent which transforms my world for all time.

Heidegger tells us that in Sein und Zeit, "we are asking about the ontological meaning of the dying of the person who dies, as a possibility-of-Being which belongs to his Being."81 In this section, we are doing exactly the same. We are not considering the death of the Other in its inauthentic, re-presen-

79   SZ 238.

80   Cf. SZ 238.

81   SZ 239.

tational nature; we are not considering the death of the Other,
simply as it influences me or my "feelings" as an individual
intending the presence of the Other.

What we are considering, is that if it is possible that I
can come to an authentic understanding of the Other person in a
relationship of solicitude as described earlier, then, the death
of that person can be understood in an equally meaningful way.

Finally, what we are considering, then, is the possibility
of an ontologically-fundamental understanding of an ontic event:-
the death of the Other with whom I stand in an authentically
solicitous relation.

(ii) Solicitude as a Projection of our Being-towards-Death: The
     temporal roots of the Belonging-together of Death and Love

"The time remains destitute not only because God is
dead, but because mortals are hardly aware and capable
even of their own mortality. Mortals have not yet come
into ownership of their own nature. Death withdraws
into the enigmatic. The mystery of pain remains
veiled. Love has not been learned... The time is
destitute because it lacks the unconcealedness of the
nature of pain, death and love. This destitution is
itself destitute because that realm of Being withdraws
within which pain and death and love belong together."82

---

82   Martin Heidegger, "Wozu Dichter?", in HW 253-254; e.t. 96-7.

Heidegger here helps to make our purpose clear. Our task is not to remain on the level of an inauthentic understanding of the death of the Other, but to reveal the ontological significance of an ontic event, by entering into a Heideggerean "remembrance" of "that realm of Being" within which "pain and death and love belong together."

Ladislaus Boros, S.J., points out that in the literature of all ages, love and death are two realities seen to be intimately related, and in fact, partial aspects of one and the same reality. Identifying the common root of love and death as a complete forgetfulness and surrender of Self, he explains how "the best love stories end in death, and this is no accident. Love is, of course, and remains the triumph over death, but that is not because it abolishes death, but because it is death itself. Only in death is the total surrender that is love's possible, for only in death can we be exposed completely and without reserve."83

There are many instances in romantic literature (Romeo and Juliet is the obvious example) of a Tristanian passion choosing death. "The writer of the Song of Songs said 'Love is as strong as death'. If this is true," Ralph Harper suggests, "then love is very strong indeed..."84 Tolstoi also will relate the two,

83   Ladislaus Boros, S.J., The Mystery of Death, p. 47.

84   Harper, R. Preface to Human Love: Existential and Mystical.

asking through a central character who is at his death-
bed: "'What is love? It is the negation of death, it is life
itself. All that I understand at all, I understand by love
alone. It includes everything. Love is God and death is the re-
absorption of an atom of love - that is myself - by the universal
and eternal source of love.'"85

In the context of "The Belonging Together of Poetry and
Death", Linda Leonard again suggests something similar. "Poetry", she writes, "brings death before us; it makes us aware of
the death that strikes deeper than the biological, of what
Heidegger calls ontological death. But to die in this sense
means to transform our relation to the world, to transform it in
such a way that we no longer put our ego demands first, and
determine from our own limited perspectives what we are willing
to accept as real and true... We have died to our particular ego
demands and now allow what is to be"86, which means that the poem
"affirms death by saying the whole"; that in order to allow the
poem to "come forth", the poet must be "ready for death"; and
finally, it means that "to receive the poem, one must surrender
to death too."

---

85   Tolstoi, Leo, <u>Anna Karenina</u>, p. 222.

86   Leonard, Linda, "The Belonging-Together of Poetry and -
     Death", in <u>Philosophy Today</u>, Vol. 19, No. 2/4, Summer 1975,
     p. 144.

Reflecting on all of this, one remembers Rilke, who speaks of the openness of the child, able to receive "Death, the whole of death... to hold it all so gently, and be good"[87] -- and then one begins to wonder just how far one wishes to take this image and indeed, whether this is really the route which we should follow, if we are to remain faithful to Heidegger.

What is most disturbing about these images, is that they may remain too metaphysical, in suggesting that both love and death are simply two different roads to a (presumably more fundamental) realm, and that the important thing is to get there, that is, whether you love or whether you die, you will in either case be open to "surrender of self" to a unifying Being-realm, which is the root of the reality of both!

This sort of metaphysical image is, of course, very far from a Heideggerean ontology, and further still from "Thought".

So, while our task is to uncover "that realm of Being... within which pain and death and love belong together",[88] to speak in terms which suggest a metaphysical realm is neither true to our desire to remain loyal to Heidegger, nor is it true to the other side of death which this kind of metaphysical interpretation cannot accommodate, and that is the aspect of death which

---

87   Rainer Maria Rilke, Duino Elegies, Translated by J.B. Leishman, and S. Spender, (NY: W.W. Norton and Co. Inc., 1963), p. 45.

88   HW 254; e.t. 96-7.

is not "good", but is absolutely and utterly "shattering" and

"unheimlich".

To uncover that realm of Being within which pain and death

and love belong together, we cannot speak in metaphysical terms,

which means that we must leap beyond metaphysics, into that realm

of belonging which can only mean the event of appropriation.

> "The event of appropriation is that realm, vibrating
> within itself, through which man and Being reach each
> other in their nature, achieve their active nature by
> losing those qualities with which metaphysics has
> endowed them."89

In seeking to uncover such a "realm" of appropriation,

Heidegger clearly distinguishes his thought from western philoso-

phies which have often understood the belonging together of man

and Being in terms of a synthetic and therefore abstract

identity.90

> "But as long as we ask our questions in this way, we
> are confined within the attempt to represent the
> 'together' of man and Being as a coordination, and to
> establish and explain this coordination either in terms
> of man or in terms of Being."91

We misunderstand the belonging together of man and Being,

Heidegger adds, anytime we "represent everything only in catego-

ries and mediations, be it with or without dialectic. Then we

---

89   ID 101-2, e.t. 37.

90   ID 87-8; e.t. 25.

91   ID 93, e.t. 30.

always find only connections that... present the belonging together of man and Being as intertwining."92

If, however, we are prepared to take the leap beyond metaphysics and systematization, then we may begin to understand the belonging together of man and Being, not in terms of a reconciliation of "the different" - "not as their synthesis, but still more primary and more originary than any thesis"93, in terms of primordial Difference itself, that is, Ontological Difference and appropriative relation. This only means that for us, the matter of thinking is "the difference as difference". With respect to the difference of Being from beings, "the matter of thinking is the Same".94

"The Same" for Heidegger is not the merely identical, for "in the merely identical, the difference disappears", whereas "in the Same, the difference appears."95 We must remember here that the "difference" is not a difference "between" two essents, consequently, our concern is not with "Der Unterschied von Sein und Seiendem", but with an Identity of Difference, of "die Ontologische Differenz". The difference, therefore, is not an analytic difference, but a difference that virtually installs itself

---

92   ID 95, e.t. 32.

93   WD 148, e.t. 241.

94   ID 112, e.t. 47.

95   ID 111, e.t. 45.

in all human life, revealing the true ontological status of man,
who is distinguished (differentiated in the sense of "Unterschied") from all other essents precisely by always having Being
on the horizon. While Being continually differentiates itself
from the essent, man too situates himself "in the differentiation
between essent and Being", so that ultimately, Ontological Difference is a lived difference, and an active differentiating (Un-
terscheidung).

> "Ontology is founded on the differentiation (Unter-
> scheidung) between Being and essent. The 'differen-
> tiation' is more appropriately called by the name
> Differenz since it announces that essent and Being are
> in a sense brought into distinction one from the other,
> separated and yet still related to one another. ...The
> difference (Unterscheidung) as difference (Differenz)
> means that a divergence (Austrag) exists between Being
> and essent."96

It may seem that we have been side-tracked from our original
concern, but that is hardly the case; for the point is, that if
the belonging together of Being and man points to no metaphysical
realm, but to an Identity in Difference, and "active
differentiating", then so too, the belonging together of death
and love of which Heidegger speaks, cannot indicate a "realm" of
Being which is a static domain, and therefore no mere identity,
but rather, it must indicate a belonging wherein each is
"separated and yet still related to one another". (See above
quote.)

---

96   Heidegger M., Nietzsche II, p. 209; translation by H.J. Sil-
      verman, p. 134, in Philosophy Today, Vol. 19, 2/4, Summer, 19

In this context, Boros' comment that love is death itself receives a wholly new meaning; for the indication of the Identity of the two can no longer imply either "mere identity" nor an analytic Unterschied, but can only mean an active, lived Differenz.

This means, in turn, that that "realm of Being" and belonging which Heidegger urges us to remember, of love and death which withdraws in a destitute time, is not a static meta-physical domain, but a differentiating which installs itself in the very structure of Dasein's Being-in-the-world. "Die ontologische Differenz", therefore, is not an isolated "realm" but the true ontological status of Dasein's finite ek-sistence in the world, and this means that it is the meaning of both Dasein's Being-towards-death, as well as his authentically solicitous relation of Being-with.

It also means that this Differenz, as lived, points to a sphere of revelation within such a genuine ontic e-vent as the death of the Other to whom I am related in authentic solicitude, particularly since the belonging together of death and love is a lived belonging which permeates the Being of Dasein, and as such, allows for an entry into an understanding of the potentiality-for-Being of the Other whom I love.

***

"All values", Bachelard reminds us, "must remain vulnerable, and those that do not are dead."[97] As part of the structure of human Being, it is "vulnerability" which is reflected in the notion of finitude and solicitude both.   Were Dasein not "vulnerable", he would be infinite rather than a finite Being-towards-death, and solicitude would be a permanent, static condi-tion, rather than an existentiale which instills itself in the structure of being-human, and finds its meaning in a history of genuine ontic moments.

Finitude, we must remember, is not a Zu-Ende-Sein, but a Sein-zum-Ende. As a state of Dasein's Being, finitude means that the Being of Dasein is rooted in the no-thingness of Being, and is reflected in all Dasein's ways of being, which means, no less, in the relation of solicitude.

To understand the "realm" of belonging of love and death as installed in human-Being and the ways of Being of Dasein, we must not seek a metaphysical domain of belonging, but we must uncover the nullity and the rootedness "within" the temporality of solicitude, as we have considered earlier the temporality of Dasein's Being-towards-death.

It must be emphasized that our understanding of solicitude at no time denies the fundamental individuation of Dasein, as presented by Heidegger and as outlined in earlier chapters.

---

97   Bachelard, Gaston, The Poetics of Space, p. 59.

"Only because Dasein is defined by selfhood can an I-Self relate 'itself' to a Thou-self. Selfhood is the presupposition of the possibility of being an 'I', which itself is revealed only in the 'Thou'".98 Not only is solicitude considered here as a way-to-be which belongs to the very structure of Dasein, but it rests on the difference and distance between persons who are ontologically defined by way of Heidegger's understanding of individuation.

Let us consider, then, where all of this leads us.

We have already shown how the roots of the phenomenon of Being-towards-death are the three temporal ecstases of the past, the present and the future. If we are to speak of a "belonging" of death and love, we must similarly uncover the temporal roots of the phenomenon of solicitude as well.

Recall that it is in the face of "guilt" that we experience the moment of already-Being-in, and that our "thrownness" is grounded in the temporal structure of the past. In a summons from the lostness in the inauthentic concerns of the "they", the call of conscience is a call to the negativity of one's existential guilt, formally defined, says Heidegger, as "Being-the-basis of a nullity"99; and this, in turn, means "never to have power over one's ownmost Being from the ground up."100

---

98   Heidegger, M. Vom Wesen des Grundes, (Bilingual translation) p. 87.

99   SZ 283.

100 SZ 284.

In solicitude, the moment of "already Being-in" or "having been" shows itself within a parallel recognition that one is not responsible for, and consequently cannot have ultimate power over the Being of the Other "from the ground up", any more than one can "have power over one's ownmost Being from the ground up." This moment of "having been", in fact, is the basic testimony to the Otherness of the Other. The Other is not my creation, not my possession, and consequently, not mine to dominate and willfully control. "Diese Fürsorge", Heidegger reminds us, "ist nicht beherrschende, sondern freigebende."101

Not only is the Otherness of the Other defined, therefore, by his biological individuality, but it is grounded in the existential structure of the very Being of the Other as an individual Dasein. This is revealed through solicitude, only when one recognizes this existential structure as part of a wider recognition of the existential Otherness and uniqueness of the Other.

Heidegger reminds us that in being open to the past, one is called by conscience from its lostness, to a remembrance of its essence as <u>thrown individuation</u>. Similarly, authentic solicitude requires a <u>respect</u> (because the Other is not my creation or mere possession) for the uniqueness and indispensability of the thrown individuation of the Other in his existential Otherness.

---

101 Heidegger, M. <u>Logik: Die Frage nach der Wahrheit</u>, p. 223.

The phenomenon of the present, Heidegger has said, reveals the resoluteness of a factical Dasein at a particular time, which brings Dasein into its true "Situation" among essents. But this means essentially, that Dasein is offered a choice either to submit to the superficial attractiveness of the concerns of "das Man", which means to sacrifice genuineness for a lostness of essence among things; or Dasein can respond with an authentic acceptance of fallenness and a letting-be of the essence of the moment.

In solicitude, there is a similar choice. One can submit to inauthenticity in two ways: either the Other can be subsumed in one's mind, among other thing-like concerns of the everyday world, which means that as a result, I take the Other for granted; or, on another level, I can submit to the tendency to approach the Other in terms of particular, analyzable characteristics rather than in terms of the mystery of his unique existence, which I am open to in a loving relation. In short, I can represent the Other.

On the other hand, in an authentic relation of solicitude, the present may take the form of the authentic existential moment (Augenblick rather than Gegenwärtigen which is a "making present" of the Zuhanden before Dasein.) Heidegger tells us that:

> "That Present which is held in authentic temporality and which is authentic itself, we call the 'moment of vision' [Augenblick]. This term must be understood in the active sense as an ecstasis. It means the absolute rapture with which Dasein is carried away to whatever

possibilities and circumstances are encountered in the Situation as possible objects of concern, but a rapture which is <u>held</u> in resoluteness".102

Such a "moment of vision" is a phenomenon which cannot be clarified simply in terms of a "now" (<u>dem Jetzt</u>) "in which" something occurs, or passes away as present-at-hand. "'In the moment of vision', nothing can occur; but as an authentic Present or waiting-towards, the moment of vision permits us <u>to encounter</u> <u>for the first time</u> what can be 'in a time' as ready-to-hand or present-at-hand."103

In the moment of solicitude, the phenomenon of the present is <u>not</u> authentically revealed by the empirically accessible presence of the Other "in" a "now", for ontologically, the present must signify more. If the present is said to take an authentic form within the "moment of vision", then in the context of solicitude, it can mean no less than that "absolute rapture with which Dasein is carried away to whatever possibilities and circumstances are encountered in the Situation". This is not to signify some "romantic rapture" with the Other but is a rapture "<u>held</u> in that resoluteness" which, Heidegger has told us, "pushes [Dasein] into solicitous Being with Others."104 Gadamer suggests that the true nature of "being present" is constituted by

---

102   SZ 338.

103   SZ 338.

104   SZ 298.

"contemporaneity", which, significantly, is not to be equated with "simultaneity" within a "now", but means instead, that something that presents   itself to us "achieves in its presentation full presentness, however remote its origin might be".105 In such a contemporaneous presence of the Other, one "endures" in the encounter, to be carried away in the recognition simply that the Other is present.

Occasionally, we may unwittingly and for no explicit reason (as Heidegger says, in the "moment of vision", no-thing can occur) suddenly come to an awareness of the wealth of unique presence of the Other -- a parent may feel this for his child-- and while this may arise in a "moment of vision", it is not a "making-present" or "re-presenting" of the Other, but involves instead a genuine openness to the possibilities encountered in the "Situation" of and with the Other.

However, this means that in order to take authentic form as more than the "just now", "the present" must be seen as tempo-ralizing itself in terms of the authentic future106 -- indeed, in terms of the dynamic unity of the three ecstases.107   To avoid "the ecstasis (rapture) of forgetting" which is a backing-away in the face of one's ownmost "been", into inauthenticity, the true

---

105 Gadamer, Hans-Georg, Truth and Method, p. 112.

106 SZ 338.

107 SZ 339.

"moment of vision" (Augenblick) requires an openness to the authentic future which, in the context of solicitude, means an openness to the authentic power-to-be-whole of the Other.

In the context of Sein und Zeit, this, of course, suggests an attitude of a free acceptance of death, as it is death which Heidegger has shown to be the only existential of totality. Does this mean, therefore, that in order that "Dasein, as Being-with, have some understanding of the potentiality-for-Being of Others"108 -- Dasein must freely accept the death of the Other?

This does sound bizarre, and indeed, as so stated, it is not our contention.

We must recall that for Heidegger, a free acceptance of death is not an acceptance simply of the fact of an occurrence (i.e. my end); it is not a Zu-Ende-Sein but a Sein-zum-Ende. To disclose Dasein's authentic power-to-be-whole is not to generalize on the basis of an empirical case-of-death of Dasein, but it is to come to an awareness of the essential temporal roots of Dasein's Being, which means, as essentially constituted by finitude.

To have some understanding of the Potentiality-for-Being of the Other, I need not necessarily envision him as "dead". On the contrary, I must come to an awareness of his authentic futurity. In fact, I must be open to the "vulnerability" of his being of

---

108   Cf. initial quote of the previous section (i); SZ 264.

which we spoke above, which is the condition for change -- the Other is not a static, substantial Whole; I must be open to the possibilities of his Situation; in short, I must be open to an understanding of the Other in terms of his fundamental Pro-ject.109

We must keep in mind that this does not mean that I must be aware simply of the "goals in life" of the Other, or his Project in terms of some explicit task to be completed. "Project", as we intend it here, signifies the underlying condition of such a notion. It signifies the unthematic understanding and care for the Other (Fürsorge) which is an essential recognition of his possibilities as possibilities. It signifies "the nullity...[which] belongs to Dasein's Being-free for its existen-

---

109   Cf. A. Paskow, "The Meaning of my Death", in International Philosophical Quarterly, Vol. 14, March, 1974, where on page 67, he suggests that one grave problem in Heidegger's discussion of death in Sein und Zeit, is that Heidegger does not sufficiently consider how "in facing my own death directly, I can for the first time identify with the other in a way that permits and even encourages the emergence of his otherness. Being capable now of listening to the call of conscience, I grasp that I have a set of basic possibilities that pertain only to me, they define my potential uniqueness. And insofar as I see in another's interior the same kind of anxiety in the shadow of his own death that I have about my own death, I may infer that he too is affected, if only subconsciously, by a potentiality-for-Being which points the way to his authentic and individual Selfhood. I thus understand that although the other is at a fundamental level similar to me, he may also be, at least potentially, different from me insofar as he is laid claim to by his conscience."

tiel possibilities"110 and the fundamental existential projection
in-the-world, which makes Dasein's world meaningful for him, in
terms of his primordial orientation and beliefs.

The past, the present and the future, therefore, each ground
the phenomenon of solicitude and make it meaningful. Clearly,
this cannot be a merely contrived imposition of the temporal
ecstases, upon the phenomenon of solicitude: Heidegger has said
that Being with Others belongs to the very Being of Dasein, which
is in turn revealed in the "Daseinanalytics" in its temporal
structure. Time is no contrived structure in this connection,
nor is it that "within which" solicitude must be situated for
purposes of analysis. Time is the horizon for all understanding
of Being-in-the-world, and for any way of interpreting it.
"Whenever Dasein tacitly understands... it does so with time as
its standpoint"111, which means that time remains the horizon, as
well, in our understanding relation with Others.

It is worth repeating in this connection, Anatole France's
remark that "we could not know love were we to live indefini-
tely", for this is attested to in the disclosure of the temporal
structure of solicitude.

Yet, our discussion here remains incomplete. We have spoken
of the temporal structure of solicitude in terms of the three

---

110 SZ 285.

111 SZ 17.

ecstases of past, present and future, but Heidegger's "way" of Thought really takes us beyond such a structure, to further depths in the primordial "giving" or "granting" which is the condition of the opening up of future, past and present. While we have, up to now, considered "true time" to be three-dimensional, the later Heidegger asks: "but from what source is the unity of the three dimensions of true time determined, the unity, that is, of its three interplaying ways of giving, each in virtue of its own presencing?"112

We recall his own response to be that true time is not three-dimensional, but four-dimensional:

> "The unity of time's three dimensions consists in the interplay of each toward each. This interplay proves to be the true extending, playing in the very heart of time, the fourth dimension, so to speak - not only so to speak, but in the nature of the matter".113

But while true time is four-dimensional, "the dimension which we call the fourth in our count is, in the nature of the matter, the first, that is, the giving that determines all."114 Remembering this, we must consider what this means with regard to our discussion of the temporal structure of authentic solicitude.

Heidegger tells us that the unity of the four-dimensional time which "we call the first, original, literally incipient

---

112   ZD 15, e.t. 15.

113   ZD 16, e.t. 15.

114   ZD 16, e.t. 15.

extending... of true time, consists in 'nearing nearness', 'nearhood' [Nahheit], an early word still used by Kant. But it brings
future, past and present near to one another, by distancing-
them."115

If the "fourth dimension" is not merely a dialectical resolution, but is "the first giving that determines all", then it is
this very interplay of "nearness" and "distancing" which must
ground each moment of solicitude as we have presented it above in
terms of the three temporal ecstases; and indeed, this is the
case.

We have said that the phenomenon of the past reveals the
thrown individuation of the Other - which means, his essential
Otherness - and consequently, my distance from him.   But such a
distance is the condition of "nearhood", because it is only
inasmuch as I am receptive to the Other (he is not my creation,
so this implies receptivity) - that I can bridge this distance in
the nearness of a genuine respect.

The phenomenon of the present brings Dasein into its true
"Situation", but there is a distance revealed when one recognizes
that the "true Situation" is the Other's situation in-the-world.
This is the condition for inauthentic re-presentation of the
Other, but the distance can be bridged again in the "nearness" of
a rare "moment of vision", as we have discussed.

---

115 ZD 16, e.t. 15.

Finally, the future _distances_ from me, the fundamental transcendental projection of the Other, within which he situates _his_ world; and yet, the nearness comes in a relation of leaping-ahead of the Other in his potentiality-for-Being to "help the Other to become transparent to himself in his care and to become _free_ for it".116   Such leaping-ahead is, in fact, an authentic _caring for_ the Other's very _potentiality-for-Being_, rather than a "what" with which he is concerned, and in this sense, is a "nearness" which respects the uniqueness and the freedom of the Other.

Significantly, then, the nearness-remoteness interplay of time's four-dimensionality is not only reflected in solicitude, but it defines it in all its modes, and in its essence. Our entire discussion of solicitude, and authentic understanding of the Other in the relation of Being-with, hinges on the funda-mental _distance between_ persons, which is the _condition of near-ness_. We are in total agreement with Heidegger when he states that man is:

> "...a creature of distance.   Only through the primor-dial distances he establishes toward all being in his transcendence does a true nearness to things flourish in him.   And only the knack for hearing into the distance awakens Dasein as self to the answer of its Dasein with others.   For only in its Dasein with others can Dasein surrender its individuality in order to win itself as an authentic self."117

---

116   SZ 122.

117   WG 131.

It is only because time is essentially the opening up of an extending which consists in the interplay of "nearness" and "distance" that the relation of solicitude, as an essentially temporal phenomenon, can be similarly defined.

But this means that solicitude, thus understood, is based on a distance wherein, to quote Simone Weil, "two friends have fully consented to be two and not one, they respect the distance which the fact of being two distinct creatures places between them."118

Solicitude, in this sense, is characterized by a lack, and yet, such a lack is indicative of the no-thingness of Sein which is not "just nothing", but, on the contrary, is the condition for a truly primordial bridging of the distance in authentic solicitude. This is so because, in such a primordial "bridging" in understanding, I do not just understand "elements" of the Others's "experiences"; I understand "nothing in particular" which, Buber has said, means "only everything".

In summary:

solicitude is a primordial encounter of "nearness", which is primordial, however, only inasmuch as it is rooted in "distance" and a lack, indicative of a core of no-thingness which means, having origins in Being itself, and in the primordial individuation (and finitude) which is the condi-

---

118 Simone Weil, Waiting for God, cited in "Simone Weil on Friendship", by A-M Sharp, in Philosophy Today, Vol. 22, No. 4/4, Winter 1978, p. 269.

tion of the possibility of nearness in contemporaneous presence within a "moment of vision"; in a respect for the uniqueness of the Other in his "thrown individuation"; and in my leaping-ahead for the Other in his fundamental Pro-ject.

Moreover, the ontological meaning of death of the Other (as "A Death" rather than a mere Todesfall) is a primordial encounter of distance, that is, of the "strange and alien [unheimlich] thing that banishes us once and for all from everything in which we are at home"119. This primordial and overwhelming encounter of the abyss is possible only on the basis of the nearness achieved in solicitude.

Before expanding on this second point in order to substantiate it, we also add the following:

that the "realm of Being" within which death and love belong together is, at the same time, "the realm of Time" - but Time as revealed by Heidegger in Zur Sache des Denkens, to be the fourth dimension of an "It-gives" which is the meaning of the Ontological Difference. As consisting of a "nearing nearness" which brings future, past and present near to one another by distancing them, Time provides the

---

119   EM 121, e.t. 133.

clue   for   an   ontologically fundamental   understanding of death and love.

Moreover, we must further keep in mind that Heidegger has said, in fact, that we are to seek that realm of Being within which pain and death and love belong together. It is our conten- tion that pain is, with Time, at the root of the ontological meaning of both death and love, and as such, grounds both in their belonging.   We say this because Heidegger tells us else- where that "we should not imagine pain anthropologically as a sensation that makes us feel afflicted."   What, then, is Pain? "Pain rends. It is the rift.   But it does not tear apart into dispersive fragments.   Pain indeed tears asunder, it separates, yet so that at the same time, it draws everything to itself, gathers it to itself... Pain is the joining agent in the rending that divides and gathers. Pain is the joining of the rift... It settles the between, the middle of the two that are separated in it.   Pain joins the rift of the difference.   Pain is the dif- ference itself."120

It is Pain, in this sense, that is at the root of the trage- dy inherent in love and death, and in their belonging - indeed, in the "Joy of Yes in the sadness of the finite"121- which is man.

---

120 US 27, e.t. 204.

121 An extraordinary description from Paul Ricoeur's Fallible Man, p. 215.

Perhaps this is why "at no time was Christ more human than when nailed to the cross with the five wounds bleeding, the stigmata, the marks of his passion.- The pursuit of the wound, the pursuit of pain, is a way a man can prove he is alive, even if only he is a prayerful witness, because pain is a living presence; it inhabits the nerve ends, the spirit, it makes a man cry out passionately, or so saps him that his cry becomes a silent, dark zero."122

(iii)   A Death.

> "Louise's baby is dead...It is not my death.
> I close my eyes, I remain motionless, but I
> am remembering things about myself, and her
> death enters into my life, but I do not enter
> into her death...
>
> The sin of being another human being..."123

Simone de Beauvoir's reminiscences have captured the signi- ficance of Heidegger's many comments in Sein und Zeit, which point to the difficulty of achieving a true understanding of death by way of the death of the Other. "The closest closeness", Heidegger points out, "which one may have in Being towards death

---

122   B. Callaghan, in an article on Cardinal Léger, entitled
       "Léger and the Lepers" in Weekend, April 28, 1979. p. 18.)

123   Simone de Beauvoir, The Blood of Others, cited in E. Marks,
       Simone de Beauvoir: Encounters with Death, p. 34.

as a possibility, is as far as possible from anything actual"124
and thus an "actual death" reveals little in terms of the Being-
toward-death which defines Dasein in its very existential structure. Even when we envision the death of the Other as a "very
real possibility", such a vision does not reveal, in fact, a true
ontological meaning, because Being-towards-death as Being towards
a possibility means more than "dwelling upon the end in its
possibility" in the sense of "pondering over when and how this
possibility may perhaps be actualized".125 Death as a
possibility is not just one more ontic "possibility among
possibilities", but refers to death as an existentiale, disclo-
sing Dasein in his ownmost potentiality-for-Being.

It is unnecessary to repeat Heidegger's entire discussion
regarding our re-presentative experience of the death of the
Other, and our encounter with "something unalive" in "the beginning of the same entity qua something present-at-hand". However,
the validity of Heidegger's comments must be kept in mind particularly now, because they will serve as a cautionary reminder of
what we do not dispute, i.e. that in most "cases of death", death
does get "passed off as... something 'actual'" as its "character
as a possibility gets concealed"126, and that in most cases,

---

124 SZ 262.

125 SZ 261.

126 SZ 253.

"recovery" from the death of the Other is such that death as an unüberholbaree possibility remains undisclosed.

Having said this, however, we recall that Heidegger has also suggested that while death individualizes, Dasein as Being-with may have some understanding of the potentiality-for-Being of Others. Moreover, he has said that our time is destitute because the essential belonging on a deepest ontological level, of love and death, has been forgotten.

While a "case of death" may tell me little about the ontological meaning of death, we have suggested that the relation of authentic solicitude opens me to an authentic understanding of the potentiality-for-Being of the Other in such a way that "asking about the ontological meaning of the dying of the person who dies, as a possibility-of-Being which belongs to his very Being"127 can be possible only if I have come to some understanding of the potentiality-for-Being of the Other, in my relation of authentic Being-with.

While it is true that authentic solicitude does reveal the possibility of a unique, ontological understanding of the Being of the Other, this does not mean, of course, that my authentic Being-with will ever allow me to die the Other's death for him, in the sense of relieving the Other of the certain, unüberholbare possibility of the impossibility of his existence. Death remains

---

127   SZ 239.

always Dasein's ownmost possibility because of this, and it remains non-relational as well, in the sense that ultimately, no relation -- not even of authentic Being-with-- can remedy or take away the death of another human being, whose very essence is defined by finitude and Being-toward-death.

Realizing this, the question to consider is whether my authentic Being-with the Other provides access for an ontological understanding of the Other's potentiality-for-Being, which is to say his Being-toward-death, as the condition of a genuine understanding of the ontic e-vent of the death of the Other. In other words, we are asking about the possibility of a significant understanding of an e-vent, the death of another human being, which understanding is accessible by virtue of a fundamental existential relation of solicitude.

In order that this ontic event reveal ontological significance, it must reveal a "realm of Being" which is not a metaphysical realm, however, but an abyss which pervades our very core.

It is clear that the death of the Other to whom I am related in authentic solicitude, is no incidental event from which I recover easily or which touches me in a superficial, passing manner. With the death of the Other, an overwhelming abyss is disclosed. The abyss which is thus disclosed in my initial encounter with the death of the Other is more overwhelming inasmuch as the Other is no longer a being, that is, he is no-being.

The Unüberholbarkeit of death shocks and overwhelms me, in the revelation of the no-thingness of existence and the ground of no-thingness which subsumes the Other. Far from signifying a beginning qua something present-at-hand, an encounter with A Death discloses sheer absence of presence, the agony of an impassable distance, and a remoteness which in most other instances, finds some balance and resolution in a counter-immersion in-the-world of our concerns.

While this may be open to dispute, it seems to me that an important reason why the corpse of the deceased person seems so "unnatural" and absurdly foreign, is because the corpse as a present-at-hand entity is not only totally devoid of the presence of the person which we felt in our solicitous relation with him when he was living, but its presence, precisely as a present-at-hand entity, seems to want to deny that very absence and no-thingness which has engulfed the nearness of presence which was the essence of solicitude; it is an unreasonable contradiction and denial of an essential nothingness of a Dasein who is-no-more, and is also a further reminder of the "impossibility of any existence at all" of the Other as a person.

In fact, the absurdity and powerlessness which I feel is the final triumph of Being, over which I have no control. "A Death" discloses the abyss, the original giving which has now "taken" the Other in such a way that for all Time, he is no-being.

The death of the Other reveals ontological meaning, not inasmuch as an occurrence, i.e. a "case of death" has now been "actualized"; such an ontic event is a revelation of more than a present-at-hand entity (i.e. the deceased), it is a revelation of the fundamental no-thingness of the finitude of human being, a nothingness which can never be grasped, can ultimately never be conquered, and to that extent, reveals once again, that man is the shepherd and the guardian, and not the master, of Being.

By way of authentic solicitude, we come to an understanding of the potentiality-for-Being of the Other. But then the Other dies, and while it is true, as Freud says about the death of a child, that "our hopes, our pride, our happiness, lie in the grave with him, we will not be consoled, we will not fill the loved one's place",128 -- yet his death reveals not just my subjective "feelings" about a loss; for the tragedy is not just my loss, but I am overwhelmed by the loss of the Being of the-Other. He is no-being, and therefore, because in a very true sense, I "am" the Other as a Being-with, his no-being opens me to the no-thingness and the mystery of Being itself.

---

128 Cited in J.G. Murphy, "Rationality and the Fear of Death", in the Monist, April 1976, Vol. 59, No. 2, p. 193.

If, in solicitude, I have come to an understanding of the Other in his potentiality-for-Being, and thereby encounter a "nearness" which is never permanent because it is rooted in a fundamental "distance", the death of the Other, initially at least129, discloses within the shattering moment of an ontic event, the awesome nothingness of that grounding distance, made all the more meaningful precisely because of that initial "nearness" of solicitude which is the condition of the possibility of the disclosure of an ontological significance of "A Death" (rather than a "case of death") of the Other.

We recall that the "nearness" which I encounter in solicitude reveals a respect for the Other in the uniqueness of his thrown individuation; it reveals a contemporaneous presence; and finally, it allows for a "leaping-ahead" for the Other in his fundamental Pro-ject.

But with the death of the Other comes the end of that project. The death of a person, unlike that of an animal, means not only the destruction of an organism, but signifies the end of a conscious history, and of a transcending, understanding appropriation of the world.

J.G. Murphy suggests that inasmuch as "persons define themselves in large measure, in terms of their future-oriented projects... then we can see wherein much of the badness of death

---

129 We shall show how "Recovery" is an important part of the meaning of the death of the Other.

lies: Death", he says, "represents lost opportunity... It is this idea that death means no more chances which tormented Ivan Ilych.. when the question suddenly occurred to him: 'What if my whole life has been wrong?'... What had appeared perfectly impossible before, namely, that he had not spent his life as he should have done, might after all be true..."130

Murphy continues by saying that since "our self-identifying projects may be bound up with persons very close to us... this explains why we sometimes see the deaths of our children or wives as a partial death of our own persons."

But "project", as we understand the term, includes more than Murphy's definition, as "the desire to accomplish something in one's profession, to provide for one's family, to achieve certain satisfactions, to redress moral injuries done, etc."131 The death of the Other does not mean just the end of some of my projects which are "bound up with persons very close to us", because "project" means something more than mere tasks and goals, "things we must do".

When we say that the death of the Other discloses the "end of the fundamental Pro-ject of the Other", we mean that in the depths of our being, we have come to an understanding that a fundamental meaning-projection of a Being-in-the-world is-no-

---

130 J.G. Murphy, "Rationality and the Fear of Death", in The Monist, Vol. 59, No. 2, April 1976, p. 197.

131 J.G. Murphy, Ibid, p. 197.

more. We are less aware of the fact that a certain task or series of tasks can now no longer be completed by the Other, as we are aware of <u>the impossibility of any existence at all</u> for the Other. The trauma of realizing that the Other will never speak again, that he will never hold me, never be close to me, that he simply is no longer, and never again will be, is so overpoweringly absurd, that at first, it is difficult to begin to comprehend at all.

Similarly, it is not just a question of <u>my</u> now not being able to do certain things which the Other could have otherwise participated in, but rather, I am made aware of the end of a project in the sense of the tragic destruction of a unique person, which brings us to a fundamental awareness once again, of the meaning of <u>his</u> thrown individuation. The <u>uniqueness</u> of the Other means, then, that not only is the life of the Other a unique presence, but equally so, our openness to the uniqueness of the Other in his thrown individuation, makes the death of such a person a unique event, entirely different from the death of any other man, because of a uniqueness revealed to me initially through solicitude. This is probably what Proust had in mind when he wrote:

> "The death of Swann! Swann, in this phrase, is some-
> thing more than a noun in the possessive case. I mean
> by it his own particular death, the death allotted by
> destiny to the service of Swann. For we talk of 'death'

for convenience, but there are... as many different deaths as there are people..."132

The death of the Other reveals not just the "end" of an "entity"; rather, the ontic event of the "end" of the Other to whom I am related in authentic solicitude, reveals the depth of not-being, and an abyss which penetrates all beings as their ontological ground.

Heidegger tells us that death is more than "an end", more than "a loss", because it reveals something other than another ontic occurrence; and so "death", as a phenomenon, must point to our Being-toward-death and as such an _existentiale_, it becomes ontologically relevant in the _Daseinanalytics_.

But while we agree that what Heidegger has said is very true, it is incomplete when it comes to the truth revealed in that singularly important, and shattering ontic event of the Other's death. Within such an event, there _can_ be other than an inauthentic significance, if there has been something other than inauthentic Being-with.

In authentic solicitude, I may come to an understanding of the potentiality-for-Being of the Other, precisely because solicitude is a projection of our Being-toward-death, i.e. it is rooted in temporality. The Other is no longer part of the anonymous "they-world", but in the nearness of an in-finite

---

132 Marcel Proust, La prisonnière in A la recherche du temps perdu, cited in Mora, J.F. Being and Death, p. 201.

presence to the Other, I become the Other through ontic e-vents of understanding.

If I say that I "become" the Other or "am" the Other, we might ask: am I the Other in the same way that I am my death?133 The answer must be no. Death is an existentiale, as is Being-with, but the Other is not an existentiale! However, in my relation of authentic Being-with and through a history of e-ventful moments of understanding, I can come to an authentic understanding of the Other in his potentiality-for-Being, and therefore, this means that in the dying of the Other person, and indeed, in the ontic event of his death, I too encounter death together with him. Simone de Beauvoir, who has understood so well "the sin of being another human being", and the difficulty of entering into the death of another person, yet in another context, strikingly shows how she "becomes" her dying mother.

> "...it was when I was at her bedside that I saw Death, the Death of the dance of death, with its bantering grin, the Death of fireside tales that knocks on the door, a scythe in its hand, the Death that comes from elsewhere, strange and inhuman: it had the face of Maman...
>
> I went home; I talked to Sartre; we played some Bartok. Suddenly, at eleven, an outburst of tears that almost degenerated into hysteria.
>
> Amazement... I had understood all my sorrows up until that night; even when they flowed over my head I recognized myself in them. This time, my despair escaped from my control: someone other than myself was weeping in me. I talked to Sartre about my mother's mouth as I

---

133   Cf. SZ 245.

had seen it that morning and about everything I had interpreted in it: greediness refused, an almost servile
humility, hope, distress, loneliness - the loneliness
of her death and of her life - that did not want to
admit its existence. And he told me that my own mouth
was not obeying me any more: I had put Maman's mouth on
my own face and in spite of myself, I copied its
movements. Her whole person, her whole being, was concentrated there, and compassion wrung my heart..."134

Related to this, it is interesting to note that throughout
this existentialist's writings, the only obsession that appears
to be as strong as the obsession with her own inevitable nothingness, is the death of Sartre.

While, as Heidegger says, death "individualizes", it also
contains another level of significance which is directly related
to the existentiale of Being-with Others.   Death, as an ontic
event, has a social significance, but this "social significance"
does not find a form only within the re-presentative significance
of rites and artificial rituals. It has an ontological "social"
significance, for those who are in an ontologically meaningful
solicitous relation.

This means that even my own death, as an ontic possibility,
may be less important to me than the realization of the effect
that my death will have upon the Others with whom I am-with. St-
Exupéry makes this clear: Lost in the Sahara with his friend
Prevot, he recalls:

---

134 Cited in E. Marks, Simone de Beauvoir: Encounters with Death,
     p. 106.

"Prevot no more than I was wringing his hands at the
sight of death the way we are told men do.   But there
did exist something that he could not bear any more
than I could.   I was perfectly ready to fall asleep,
whether for a night or for eternity... But that cry
that would be sent up at home, that great wail of
desolation, that was what I could not bear.   I could
not stand idly by and look on at disaster.   Each second
of silence drove the knife deeper into someone I
loved. At the thought, a blind rage surged up in
me..."135

For the "survivors", death as this kind of ontic event

reveals the no-thingness which is at the root of all existence;

and the "nearer" the "nearness" in solicitude, the more overwhel-

ming is the "absence" of the Other in his death. The nothingness

plunges the Other into non-existence, non-being, and thereby

plunges me into a dread and a revolt of existence itself. As

Edna St. Vincent Millay points out in her well-known poem, "Dirge

Without Music", "A formula, a phrase remains-/ but the best is

lost", and "I am not resigned"; the vividness of this realization

that the world of the Other is no more, makes a mockery of all

logic; as Rilke says, "what removes us in death, nothing

unveils."136 It is one time when Being's revelation is far from

sublime and "blue" in the sense of an "arrival at the quieter

sojourn".137

---

135 Antoine de Saint-Exupéry, "Prisoner of the Sand" in Wind,
     Sand and Stars, translated by Lewis Galantière (New York:
     Harcourt, Brace and World, 1967), p. 157.

136 Rilke's Sonnet to Orpheus, as quoted by Heidegger, in HW 255,
     P.L.T. 97.

137 US 69, e.t. 187.

The depths of this emptiness, and the unfathomable chaos of
nothingness throws me into the closest comprehension perhaps of
what Levinas will have called the il y a - an existence without
world, a night without beings; and it is only Recovery, in the
sense in which we shall now present it, that brings us back from
the deepest sense of despair.

(iv) Recovery.

> "My uncle Maurice, having existed entirely on fresh
> green salad for two or three years, had died of stomach
> cancer after the most hideous sufferings. My aunt and
> Madeleine had mourned him long and loud. But
> eventually, they found consolation, and life at La
> Grillère became much gayer than it had been in the
> past."138

The fact that one recovers from the death of the Other, and
that "life goes on" as before (or, as the quote above shows,
perhaps goes on better than before) provides a large measure of
justification for Heidegger's contention that in the dying of the
Other, we simply experience a "change-over of an entity from
Dasein's kind of Being (or life) to no-longer-Dasein"139 and that
this means no more than the "beginning of the same entity qua
something present-at-hand."   I may be-with the Other in my
thoughts, but since "the deceased himself is no longer factically
'there'", and since Being-with means "Being with one another in

---

138 Simone de Beauvoir, cited in E. Marks, op.cit., p. 35.
139 SZ 238.

the same world", this only goes to show that my conceptual representation of the Other after his death, is far from being ontologically relevant.

Moreover, the fact that we recover from the deaths of Others also reminds us that there is an ontological necessity (Notwendigkeit, as discussed in Part One) of individuation which is revealed in the meaning of Dasein as a transcending Being-in-the-world. The fact that Dasein "continues to exist as before" apparently testifies to his "individuation" as an intentionally-projecting ek-sistence, and indeed, the fact that one does continue to function as before, notwithstanding the loss of the Other, may even bring into question the truth of our assertion that solicitude can be truly authentic at all. That I "continue to exist as before" may well suggest that my relation with the Other was not fundamental, in fact, but of incidental or secondary importance. What is primary in any "Daseinanalytic", it may then be concluded, is Dasein itself as an intentional appropriation of essents — and the phenomenon of "recovery" simply proves this once again.

Yet we recall that Heidegger has not spoken of Dasein simply as an intentional Being-in-the-world, but that even in his early works, he insists that "intentionality is only possible, if Dasein as such in itself [als solches in sich selbst] is trans-

cendental."140   Transcendence is not only the condition for
Being-with, but   transcendence itself is only possible insofar as
the Being of Dasein is grounded in Time.141   In order to go-
beyond intentionality, to more fundamental ontological roots,
Heidegger shows temporality to be the meaning of transcendence
and individuation.   Our own presentation of the meaning of authentic solicitude has been geared to remain faithful to Heidegger's understanding of individuation, and so it is unnecessary to
repeat how we feel that authentic Being-with is a true possibility.

The question to ask at this point, however, is whether it is
possible to respect the   ontological   meaning   of Dasein's
individuation, and yet, in recalling the funamental ontological
meaning of Time in which individuation and transcendence are
rooted, can we uncover an authentic mode of "Recovery" which will
be distinct from the inauthentic mode of a lostness among the
world of everyday concerns -- and which will therefore respect
and "care" for, in the sense of "shelter", the relation of
solicitude and the depth of significance of a genuine ontic
event, "A Death"?

The very word "Recovery" is most commonly translated by the
German "Erholung" (f), which suggests rest, recuperation, and

---

140   GP 447.

141   GP 447.

rehabilitation. To recover from an illness, then, or from the death of the Other, is translated as "sich erholen". In what sense is recovery a "coming round to oneself", or a "getting" hold of oneself?

We recall that Dasein as a Self is neither a Subjekt, nor does one stand alone in any ontic sense, but rather, Dasein is a Being-in-the-world. As a Being-in-the-world, Dasein ek-sists among a world of things -- either inauthentically, or in privileged moments, authentically.

As "inauthentic", Dasein can recover from a death by immersing itself in the everyday, comfortable concerns of the "they-world", and in large part, recovery consists of just that.

But Heidegger himself has said that death can call man to a more authentic "sparing", caring and sheltering of the things-that-are. In "getting" hold of oneself, can recovery from a death not also bring me to a more authentic "sparing" of the things-that-are?

We have shown solicitude to be an encounter with "nearness", rooted in a primordial "distance" of an Ab-grund; and we have shown how "a death", as an ontic event, reveals a nothingness which is all the more "unheimlich" and strange because it emerges from an initial "nearness" of presence in solicitude.

The root of the belonging of solicitude and death, we have identified as Time -- the four-dimensional "realm", which is, for all intents and purposes, "the first".

It is our contention now, that Recovery, in an authentic
sense of the word, is essentially related to Time.

We say that "time heals all", and this casual remark is far
from insignificant. Out of the overwhelming depths of no-
thingness, we are called back to a dwelling among things, within
a "Recovery" which, as a "getting" hold of oneself, is a return
to an awareness of our temporal Being. But the roots of this
temporality, in the most fundamental meaning, lead to a four-
dimensional realm of a revealing/concealing essence of the "It
gives".

Recovery, then, is the restoration for Dasein of the balance
of a nearness/remoteness essencing of Being, which is Time itself.

As I "get" hold of myself within a Recovery which is essentially related to Time, the temporality of my Being-in-the-world
reveals again the forms of the past, the present and the future.

If the phenomenon of the past discloses the ontological
significance of the uniqueness of every thrown individuation,
then too, it is the condition of my realization that while the
Other is-no-more, I, as the thrown individuation which I am, must
continue to Be in-the-world. "Getting" hold of myself involves a
"coming round" to the meaning of my own individuation once again,
so that as I "recover", the absence and no-being of the Other
begins to be balanced in the realization of the need (Not) that I

continue-to-Be in-the-world as the Self which, in the deepest ontological sense, Heidegger has shown that I am.

This involves, as well, the understanding that my present "Situation", and the possibilities which are handed over within this Situation, are now part of my new reality. The Other is-no-more, but still, I-am-in-the-world, and as so situated, I understand from the ecstasis of the present, new possibilities which again, constitute the meaning of a world which no longer belongs to the Other, and yet continues to belong to me by virtue of my temporal, ek-sistential situatedness.

Indeed, this is all part of an equally important disclosure, through the form of the future ecstasis, that my future pro-jections in-the-world will continue, despite the loss of the Other, and that, as a futurally-projecting individuation, I must continue to ek-sist.

But if such "getting" hold of onself in Recovery involves a coming round to oneself by virtue of the temporal roots of my individuation, doesn't this mean that my relation of solicitude with the Other was, in fact, incidental rather than fundamental, and therefore, his death was not truly significant or ontologically meaningful?

In answer to this question, we must keep in mind that if the temporal roots of my existential structure explain how I must continue to ek-sist in "getting" hold of myself in Recovery, so too, we recall that the relation of solicitude is grounded in temporality, and moreover, that Being-with, as an _existentiale_, is of the very essence of my temporal Being-in-the-world. Therefore, while Recovery -- as essentially related to Time -- means a "getting" holding of _myself_ inasmuch as I continue to ek-sist as a transcendental individuation, that very Recovery, as related to Time, also is the condition for a kind of ontological "meaning-presence" of the Other, even in his absence.

Indeed, once one realizes that the phenomenon of the _past_ reveals the truth of _my_ thrown individuation, but by the same token, shows that the individuation has-been fundamentally in-fluenced by _the Other_; once one realizes that the phenomenon of the present discloses _my_ own situatedness in a world of things- but that even in the presence of this world of things, _the Other_ can (in a sense which we will explain) leave _his_ _"presence"_ in things behind; and finally, once one realizes that while my ek-sistential pro-jects are _my own_ - yet (since time is a continuum) my future is essentially affected because of my past relation with the Other - _then_, we realize that Recovery need not be merely a phenomenon of "coming round to oneself" in the sense of "getting" hold of an individuation which is isolated and remains uninfluenced by its relation of having-been with the Other.

On the contrary, my "getting" hold of myself also includes another aspect: as authentic, Recovery is grounded in the revea-ling/concealing essence of four-dimensional Time. Can it be, then, that while I "get" hold of myself within the disclosure of the truth and the necessity of my individuation, at the same time, assuming that I had come to an authentic understanding of the potentiality-for-Being of the Other, I am not an individuation in the ontic sense of being isolated from the Other, and consequently, authentic Recovery also leaves room for an essential Remembering of the Other?

To be sure, "Time heals all" in the sense that it is the root of the necessity [Notwendigkeit] of our return from the depths of the chaos of no-thingness which overwhelmed my world in the face of a death, to the true implications of the meaning of one's individuation, and to a "nearness" among things. From the Ab-grund of the night of death, my state-of-Being is "balanced" within my own resumption of activities in-a-world of essents.

But Recovery, so understood, is never complete. In this sense, Recovery is Pain-ful, that is, grounded in Pain (and therefore Time) as the dif-ference.

On the road to a "getting" hold of oneself, there may be an inauthentic "lostness" among the "they-world" world of essents, and then one may believe that he has "recovered" from the death of the Other in his forgetting of the Other - and therefore, a forgetting of his death.

However, it is of the essence of Recovery (i.e. Recovery from the death of the Other to whom I have been related in authentic solicitude) that, as there is never a total and completed remembering, there is never a total forgetting, even within a total immersion in the world of essents. Indeed, if Recovery, as grounded in Pain and Time as the Dif-ference, is not a completed state, then this explains the varying degrees of Recovery among different people, and explains as well how sometimes, one may in fact never fully recover from the death of the Other. In describing his mourning over his late wife, C.S. Lewis admits that "in grief, nothing 'stays put'. One keeps on emerging from a phase, but it always recurs. Round and round. Everything repeats...I thought I could describe a state; make a map of sorrow.   Sorrow, however, turns out to be not a state but a process. It needs not a map, but a history, and if I don't stop writing that history at some quite arbitrary point, there's no reason why I should ever stop."142

Heidegger has already taught us that it is of the essence of Time that the past is not simply dead and gone, for Time is a "happening". The "past", then, includes the Other, so that the Other is not "just dead and gone" for me, in terms of an ontological meaning-presence which the Other continues to radiate for me.   As there is an equiprimordial absence of Others even in their presence in the relation of solicitude, so too, even in their absence, there is a "presence". As Heidegger himself has remarked:

"Absence reveals presence,

---

142 C.S. Lewis, A Grief Observed, p. 46-7.

Death brings nearness."143

The cynic   (or the   empiricist!) may   wish to   say that such statements   are   confusing   reality   with thought, that any "presence" of the Other to me after his   death, is   a conceptual presence,   fabricated   by   the   subject's   mind.   Indeed, Heidegger himself has pointed out that the death of the Other   is the occasion for a re-presentative grasp of the Other as now a no-longer-living, and therefore, present-at-hand   entity to   be manipulated in an essentially inauthentic manner.

But we must keep in mind that memory and imagination, on the level of pre-ontological understanding, involve more than merely conceptual constructs, and I think that no-one makes this clearer than Gaston Bachelard, who   reminds us   in his   Poetics of Space, that   while   "we   retain   images   in   our   memory   - the image is everything except a direct PRODUCT of the imagination."144   There is something essentially "poetic" about imagination, wherein "the function of the real and the function of   the unreal   are made to cooperate... Actual   conditions   are   no   longer determinant." In this "poetic" sense, "imagination takes its place on   the margin, exactly   where   the   function   of   unreality comes to charm or to

---

143   "Abwesen entbringt Anwesen, Tod   erbringt Nähe".   Heidegger, M.,   Derrière   le   miroir: Homage   à   Georges   Braque. 1963. Cited in Hirsch,   E.   "Remembrances   of   Martin   Heidegger in Marburg",   in   Philosophy   Today,   Vol. 23,   No. 2/4,   Summer 1979, p. 168.

144   Bachelard, Gaston, Poetics of Space, p. xxx.

disturb, always to awaken, the sleeping being lost in its automatisms."145

Lest this interpration of imagination appear arbitrary, Bachelard replies that while it is true that "space that has been seized upon by the imagination cannot remain indifferent space subject to the measure and estimates of the surveyor," yet, such space is seen to "concentrate Being within limits that protect."146

Our "imagining" remembrances of the past with the Other, therefore, are not simply conceptual, re-presentative constructs, or if they are, they are meaningless. This is why when we try and remember the Other in terms of mere particular characteristics - what did he look like? exactly what colour was his hair? how tall really was he? - such representative thought about the Other "lacks imagination", and therefore ontological meaning and truth. This is why a photograph of the deceased can be surprisingly devoid of content and significance; while it portrays the physical features correctly, it may miss the essence of that spirit with whom I shared my life.

Indeed, such a portrayal can be far less meaningful perhaps than the meaning-presence of the Other which one may sense in the presence of certain special Things. What I mean by this is that

---

145 Ibid, p. xxxi.
146 Ibid, p. xxxii.

since the past is not "just dead and gone", but lives in the present, it is often the case that I can remember the Other in a genuine sense, with a much greater vivacity and depth than in my conceptual re-presentation of him, in the presence of certain "historical memorabilia". Just as in birth, there is not just a new entity but a new personal history, so too death is not just the end of an entity because "in death, men leave their presence in things behind" in historical memorabilia and in similar Things which are "filled with gods". Others are not merely "reflected there; they are present there."147

Professor John Caputo has pointed out how there is an Italian custom at funerals, that the deceased be kept within the home for a certain length of time after his death, because there is a sense in which the presence of the person is embedded in the home. The significance of the home, as related to the death of a human being, is reflected in many customs of varying traditions. Another example is how in Camaroon, dead family members are typically buried in front of the house. Paul-Emile Cardinal Léger reports how through this custom and "through faith, you can help them keep the dead more present and they are present...

---

147 Remarks made by John Caputo, in his Address on the "Presence of the Other", presented to the American Catholic Philosophical Association Convention in Toronto, Canada, April 22, 1979.

There is no cemetery here. They are living with their dead."148
Needless to say, a "home" is here more than the physical construction of a house, and while anyone familiar with Heidegger
must recognize the poetic significance of "dwelling" in the home,
again I must recall Bachelard's reminder too, that a "house which
has been experienced is not an inert box.   Inhabited space
transcends geometrical space".149 The house as a "living value"
once again "must integrate an element of unreality".150

I dwell on the importance of this notion of a house or a
home because it is one of the most significant examples of our
Situation of Recovery in the presence amidst things.   The actual
physical presence, or the conceptual reconstruction of the house
in my mind, fails to capture the presence of the Other, as he
appears in the "unreal imaginings" or, in Heidegger's terminology,
in a "poetic remembrance" of the Being of the house, where there
is disclosed (much more so than in our conceptual re-construction
of particular characteristics) an ontologically meaningful
presence of the Other, with whom I may have once dwelled-there.

But all of this is meaningful only if I had come to an
understanding of the potentiality-for-Being of the Other in an
in-finite relation of solicitude.

---

148   quoted in B. Callaghan, "Léger and the Lepers", in Weekend,
      April 28, 1979.

149   Bachelard, G. op.cit., p. 47.

150   Ibid, p. 59.

As noted, the house is just one (though a fundamental) example of the presence of the Other in things; there may be others. Sometimes we know that the Other had a favourite piece of jewelry, or a special book, or any other similar "thing", which is meaningful in my Recovery not as the cause of a willful re-presentation of the Other as a now present-at-hand entity, but it is meaningful only inasmuch as the "thing" shelters the Other's "presence" there.

Indeed, this suggests, too, a deep significance of the gravesite: it is a symbol and a testimony to the Other's pre-sence, not simply in the sense that the Other is present "for me" in any psychological sense, or in my conceptual reminiscences, but rather, there is still "place" for the Other. Recovery brings me back from the depth of no-thingness in the preservation and "making room" for the Other's "space".

Despite such a "presence", however, in Recovery, I realize that the future is one which is devoid of the "factical" presence of the Other and in this sense, my "way" is now mine alone. From an "imagining" remembrace of the past through the Presence of the Other among Things, my Recovery in future, as related to Time, to finitude, and to Pain as the difference, discloses this obviously central factor as well.

Yet, it is always balanced by a Remembrance that such an open future is never uninfluenced by past or present, and in this sense, as one seeks to "continue life in the way that the Other

will have wished", my future is never uninfluenced by the Other.

C.S. Lewis ·is worth quoting one more time, from his moving

work, A Grief Observed:

> "Getting over it so soon? But the words are ambigu-
> ous. To say the patient is getting over it after an
> operation for appendicitis is one thing; after he's had
> his leg off it is quite another... Presently he'll get
> back his stength and be able to stump about on his
> wooden leg. He has 'got over it'. But he will
> probably have recurrent pains in the stump all his
> life, and perhaps pretty bad ones; and he will always
> be a one-legged man. There will be hardly any moment
> when he forgets it. Bathing, dressing, sitting down,
> and getting up again, even lying in bed, will all be
> different. His whole way of life is changed. All
> sorts of pleasures and activities that he once took for
> granted will have to be simply written off. Duties
> too, At present I am learning to get about on
> crutches. Perhaps I shall presently be given a wooden
> leg. But I shall never be a biped again."151

So that in this revealing/concealing interplay of a World,

and in this circling of presence in absence, from the depths of

no-being in the encounter with A Death, one "gets" hold of oneself

- one recovers.

**

151 C.S. Lewis, op.cit., p. 43.

CHAPTER THREE

THE PHENOMENON OF IMMORTALITY

A.   The Possibility of My Own Immortality

        "What if death is the end?
        What then?"[1]

While the metaphysician or the theologian may wish to con-
clusively establish the certainty of man's immortality, the
phenomenologist's task is a more modest one: rather than seek to
prove the fact of immortality, the phenomenologist will seek to
describe the phenomenon, as it is meaningful to the human
understanding. Instead of re-presentative certainty, he will
seek to describe immortality as it reflects man's existential
search for significance and meaning.

        Jean-Paul Sartre provides an interesting example in his
Being and Nothingness, which begins to describe the essence of
consciousness as "no-thing". He describes the case of counting
cigarettes in a cigarette box. My positional consciousness is
directed towards the cigarettes, and I note that there are a
dozen cigarettes in the box. As I am counting, someone enters
the room and demands to know what I am doing. At once, I am able

---

1   From "The Mouse", a film written and narrated by Gregory
     David Armstrong, visual conception by Gord Creelman, pro-
     duced at York University, Toronto, Canada. 1984.

to reply: "I am counting". What this shows for Sartre is that while my positional consciousness is directed   towards the cigarettes, nevertheless my non-positional consciousness reflects a pre-reflective awareness of the fact that I am, in fact, counting.   "There is", says Sartre, "a pre-reflective cogito which is the condition of the Cartesian cogito", for it is precisely the "non-thetic consciousness of counting which is the very condition of my adding".2   Further on, it becomes evident that no matter how I try to delimit and capture that non-thetic consciousness, it is impossible to do so: the minute the non-thetic is reflected upon, it is no longer non-positional, but is the condition of the reflection once again.

Whether one wishes to accept the Sartrean ontology (I do not!), nevertheless Sartre's example nicely describes the pre-reflective awareness of the world which is the condition of explicit, re-presentative thought.   It is not unlike the case where when one plays a musical instrument and tries to reflect excessively on the music and the notes: the creativity of the performance is destroyed, the reflection changes the spontaneity of the pre-reflective, creative act.

Victor Frankl points to something similar when he suggests that the spiritual basis of human existence is ultimately "un-conscious".   Quoting the Indian Vedas, he writes: "That which

---

2   Sartre, Jean-Paul, <u>Being and Nothingness</u>, p. 13.

does the seeing, cannot be seen; that which does the hearing, cannot be heard; and that which does the thinking, cannot be thought".3

In his fascinating volume entitled The Unconscious God, Frankl argues that this "pre-logical spiritual unconscious" at the root of human existence, as a true "Urphänomenon", helps to explain an essential, "unconscious religiousness" of man. He writes:

"It is true that man is responsible for himself, but ultimately, he is not responsible before himself. Not only man's being free, but also his being responsible requires an intentional referent...

...existential analysis has uncovered, within the spiritual unconscious, unconscious religiousness. This unconscious religiousness, revealed by our pheno-menological analysis, is to be understood as a latent relation to transcendence inherent in man... However one wishes to formulate it, we are confronted with what I should like to term 'the transcendent unconscious', as part and parcel of the spiritual unconscious."4

Frankl finally concludes, then, that "this concept means no more or less than that man has always stood in an intentional relation to transcendence, even if only on an unconscious level. If one calls the intentional referent of such an unconscious relation 'God', it is apt to speak of an 'unconscious God'. This, however, in no way implies that God is unconscious to

---

3   Frankl, Victor, The Unconscious God, p. 31.

4   Ibid, p. 57, 61.

himself, but rather that God may be unconscious to man and that man's relation to God may be unconscious".5

Referring back to our discussion of the terminal patient's "acceptance" of his death, perhaps it is no coincidence that from writers like Kübler-Ross to the staff of the Windsor Hospice, these people "can't help noticing that agnostics have a 'terrible time' facing death, and those with strong faith seem to fare best."6   Why is this so?

In previous chapters, we have described a near auto acci- dent, and the pre-reflective, spontaneous need to be which over- takes my whole way of being-in-the-world, as I seek to avoid catastrophe. That need was seen to be grounded in transcendence, in temporality and in the existential structure of being-human as futurally-projecting. Further on, we have described the denial of one's terminal illness as grounded in a similar "need to be", and in terms of the difficulty of understanding that some day soon, I will have no future, I will-not-be. The denial was seen to be not reducible to an inauthentic escape, but rather, as an expression of the ek-sisting activity of being-human, a disclosure

---

5   Ibid, p. 61-2.

6   Report from the staff of the Windsor Hospice, quoted by Bryan
     Johnson, "Helping the Dying to Live", The Globe and Mail,
     September 15, 1985. p. 10.

of the transcendental roots of a temporalizing Da-sein, pro-jecting meaning into the future.

It seems to me that faith in immortality is a similar expression, to use Frankl's words, of an "unconscious intentionality", or better, it is a quite authentic expression of a transcendental understanding defined by a pro-jecting, temporal essence of being-human. To have faith in immortality is not to automatically, _in_authentically deny one's finitude; on the contrary, one is able to acknowledge one's imminent death, but nevertheless, on an existential level, to hope and believe that in some sense, understanding, comprehension will not totally disappear. Inasmuch as I am, and inasmuch as I have-been, my essence is of a Being-there: I am not a present-at-hand object which will cease to be. I am a transcendental activity of understanding, which hopes and perhaps finds some peace in a "subconscious" desire to continue to be, even after the physical death of my self.

Perhaps this also helps to explain Lucretius' famous remark of how we regard as bad, a future in which we will not exist, but none of us lament in this way, the fact that there was a time before our birth when we did not exist.

Needless to say, I cannot argue here for the objective, actual truth of immortality. Neither is that my intention. I simply would like to consider the possibility that faith in immortality is not a mere "inauthentic" escape, as implied by so many existentialists, but is an ex-pression of a human need-to-be, which is essential to my horizontal, transcendental, futural activity of com-prehending the world into which I am thrown. As such, it is not to be deplored by contemporary philosophers, but perhaps is to be seen instead as an authentic existentiale.

B.   The Immortality of the Other

I have made reference in previous chapters, to a meaning-presence of the Other, which remains with those with whom the Other has been in a relation of authentic solicitude. As should have been evident, that "presence" was not intended to signify an "other-worldly" presence, but again, referred to the meanings pro-jected by me upon my world.

In connection with our thinking-through of the phenomenon of the "immortal" presence of the Other, I find it useful to bring to mind the German translations: "immortality" can be translated either as "Unsterblichkeit", or "Unvergänglichkeit".

"Unsterblichkeit" or, to hazard a contrived-sounding word, "un-mortality", seems to suggest the notion of a metaphysical or religious presence of an undying soul, and as such, it seems to me to come too close to denying the essential finitude and temporal structure of human-being. It suggests a vision of a static, never-ending presence of the deceased, which goes against the dynamic personality I knew while he was still alive. It comes too close to a re-presentative objectification of a living reality, which now may be seen, as Heidegger has said, as a Present-at-hand corporeal Thing. It is, by no means, a satisfying interpretation of any sort of genuine presence of the Other to my imagination, after his death.

On the other hand, "Unvergänglichkeit" seems to me to sug-gest that the meaningful Presence of the Other, even after his death, is un-passing, un-transitory, and un-fugitive. In what sense can we say that the presence of the Other is "un-transi-tory", when in fact, he has been reduced, physically speaking, to cinders or dry bones?

The poet George Eliot has written: "O may I join the choir invisible/ Of those immortal dead who live again/ In minds made better by their presence". Is it sufficient to say that it is just my "mind made better" by the Other to whom I have been related in authentic solicitude? Is it just a possession that I now have, and did not have before having known the Other? I believe it is something more that defines the "Unvergänglichkeit" of the Other -- but what is this "something more"?

In answer to this question, some key points may be raised.

It is interesting to note how when I wilfully try to extort an image of the deceased to my mind, when I deliberately try to elicit such memories, they arise as false. They are contrived, and one feels profound dissatisfaction in the inauthentic conju-ring up of a mundane misrepresentation of the one I loved.

At other moments, however, when one least expects it, an image is presented to the transcendental imagination spontaneously, without warning, and that image is a genuine illumination of the presence of the Other, with whom I stood in an in-finite relation. What is the source of that image? It is definitely not my purposeful, manipulative willing. Perhaps, as we have described previously, a "thing" (such as a piece of jewellery, or a home) may elicit a meaning-presence of the Other, but while such a "thing" may activate the memory, what is it that sustains that memory as truly no less than the very sort of mysterious Presence which we shared while he was still alive? The grace of that presence to my imagination is much more significant than one more "memory" among others. Rather, it overtakes my world, as the Other is momentarily re-born within me.

I will deliberately avoid any suggestion of "telepathy" with the deceased, because I believe the notion suggests a representative presence of the Other, which is completely outside of the description of the meaningful presence of the Other which I am yet only beginning here. However, neither is the "un-transitoriness" of the Other to my imagination, an incidental image which remains in my "mind" after the deceased is gone. Rather, the "presence" of the Other, as "Unvergänglich", is such that my being is illumined by that presence, unexpectedly rising to the surface in moments of appreciation, because the in-finite relation between myself and the Other does not die so easily as the physical being of one's body: it remains as a haunting, mysterious presence, defining my being-in-the-world for as long as I live, and until I too, meet my own death one day.

**

PART THREE

ONTIC/ONTOLOGICAL IMPLICATIONS

INTRODUCTION

It is useful at this stage, to review some central points in our discussion, in order to then consider some of the implications of our argument.

In Part One, we have set out Heidegger's own understanding of the meaning of death as the possibility of the impossibility of any existence at all. That this possibility is not just one more ontic possibility among possibilities is clear, in light of the fact that death is not just a <u>Zu-Ende-Sein</u> but a <u>Sein-zum-Ende</u>. The ontological meaning of the phenomenon of death is revealed, therefore, in terms of Dasein's <u>Being-toward-death</u>, a mode of ek-sisting which, as "ownmost" and "non-relational", is rooted in the temporal structure that reveals Dasein in its essential finitude.

In addition, we have considered comments made by Heidegger in the later phases of his thought, comments which show how in death, Dasein "shatters" against Being, as the "supreme concealedness of Being crystallizes". The later Heidegger understands death as the shrine of Nothing, and therefore, as the shelter of Being, for death is now seen to be capable of the greatest lighting-up of Being in its truth.

It is clear that Heidegger's "raising anew" of the question of the meaning of <u>Being</u> supports the entire development of his "way" of thought on the phenomenon of death, and that equally

important is the new meaning and ontological significance revealed of True _Time_. Being-towards-death is understood in terms
of the essentially finite, temporal structure of Dasein's ek-
sistence, which, upon further investigation, leads to an "Ab-
grund" of the It-gives Being, It-gives Time, that are at the core
of Heidegger's understanding of Ontological Difference, and a
revealing/concealing essence of Being disclosed through death.

Part Two raises the question of the _full_ _ontic_ significance
of death, not as an inauthentic "case of death", re-presented in
a calculative way, but as a prism or "happening" of the e-vent of
Being itself.

Initially, we have considered the determinate possibility of
one's own death, as revealed through the perspective of terminally ill patients. Focussing on the matter of Time, we have
explored how past, present and future "congeal" within a moment
of truth, whereby my death is no longer a vague possibility of
the future, but, through its determinacy, changes the temporal
and ontological meaning of the remainder of my life. Through an
examination of the terminal patient's sensibilities, we saw the
Ontological Difference revealed in the very struggle to come to
terms with the full significance of this overwhelming ontic
possibility, this e-vent of my own death.

Chapter Two of Part II provides another perspective on death
as an ontic e-vent, that is, through the death of the Other to
whom I am related in authentic solicitude. Authentic solicitude

is shown to be an ontological relation "between" Daseins, whose "essence" has already been disclosed by Heidegger as "Being-with, which understands primordially." The ontological (and therefore temporal) roots of the solicitous relation are revealed as the condition of both, understanding and communication between Daseins, as well as a continued respect of the ontological significance of Dasein's own individuation. Having shown how one can come to an authentic awareness of the potentiality-for-Being of the Other, and having revealed the essential belonging of pain and death and love, the stage was set for a discussion of the possibility of an ontological understanding of another ontic e-vent: the death of the Other. The possibility of such an under-standing of "A Death" was again revealed to be rooted in Time which, as related to Pain and the Dif-ference, also helped to explain the essence of genuine Recovery.

The question to consider now is: if death, as an ontic e-vent, can reveal ontological significance, what kind of impli-cations does this have for the meaning of the Heideggerean onto-logy?

**

CHAPTER ONE

ONTOLOGY AS CONCRETE

That Heidegger's primary concern throughout the entire
development of his thought, is to "raise anew the question of the
meaning of Being"1, in fact has been the cause of a wide variety
of interpretations of his thought, which means that there has
been a great deal of misinterpretation as well. His originative
style of writing has even prompted many readers to conclude that
Heidegger's "mysticism" is a relinquishment of strict scientific
certitude in favour of an illogic - so that his thinking is far
from rigorous.

Other (not unrelated) comments accuse Heidegger of placing
such a priority on "Being" that man becomes a mere passive reci-
pient of Being's grace2, as his true nature is ultimately forgotten; or else, such a separation is said to develop between Being
and beings (thus between Being and man as well) that Heidegger's

---

1   SZ 1.

2   In reply to this rather common accusation, we must recall
     Heidegger's own reply that while man, as open to Being, is
     open to the nothingness of his existence, "this 'nothing-
     ness' is no cause for pessimism or sadness. It only helps
     to realize that there can be real productivity only where
     there is resistance, and thus it is up to philosophy to turn
     man around, from the passive [faulen] preoccupation with the
     products of the spirit, back to the hard severity of his
     destiny." (Translation by C. Hamburg, "A Cassirer-Heidegger
     Seminar", in Philosophy and Phenomenological Research,
     Vol. 25, 1964, p. 220.

"raising anew" of this question becomes an abstract metaphysical exercise, and therefore, is quite irrelevant.

One such typical commentator is Lambert van de Water, who writes that the "anxious desire to give priority to that which is, to escape in this way from the deepest forgetfulness of Being characteristic of metaphysics, which confused Being and beings, misleads Heidegger and causes him to fall into an empty and abstract 'Being'! As a disciple of Husserl, he intends to philosophize by starting merely from the things themselves, but in fact he does it in such a way that they ultimately escape him... The final result of all this is that anything precise can no longer be said about Being. Even the word 'Being' is still too concrete, it is too much of a being; therefore it is better to drop it... Being as a formal <u>an sich</u> has turned into a third something, that stands above object and subject, and consequently also above everything which is. Because this Being has neither name nor content, and is only itself, the Being of each being is likewise empty."3

Inasmuch as "Being as ground 'is' the 'over-against' of the being that is man, in such a way that it utters itself first out of nothingness, Being is the antithesis of beings, primarily human beings"4, and the worst of it, concludes van de Water, is

---

3   Van de Water, L., "Being and Being Human: An Impasse in Heidegger's Thought?", p. 395-7.

4   <u>Ibid</u>, p. 393.

that Heidegger does not really provide a "synthesis" to account for the interweaving of man and Being.

We have already discussed in previous chapters, how and why Heidegger repudiates this notion of a synthetic resolution of man's belonging to Being. Clearly, commentators such as van de Water have not paid heed to Heidegger's own warnings: "Let us note well - the presence of what is present, and not what is present as such and not Being as such, nor both added together in a synthesis, but: their duality, emerging from their unity kept hidden, keeps the call [unto Thought]."5

But even if one does not wish to go as far as van de Water, an easier assumption to make is that since Heidegger is concerned to raise anew the forgotten question of the meaning of Being, the ontological ground of beings is such that authenticity must be confined to ontological awareness, which seems to mean that ontic concerns are necessarily _inauthentic.

We have offered in this volume, the example of the determinate e-vent of death, in order to show how an ontic event need not be restricted to inauthentic, re-presentative interpretations, but on the contrary, may reveal ontological significance.

But how consistent is this with what Heidegger himself has had to say, on the relation of the "ontic" with the "ontological"?

---

5   WD 148, e.t. 242.

That the "ontic" is not to be merely subsumed within the notion of inauthenticity is clear from quite a number of statements, more often than not, made by Heidegger in the context of his discussions of Ontological Difference. He writes: "Let us think Being, and in Being of the difference, and in the difference of perdurance in terms of that character of Being through which Being has cleared itself as logos, as the ground." Such a thinking of the difference as perdurance – "the perdurance that begins the history of metaphysics, governs all of its epochs, and yet remains everywhere concealed as perdurance" -reveals that:

> "What is held apart is held in the tension of perdurance in such a way that not only does Being ground beings as their ground, but beings in their turn, ground, cause Being in their way. Beings can do so only insofar as they 'are' the fullness of Being: they are what is most of all."6

We must not forget that Heidegger's interpretation of a "thing" reveals a gathering which appropriates the fourfold: "it gathers the fourfold's stay, its while, into something that stays for awhile". While the gathering is "into a single time-space, a single stay", the thing is not just an ob-ject (which suggests inauthenticity) but rather, its "presencing is the true, giving gathering of the onefold fourfold."7

Equally important, we must not lose sight of the fact that Heidegger's own "raising anew" of the question of the meaning of

---

6   ID 137, e.t. 68-9.

7   VA 172, e.t. 174.

Being began by way of a "certain special entity, Dasein".8 In the

Grundprobleme der Phänomenologie volume, Heidegger reiterates the

centrality of this special "entity", reminding the reader that:

> "Sein gibt es nur, wenn Seinsverständnis, d.h. Dasein
> existiert... Die Ontologie hat zur Fundamentaldisziplin
> die Daseins-Analytik.   Darin liegt zugleich: Die Onto-
> logie lässt sich selbst nicht rein ontologisch beg-
> ründen .   Ihre eigene Ermöglichung wird auf ein Seien-
> des,   d.h. Ontisches   zurückverwiesen: das   Dasein.
> Ontologie hat ein ontisches Fundament..."9

Indeed, Heidegger writes too, that "man is never absolute

and infinite in the creativeness of Being itself, but only inso-

far as he is engaged in comprehending it. This infinite of the

ontological is   essentially tied to the experience of the

ontic."10   Instead of "just being determined in its essence by

what is called 'spirit' and 'life', [Dasein] is the original

unity and structure of the immanent commitment of man who, bound

to his body, is thereby bound to 'what there is' [Seiendem] in

the sense that existence (being thrown into what there is) breaks

through to it."11

This means, then, that:

---

8   SZ 39.

9   GP 26.   Emphasis mine.

10   "A Cassirer-Heidegger Seminar", translated by C.H. Hamburg,
in Philosophy and Phenomenological Research, Vol. 25, 1964,
p. 216.

11   Ibid, p. 219.

"Kein Verhalten zu Seiendem existiert, das nicht Sein
verstünde. Kein Seinsverständnis ist möglich, das
nicht in einem Verhalten zu Seiendem wurzelte."12

Being and beings belong together, therefore, in their es-
sence, and this belonging is the meaning of the Ontological
Difference itself. As Heidegger says in "Was ist Metaphysik?",
"Being 'never is' [nie west] without beings". The Ontological
Difference, therefore, is no abstract metaphysical realm but in
an important sense, requires beings in order to be. "Der
Unterschied von Sein und Seiendem ist, wenngleich nicht aus-
drücklich gewusst, latent im Dasein und seiner Existenz da. Der
Unterschied ist da, d.h. er hat die Seinsart des Daseins, er
gehört zur Existenz."13

To raise anew the question of the meaning of Being, then,
means more than to meditate on a transcendent, metaphysical realm
within a mystical awe, and at the expense of "the structures of
concrete existence"14, for "there is no problem more elementary
and concrete than that of Being".15 In response to commentators
like van de Water, or C.W. Richey who cynically concludes that
"when we contemplate the works of Heidegger, we must keep in mind

---

12   GP 466. Emphasis mine.

13   GP 454.

14   Cf. W. Kluback, and J.T. Wilde's introductory comments
      entited "A Heideggerean Limitation", in Heidegger's The
      Question of Being, esp. pp. 15-17.

15   Heidegger, M. in "A Cassirer-Heidegger Seminar", in op.cit.,
      p. 217.

the image of a priest, the guardian of an archaic temple, whose utterances are the 'dictating of Being as such'... Plato had thought that philosophy begins in wonder, but Heidegger has decided that it ends there"16 -- it is interesting to note Heidegger's advice to one of his students in Freiburg17, advice which reflects his conviction that the _rigour_ of originative thought does not begin or end in a passive awe in the face of Being, but requires a discernful and "sobering" understanding of origins. His advice to Kluge is not to go to a temple to contemplate Being, but to read Aristotle: "Die meisten scheuen heute diese nüchternen Sachen, darum entsteht auch so wenig Ursprüngliches."   Indeed, Heidegger's advice continues in the suggestion that aside from these studies, the student must "eine ganz konkrete handwerkliche Arbeit... nehmen, damit Sie mit den prinzipiellen Fragen nicht ins Schwimmen und Gleiten geraten! Wir müssen die wesentlichen Dinge sparsam behandeln, sonst werden sie leicht abgenützt."

After careful study of Heidegger, I am convinced that his intention has never been to think Being at the expense of beings, and that therefore, the ontic dimension is not just something "inauthentic" which is to be cast away in "theaters of speechless-

---

16   Richey, C.W. "On the Intentional Ambiguity of Heidegger's
      Metaphysics", p. 1145.

17   Letter to H. Kluge of Sweden, dated 02 August, 1952. Pro-
      vided to me by Mr. Kluge in Freiburg-im-Breisgau, in 1976.

ness" before the luminosity of a transcendent realm. Heidegger's primary task has certainly been to raise anew the question of the meaning of Being, but not so that philosophy will "end in wonder"; rather, our technological epoch has indeed forgotten that a "thing" can be much more than a res or an ob-ject, and this is so, because we have forgotten to think originatively and to even question the meaning of Sein as other than an abstract concept.

In other words, a re-thinking of the meaning of Being certainly takes us beyond re-presentational concerns and our everyday lostness amid present-at-hand entities, but a more originative thinking of Being is not the condition for a relinquishing of the world; it is the condition for a more careful handling of "die wesentliche Dinge" and an ontological depth of meaning, even within our ontic concerns with "essents" and "things" which are in the world. Heidegger himself will tell us that before the "participation of the one, a particular being, in the other, Being," can be conceived and dealt with, the "duality of individual beings and Being must first lie before us openly, be taken to heart and there kept safely... What is the call that speaks to us from Parmenides saying? 'Let lie before you, and take to heart, beings in being!'"18

_____

18   WH 136, e.t. 223.

We must   not forget that ontology is "nicht rein ontologisch begründen"19, but that Being shows itself while hiding itself in a "thing" such as a work of art, which "opens up a _world_ and keeps it abidingly in force."20

"Art lets truth originate"21 so that abstractions are suddenly e-ventful by virtue of their appearance in the horizons of a personal universe. Empty abstractions are suddenly concrete, made manifest in the revelation of that single, exceptional moment now captured as a work of art. While it is true that "Art is the origin of the art work and the artist"22, this does not mean that the artist is a passive instrument of some cosmic destiny, but rather, there corresponds to the self-forgetfulness of the artist a calling to respond with   his very Being, to release the creative power which will pose a challenge and a risk to him, to not only imitate but to capture the mystery of the world in the heightened truth of its Being.

Therefore, Heidegger says that "truth happens in Van Gogh's painting. This does not mean that something is correctly portrayed, but rather that in the revelation of the equipmental

---

19   GP 26.

20   HW 33, e.t. 44.

21   HW 64, e.t. 77.

22   HW 46, e.t. 57.

being of the shoes, that which is as a whole, world and earth in their interplay, attains to unconcealedness."23

Art is more than a passive acceptance of an unlimited universal appeal; it is more than a "remote imitation of the infinite play of the world" (F. Schlegel), for it is a challenge to create, requiring a response wherein both the vision and the artist's very essence as a creator will be ful-filled. A true work of art does not just open one to the un-expressible possibilities of Being which is its source, but as an e-ventful happening, it arises within an inspiration which asks to be given a particular form within the horizon of a Bereich, a form which will "add" to the truth of that mysterious source in making it meaningful.

Heidegger's comments about a work of art tell us much about Being as it "hides itself" in its revelation, but they also tell us a great deal about the way of Being's revelation in concrete things. As David Starr points out,24 "the insight which Heidegger seems to share with Pindar, Heracleitus, and Lao Tzu, is that if the source of authentic thinking cannot ultimately be expressed, it may nevertheless express itself in us, in our own act of thinking, and having expressed itself, we may within limits give

---

23   HW 44, e.t. 56.

24   Starr, David, Entity and Existence, p. 220.

conceptual form to the deposit, to the expression."25 There can be "no Disclosure without man's dis-closure (Ent-schlossenheit) to it"26, and therefore, there is a wide gap separating meta-physics and ontology, as Heidegger understands them. Again, the Ontological Difference and appropriation reveal a belonging of man to Being wherein "the very unity or identity of thinking and Being at which Heidegger's thought aims is not an integration of Dasein with a supra-temporal, immutable Presence, but rather, an active reintegration of existing Dasein with the intrinsic temporality of his own way of being."27

There is no metaphysical priority of an abstract realm, but rather, "the correlation is between thought and the Being of beings, where the 'of' points in both directions at once."28

Once one realizes that Heidegger himself expresses the dependence of the Seienden upon das Sein, as well as das Sein's revelations in the Seienden, such reciprocity suggests that the Seienden need not only delimit and thereby be subject to re-presentation, but may - and do - express Being. The "ontic", therefore, need not suggest the merely inauthentic, but inasmuch

---

25   - although never completely, or "finally", we must remember,
      because to do so would be to transform the "thing" into an
      ob-ject again.

26   Versényi, L. Heidegger, Being and Truth, p. 156.

27   Starr, David, op.cit., p. 221.

28   Richardson, W.J.   Heidegger: through Phenomenology to Th-
      ought, p. 605.

as it reveals Being in a density of heightened truth, suggests the challenge of a concrete ontological understanding of a lived happening.

Indeed, once we realize that "Die Ontologie lässt sich selbst nicht rein ontologisch begründen", and that to somehow think Being "directly" or abstractly to the exclusion of beings would mean to make Being an ob-ject directly conforming to reason, then we realize that Being is in fact a dynamic and unsettling presence which shows itself in beings, yet never completely.

In other words, if my awareness of Being is not by way of a direct knowledge through reason, but is intimately related to my being-in-the-world, then what we are saying is that the concrete relation and "dense" revelation of Being within the ontic domain, forms the counterpart of ontology as unified within the single, concrete moment, understanding "moment" to be a free, historical articulation which de-cides something, and gives a fundamental significance and commitment to a presence which perdures. Such a moment is thus a particular ontological ex-pression, which may find a form within the poem, within the work of art, or within the strangely disquieting ontic event of "a death".

The important point, however, is that it is not only consistent with Heidegger's ontological investigations to include an enquiry into the meaning of Being's revelation within the concrete moment, but it is demanded by them. In raising anew the question of the meaning of Being, in other words, we must not forget that reciprocal challenge of raising anew the question of the meaning of ontic authenticity - or the "genuineness" of the moment.

Heidegger's references to this notion of "genuineness" do, in fact, suggest a specificity and ontic "channelling" of authentic understanding. For example, we recall that in Sein und Zeit, Fear is shown to be a state of mind and an existential possibility which reveals Dasein in the Being of its "there". While "modifications" of such possibility are "not to be under- stood in an ontic sense as some factical 'individualized' dispo- sition"29, yet Heidegger does speak of a "specific genuineness" of fearing-about Others, or "fearing for" them (Fürchten für sie), inasmuch as "the Dasein-with for which it fears is affec- ted".30   Just as the notion of authentic Dasein-with is far from adequately developed in Sein und Zeit, neither is this notion of fearing-for; but this does not prevent us from asking: if there can be a "specific genuineness of fearing about" Others, is it not equally legitimate to suggest that there can be a "specific genuineness of understanding" of the death of the Other, and that this understanding (as genuine) is more than some "factical 'individualized' disposition", rooted in re-presentative inauthenticity?

---

29   SZ 142.

30   SZ 142.

In any case, it is unfair to condemn Heidegger as having
lapsed into what Levinas called an "ontological imperialism"
because the domain of the ontic is not reducible to "the inauthentic" but may rather reveal a genuine understanding of a
unique moment which gathers Being and shelters its revelation in
order that truth may happen. We must recall Heidegger's
statement that "if we are enquiring about the meaning of Being,
our investigation does not then become a 'deep' one [<u>tiefsinnig</u>],
nor does it puzzle out what stands behind Being. It asks about
Being itself insofar as Being enters into the intelligibility of
Dasein. <u>The meaning of Being can never be contrasted with
entities.</u>"31

But while we know that Heidegger has himself spoken of a
reciprocity of the ontic and the ontological, what is the essence
of this reciprocity?

It is clear that the reciprocal relation between Being and
beings cannot require some sort of dialectical synthesis, but nor
does it suggest a metaphysical "participation" of beings in a
transcendent Being-realm.

If we are to go-beyond such interpretations to their ground,
and if we are to retain the true sense of the belonging of Being
to beings which is the very meaning of appropriation, then the
clue, Heidegger tells us, to the understanding of the meaning of

---

31   SZ 152.

such a reciprocity is the description of a relation of "a remarkable 'relatedness backward or forward'"32 wherein "each of the two members of the relation between man's nature and Being, already implies the relation itself."33 While not reducible to a "circulus vitiosus" on the level of logical analysis, yet there is a suggestion of a "circling" of Being and beings around each other.

We recall the all-important "hermeneutic circle" introduced by Heidegger in Sein und Zeit. "When it is objected that the existential Interpretation is 'circular', it is said that we have 'presupposed' the idea of existence and of Being in general, and that Dasein gets Interpreted 'accordingly', so that the idea of Being may be obtained from it."34 In response to such an objection, Heidegger replies that "'the circle' in understanding belongs to the structure of meaning, and the latter phenomenon is rooted in the existential constitution of Dasein - that is, in the understanding which interprets. An entity for which, as Being-in-the-world, its Being is itself an issue, has, ontologically, a circular structure." Consequently:

> "What is decisive is not to get out of the circle but
> to come into it the right way. This circle of
> understanding is not an orbit in which any random kind
> of knowledge may move; it is the expression of the

---

32   SZ 8.

33   WD 74, e.t. 79.

34   SZ 314.

existential fore-structure of Dasein itself. It is not to be reduced to the level of a vicious circle, or even of a circle which is merely tolerated. In the circle is hidden a positive possibility of the most primordial kind of knowing".35

The basic activity through which man understands and interprets his experience is, therefore, essentially circular, expressing the ecstatic unity of a Dasein which makes the past present, in its pro-jecting toward the future. This "circularity" of temporal understanding is also reflected, not surprisingly, at the level of the Ontological Difference itself. Understanding is "circular" but since Ereignis means, above all else, that Being and man are appropriated to each other as belonging, then Heidegger writes:

"Being grounds beings, and beings, as what is most of all, account for Being. One comes over the other, one arrives in the other. Overwhelming and arrival appear in each other in reciprocal relation. Speaking in terms of the difference, this means: perdurance is a circling, the circling of Being and beings around each other."36

While we must do so cautiously, I believe that exploring this notion of circularity can yield interesting and rather suggestive results.

Heidegger warns us that "if we note that 'circularity' belongs ontologically to a kind of Being which is present-at-hand (namely, to subsistence [Bestand]), we must altogether avoid

---

35   SZ 153.

36   ID 138, e.t. 69.

using this phenomenon to characterize anything like Dasein ontologically."37

However, assuming that the ontic domain may suggest something other than the present-at-hand, i.e. a genuineness of a
gathering presence within the concrete moment or "thing", perhaps
this notion of circularity provides an important clue to the
continuing enquiry into the meaning of both ontic/ontological
reciprocity, as well as the meaning of ontic genuineness.

We can turn for some help in this connection, once again to
Gaston Bachelard, who devotes an entire (yet all too short)
chapter of his Poetics of Space to the "phenomenology of roundness".

He begins by citing Karl Jaspers, who on page 50 of his Von
der Wahrheit, writes: "Jedes Dasein scheint in sich rund".
Reducing Jaspers' formula by one word, in order to make it "phenomenologically purer", Bachelard declares therefore: "das Dasein
ist rund, Being is round. Because to add that it seems round is
to keep a doublet of being and appearance, when we mean the
entire being in its roundness."38

Without much commentary, Bachelard cites Van Gogh who said
that "Life is probably round"; he cites Joë Bousquet's statement: "He had been told that life was beautiful. No! Life is

---

37   SZ 153.

38   Bachelard, Gaston, The Poetics of Space, p. 234.

round!"; and finally, he concludes with a statement by La Fontaine that "a walnut makes me quite round".39

While the sources appear quite unrelated, Bachelard explains that "when two strange images meet, two images that are the work of two poets pursuing separate dreams, they apparently strengthen each other.   In fact, this convergence of two exceptional images furnishes, as it were, a countercheck for phenomenological analysis. The image loses its gratuitousness; the free play of the imagination ceases to be a form of anarchy."40 Exploring the underlying meaning of this convergence of images of roundness, Bachelard then tries to establish what important truth these remarks in fact reveal.

Needless to say, upon logical analysis again, the declaration "das Dasein ist rund" appears to be a somewhat arbitrary, and even puzzling remark.   "No doubt there are those who will want to 'understand', whereas the image must first be taken at its inception.   Others will declare ostentatiously that they do not understand, and will object that life itself is certainly not spherical... From every side, objections accumulate to put a quick end to the discussion"41 - yet, this does not prevent such "joy to the ear" when the philosophy professor begins his course

---

39   Ibid, p. 232.

40   Ibid, p. 59.

41   Ibid, p. 223.

with that very declaration: Being is round.   "Then wait for the
rumblings of this dogmatic thunder to die down, while his
disciples beam with ecstasy."42

This declaration, Bachelard suggests, is not to be explained
by way of a step-by-step argumentation, because it is not to be
understood by way of an empirical analysis, nor is it graspable
by way of a mathematical, calculative mode of thought. "It is
evident that when a geometrician speaks of volumes, he is only
dealing with the surfaces that limit them. The geometrician's
sphere is an empty one, essentially empty. Therefore, it cannot
be a good symbol for our phenomenological study of roundness."43

In order to understand how Being is round, Bachelard suggests that one must be, not a mathematician, but a "dreamer of
words": "...what calm there is in the word round. How peacefully
it makes one's mouth, lips and the being of breath become round.
Because this too should be spoken by a philosopher who believes
in the poetic substance of speech."44

Understanding of Jaspers' declaration then demands an essentially _poetic_ way of thinking. The expressions cited by Bachelard do not "come from immoderations of language, any more than
they do from linguistic clumsiness.   They are not born of a

---

42   _Ibid_, p. 239.

43   _Ibid_, p. 235.

44   _Ibid_, p. 239.

desire to astonish others. In fact, despite their extraordinary
nature, they bear the mark of primitivity. They suddenly appear
and in a twinkling, they are completed."45

What does this poetic way of thinking, however, tell us
about the phenomenology of roundness?

The poet, we learn, is one who knows that "when a thing...
becomes round, it assumes a figure of being that is <u>concentrated</u>
<u>upon itself... The world is round around the round being</u>",46-and
no-one understand this better than Rilke who, in his <u>Poèmes</u>
<u>francais</u>, shows how the walnut tree "lives and commands atten-
tion. Here, around a lone tree, <u>which is the center of a world</u>,
the dome of the sky becomes round, in accordance with the rule of
cosmic poetry." On page 169 of this collection, we read:

> Arbre toujours au milieu
> De tout ce qui l'entoure,
> Arbre qui savoure
> La voûte des cieux.
>
> (Tree always in the center
> Of all that surrounds it
> Tree feasting upon
> Heaven's great dome.)

For Bachelard, from verse to verse, as the poem grows, it
"increases Being":

> Dieu lui va apparaître
> Or, pour qu'il soit sûr,
> Il développe en rond son être,
> Et lui tend des bras mûrs.

---

45   <u>Ibid</u>, p. 233.

46   <u>Ibid</u>, p. 239. Emphasis mine.

Arbre qui peut-être
Pense au-dedans
Arbre qui se domine
Se donnant lentement
La forme qui élimine
Les hasards du vent!

(One day it will see God
And so, to be sure,
It develops its being in roundness
And holds out ripe arms to Him.

Tree that perhaps
Thinks innerly
Tree that dominates self
Slowly giving itself
The form that eliminates
Hazards of wind!)

The final entry in Bachelard's Poetics of Space concludes with his insistence that if he were ever able to group together all the images of being that, in spite of everything, illustrate "permanence" of being, Rilke's tree would begin an important chapter in his album of "concrete" philosophical thought. "I shall never find a better document", he writes, "for a phenomenology of a being which is at once established in its roundness and developing in it. Rilke's tree propagates in green spheres a roundness that is a victory over accidents of form and the capricious events of mobility. Here becoming has countless forms, countless leaves-- but being is subject to no dispersion."47

---

47   Ibid, p. 240-1.

Without agreeing (and without disagreeing!) with Bachelard's comments on the phenomenology of roundness, we introduce them because they point to an important element of the concrete, ontic moment. A philosopher, a painter, a poet, and an "inventor of fables" have each supported the thought that "Being is round", and it is "up to us now to use them in order to learn how to gather Being together in its center."48

We have suggested that the ontic event of death can have ontological significance. Perhaps we can now add that when experienced "from the inside, devoid of all exterior features"49, this ontic event is not just re-presentative of a "case of death" or a mental picture of death, but inasmuch as it is an encounter with A Death and the full implications of finite existence, at that moment, nothing else is real or meaningful, and in this way, in the fullness of the realization of the overpowering and "shattering" significance of death, all Being is concentrated there, in the dense revelation of a pure happening.

The symbol or image of roundness presented by Bachelard, while not meant to be empirically verifiable, is suggestive of a new level of meaning of an ontic "sheltering" of Being. In the circling of Being and beings around each other at certain moments, there can be a con-centration of Being in the fullness of a

---

48   Ibid, p. 234.

49   Ibid, p. 234.

concrete e-vent. It must be emphasized that this is not meant to suggest any new metaphysical truth; as Bachelard points out, he is speaking about a phenomenology of roundness, and so he is thereby evolving a new image which helps to put into perspective the fullness and the depth of meaning accessible within an "ontic" revelation.

Not that this must ever be at the expense, of course, of a fundamental, Heideggerean ontological questioning. Heidegger has begun the essential process of "raising anew" the question of the meaning of Being, and it must by no means be abandoned, or under-valued.

However, my firm belief is that in order to strengthen it, we must at the same time come to a more fundamental understanding of the ontic domain because through the "theaters of spe-echlessness" in the light of Being, there is a depth of signi-ficance revealed by "the thing" and in order to guard Being, we must learn to "save" and to "shelter" things in such a way that they are not simply reduced to present-at-hand entities but may lead us to a respectful preserving of the things-that-are.

Moreover, in addition to an increasing respect for the things-that-are, it seems to me that the Heideggerean ontology is the necessary condition for a deeper respect and understanding of other Daseins, that is, it is the condition for a more funda-mental understanding of authentic solicitude. This is not unre-lated to a sheltering of the things-that-are, and this is most

evident when one comes to realize how the manipulative, calculative and essentially selfish interpretation of Being-with in our
society is supported within a subjectivistic epoch which seeks to
master and control all essents through technology. Once we learn
to respect, and to "save" the things-that-are in the world, then
too perhaps we may learn the true meaning of an in-finite respect
for the Other as well.

Indeed, this is all part of the challenge of raising anew
the question of the meaning of Being in such a way as to ensure a
depth of questioning of Being, as well as of man as the location
of the truth of Being. This volume has shown how the event of
death opens us to the essential finitude and to the uniqueness
and irreplaceability of each and every transcendental individuation which is the "special" essent precisely because it is open
to Being in such a way as to be capable of a care-ful sheltering
of the things-that-are.

While finite, then, man is yet capable of in-finite understanding; in Rilke's words, man remains essentially

> "...the pause between two notes that fall
> into a real accordance scarce at all:
> for Death's note tends to dominate -
>
> Both though, are reconciled in the dark interval,
> tremblingly.
> And the song remains immaculate."
>
> -   Rilke, The Book of Hours, I.

**

CHAPTER TWO

Postscript:

IS PHENOMENOLOGY

STILL TOO METAPHYSICAL?

Heidegger has sought to go-beyond metaphysics, although, as Mrs. Heidegger scolded him, he sometimes did continue to be "zu metaphysisch!"

Heidegger has achieved an immense success in "raising anew the question of the meaning of Being" in such a way that we have, indeed, leapt forward, or perhaps backward, to the ground of the meta-physical tradition, to uncover the mystery and grace of a source which, while remaining hidden, nevertheless reveals itself to the privileged human understanding.

Heidegger's accomplishments themselves cannot be overestimated.

But at certain moments, when Heidegger refers to Being as a "realm", or as "the dimension, insofar as it measures out, apportions, world and thing, each to its own"[1], one feels the need to go yet further, to leave behind such references to Being as a "realm" or a "dimension", which comes too close to meta-physical language of an abstract, general region, after all,--

_____

[1]   US 25, e.t. 203.

and consider instead, the appropriative intermingling of Being and beings, to consider instead the wider significance of the Ontological Difference.

As we have seen, an ontic e-vent may reveal Being, and indeed, may be a happening whereby Dasein's perception of primordial Time, within the horizon of his understanding, fundamentally alters through the congealing of past, present and future within the region of that e-vent.

While Heidegger did begin in his later Thought, to meditate on the essence of the Thing, he left us with an unresolved challenge: a challenge to investigate further, against the backdrop of his discussion of Ontological Dif-ference, the myriad of ontic e-vents which themselves, and in their own unique way, reveal Being. He has left with us a challenge to consider in further detail Jeweiligkeit, how Being "whiles". It is part of the phenomenological challenge proposed initially by Edmund Husserl, of investigating the lived-world, in order to describe it and understand the complexity of human experience within it.

As a concomitent challenge to make phenomenology and ontology concrete, I hand over to the reader a task in the memory of Martin Heidegger. Gaston Bachelard reminds us that "there is no dearth of abstract, 'world-conscious' philosophers"; let us ourselves learn from Heidegger's Thought on the question of the meaning of Being, let us respect all that he has taught us, and then let us move forward to unravel the mystery of how Being is revealed within different, ontic events. After all, let us not be hasty: let us remember that it is the ontic e-vents which make each of our lives unique, and meaningful. Can we not investigate such uniqueness of meaning, without restricting ourselves to obsolete categories of particularity, and without thoughtlessly equating the "ontic" with the "inauthentic", but instead, open ourselves to the meanings revealed within moments which speak Being?

This book has been one author's preliminary attempt to answer to this challenge.

There is yet much, much more to be done.

-o0o-

BIBLIOGRAPHY

This Bibliography is not an exhaustive listing by any means, but contains only those texts which have been referred to in the course of the. research for this work. Except in the case of Bilingual editions which have been cited in the volume and are marked below with an *, both German and English page references are cited within the text. The English translations which have been quoted are from the published works as listed below, but where they were not available in print, translations are my own.

PRIMARY SOURCES
Readings by Martin Heidegger

"Arbeitsgemeinschaft Cassirer-Heidegger", Printed in Schneeberg, G. Erganzungen zu einer Heidegger-Bibliographie, Bern, 1960, pp. 17-27. Translated by Carl H. Hamburg, "A Cassirer-Heidegger Seminar" in Philosophy and Phenomenological Research, Vol. 25, 1964, pp. 208-222.

Aus der Erfahrung des Denkens. Pfüllingen: Neske, 1954. Translated by A. Hofstadter, "The Thinker as Poet", in Poetry, Language, Thought. New York: Harper and Row, 1971.

"Brief" an Richardson, as "Vorwort" in Richardson W.J., Heidegger: Through Phenomenology to Thought, The Hague: Martinus Nijhoff, 1963.

Der Feldweg. Frankfurt: Klostermann, 1953. Translated by T. O'Meara, "The Pathway", in Listening II, 1967, pp. 88-91. Dubuque, Iowa.

Der Satz vom Grund, Pfüllingen: Neske Verlag, 1957.

Der Spiegel Interview, Translated as "Only a God can Save Us", in Philosophy Today, Vol. 20, Winter 1976, pp.267-284.

Die Frage nach dem Ding. Tübingen: Niemeyer, 1962. Translated by W.G. Barton Jr., and V. Deutsch, What is a Thing? Chicago: Henry Regnery Co., 1967.

Die Kunst und der Raum. Erker-Verlag St. Gallen, 1969.

Die Technik und die Kehre. Pfüllingen: Neske, 1962. Translated by William Lovitt, "The Turning" (and "The Question Concerning Technology") in The Question Concerning Technology and Other Essays, New York: Harper and Row, 1977.

Einführung in die Metaphysik.   Tübingen: Niemeyer, 1953.   Translated by Manheim, R.   Introduction to Metaphysics, New
Haven: Yale University Press, 1959.

Erläuterung   zu   Hölderlins Dichtung.   Frankfurt: Klostermann,
1944.   Translated by Douglas Scott, "Remembrance of the
Poet", (Heimkunft) and "Holderlin and the Essence of Poetry", (Hölderlin und das Wesen der Dichtung), in Brock,
W. Existence and Being, Chicago: Henry Regnery Co., 1949.

Gelassenheit. Pfüllingen: Neske, 1959. Translated by Anderson,
J., and Freund, E.H., Discourse on Thinking, New York: Harper and Row, 1966.

Grundprobleme der Phänomenologie. Frankfurt am Main: Vittorio
Klostermann, 1975.

"Hölderlins Erde und Himmel", Hölderlinn Jahrbuch, Tübingen,
1960.

Holzwege.   Frankfurt: Klostermann, 1950.   English translations
are as follows:

    A. Hoffstadter, "Origin of the Work of Art", and "What are
    Poets For?" in Poetry, Language, Thought, New York: Harper
    and Row, 1971.

    Greene, Marjorie, "The Age of the World View", in Measure,
    II. 1951.

    William Lovitt, "The Word of Nietzsche: God is Dead" in The
    Question Concerning Technology and Other Essays, New
    York: Harper and Row, 1977.

    K.R. Dove, "Hegel's Concept of Experience", including sec-
    tion from Hegel's "Phenomenology of Spirit", in Hegel's
    Concept of Experience, New York: Harper and Row, 1970.

Identität und Differenz.* Pfüllingen: Neske, 1957. Translated
by Joan Stambaugh, Identity and Difference, New York: Harper
and Row, 1969.

Kant und das Problem der Metaphysik. Frankfurt: Klostermann,
1951.   Translated by James S. Churchill. Kant and the
Problem of Metaphysics, Bloomington: Indiana University
Press, 1962.

Logik: Die Frage nach der Wahrheit. Frankfurt: Klostermann,
1976.

Martin Heidegger zum 80. Geburstag. Containing "Vom Geheimnis des Glockenturms", "Der Feldweg", "Gelassenheit", "Ein Wort des Dankes", "700 Jahre Messkirch", "Uber Abraham a Santa Clara", "Ein Geburtstagsbrief des Bruders". Frankfurt: Klostermann, 1969.

Nietzsche, Vol. 1 and II. Pfüllingen: Neske, 1961. Vol. II, chapters 8-10, translated by Joan Stambaugh: "Metaphysics as History of Being", "Sketches for a History of Being as Metaphysics", "Recollections", in The End of Philosophy, New York: Harper and Row, 1973.

Phänomenologie und Theologie. Frankfurt: Klostermann, 1970. Translated in The Piety of Thinking, with notes and commentary by James G. Hart and J.C. Maraldo, Bloomington: Indiana University Press, 1976.

Platons Lehre von der Wahrheit, Mit einem Brief über den "Humanismus" (1946). Bern: Francke, 1947. Translated by William Barrett and Henry D. Aiken, eds., in Philosophy in the Twentieth Century, 2 vols. New York: Random House, 1962. Vol. 2.

Sein und Zeit*. Tübingen: Niemeyer, 1927. Translated by John Macquarrie and Edward Robinson, Being and Time, New York:-Harper and Row, 1962.

Unterwegs zur Sprache. Pfüllingen: Neske, 1959. Translated by Peter D. Hertz and J. Stambaugh, On the Way to Language, New York: Harper and Row, 1971. The essay "Language" is translated by A. Hofstadter in Poetry, Language, Thought, New York: Harper and Row, 1971.

"Versuch einer zweiten Bearbeitung. Einleitung. Die Idee der Phänomenologie und die Ruckgang auf das Bewusstsein", in Band IX of Husserliana, pp. 256-263. Translated by John N. Deely, and J.A. Novack, "The Idea of Phenomenology" in The New Scholasticism, 1970, pp. 325-344.

Vier Seminare. Frankfurt: Klostermann, 1977.

Vom Wesen des Grundes*. Frankfurt: Klostermann, 1955. Translated by T. Malick, On the Essence of Reasons, Evanston, Ill: Northwestern University Press, 1969.

Vom Wesen der Warheit. Frankfurt: Klostermann, 1943. Translated by R.F.C. Hull and Alan Crick, "On the Essence of Truth", in Brock, W. Existence and Being, Chicago: Henry Regnery Co., 1949.

Vorträge und Aufsätze.   Pfüllingen: Neske, 1954. English trans-
    lations are as follows:

    "Building, Dwelling and Thinking"; "The Thing"; "Poetically
    Man Dwells", translated by A. Hofstadter, in Poetry, Langu-
    age, Thought, New York: Harper and Row, 1971.

    "Die Frage nach der Technik", translated by William Lovitt,
    The Question Concerning Technology and Other Essays, New
    York: Harper and Row, 1977.

    "Overcoming Metaphysics", translated by Joan Stambaugh, in
    The End of Philosophy, New York: Harper and Row, 1973.

    "Who is Nietzsche's Zarathustra?", translated by B. Magnus,
    in Review of Metaphysics, Vol. XX, 1967, p. 411-31.

Was Heisst Denken?   Tübingen: Niemeyer, 1954. Translated by
    J. Glenn Gray, What is Called Thinking? New York: Harper and
    Row, 1968.

Was ist das - die Philosophie?* Pfüllingen: Neske, 1956. Trans-
    lated by W. Kluback and Jean T. Wilde, What is Philosophy?
    New York: Twayne, 1958.

Was ist Metaphysik? Frankfurt: Klostermann, 1955. Translated by
    R.F.C. Hull and Alan Crick, in Brock, W. Existence and
    Being, Chicago: Henry Regnery Co., 1949.   Introduction
    translated by Walter Kaufmann, "Way Back into the Ground of
    Metaphysics", in Existentialism: From Dostoevsky to Sartre,
    New York: Meridian, 1957.

"Wissenschaft und Besinnung", Börsenblatt für den Deutschen
    Bucchhandel, Frankfurt: 1954. Translated by William Lovitt,
    "Science and Reflection", in The Question Concerning Techno-
    logy and Other Essays, New York: Harper and Row, 1977.

Zur Sache des Denkens.   Tübingen: Neske, 1969. Translated by
    Joan Stambaugh, On Time and Being, New York: Harper and Row,
    1972.

Zur Seinsfrage.*   Frankfurt: Klostermann, 1956. Translated by
    W. Kluback and Jean T. Wilde, The Question of Being, New
    York: Twayne, 1958.

SECONDARY SOURCES

A. BOOKS

Ariées, Philippe, Western Attitudes toward Death: From the Middle
     Ages to the Present, Translated by P.M. Ranum, Baltimore and
     London: John Hopkins University Press, 1974.

Bachelard, Gaston, The Poetics of Space, Translated by Maria
     Jolas. Boston: Beacon Press, 1964.

Becker, Ernest, The Denial of Death, New York: The Free Press,
     1973.

Binswanger, L. Grundformen und Erkenntnis menschlichen Daseins,
     2te. Aufl., Zurich: 1953.

Boros, Ladislaus, S.J. The Mystery of Death, New York: Herder and
     Herder, 1965.

Brown, James, Kierkegaard, Heidegger, Buber and Barth: Subject
     and Object in Modern Theology, New York: Collier Books,
     1962.

Buber, Martin, Between Man and Man, New York: Macmillan Publi-
     shing Co., 1965.

-------- I and Thou, Translated by Walter Kaufmann, New York:
     Charles Scribners Sons, 1970.

Cedrins, Janis, "Gedanken über den Tod in der Existenz-philoso-
     phie", (Doctoral dissertation, University of Bonn, 1949.)

Crossan, John Dominic, The Dark Interval: Towards a Theology of
     Story. Niles, Illinois: Argus Communications, 1975.

D'Arcy, M.C. The Mind and Heart of Love, New York: Meridian
     Books, 1956.

Deely, J.N. The Tradition via Heidegger: an Essay on the Meaning
     of Being in the Philosophy of Martin Heidegger, The Hague:
     Martinus Nijhoff, 1971.

Demske, James M., Being, Man and Death. Kentucky: University
     Press of Kentucky: 1970.

Euripides, The Bacchae. Translated by Paul Roche, in Three Plays
     by Euripides, New York: W.W. Norton & Co., 1974.

Frankl, Victor, The Unconscious God. New York: Simon and Schuster, 1975.

Frings, M.S. (ed.) Heidegger and the Quest for Truth, Chicago: Quadrangle Books, 1968.

Fürstenau, P. Heidegger: das Gefüge seines Denkens. Frankfurt-am-Main, 1958.

Gadamer, Hans-Georg, Truth and Method, New York: The Seabury Press, 1975.

Godfrey, Dave, Death Goes Better with Coca-Cola, Toronto: Anansi, 1967.

Harper, Ralph, Human Love: Existential and Mystical, Baltimore, Maryland: John Hopkins Press, 1966.

Heineman, F.H. Existentialism and the Modern Predicament, New York: Harper and Row, 1953.

Hobbes, Thomas, Leviathan, New York: Macmillan Publishing Co., 1962.

Husserl, Edmund, Ideas: General Introduction to Pure Phenomenology, Translated by W.R. Boyce Gibson, London: Collier-Macmillan Ltd., 1931.

Kant, Immanuel, Critique of Pure Reason, Translated by Norman Kemp Smith, New York: Martin's Press, 1965 (1929).

Kastenbaum, Robert, and Aisenberg, Ruth, The Psychology of Death New York: Springer Publishing Co., 1976.

Kübler-Ross, Elisabeth, Death: the Final Stage of Growth. Englewood Cliffs, New Jersey: Prentice-Hall, Inc., 1975.

-------- On Death and Dying, New York: Macmillan Publishing Co., 1969.

Langan, Thomas, The Meaning of Heidegger, New York and London: Columbia University Press, 1961.

Lehmann, Karl, Der Tod bei Heidegger und Jaspers. Heidelberg: Evangelischer Verlag Jakob Comtess, 1938.

Levinas, E. Totality and Infinity. Translated by Alphonso Lingis. Pittsburgh: Duquesne University Press, 1969.

Lewis, C.S. A Grief Observed. London and Boston: Faber and Faber, 1961.

Löwith, Karl, Denker in dürftiger Zeit. Frankfurt: Fischer, 1953.

Lynch, Lawrence E. Language and Being. An Etienne Gilson Tribute. Milwaukee: The Marquette University Press, 1959.

Macomber, W.B. The Anatomy of Disillusion: Martin Heidegger's Notion of Truth. Evanston: Northwestern University Press, 1967.

Marcel, Gabriel, Presence and Immortality. Pittsburgh, Pa: Duquesne University Press, 1967.

Marks, E. Simone de Beauvoir: Encounters with Death. New Brunswick and New Jersey: Rutgers University Press, 1974.

Marx, Werner, Heidegger and the Tradition. Evanston, Ill: Northwestern University Press, 1971.

McCormick, Peter, Heidegger and the Language of the World. Ottawa: University of Ottawa Press, 1976.

Mehta, J.L. The Philosophy of Martin Heidegger. New York: Harper and Row, 1971.

Merleau-Ponty, Maurice, Phenomenology of Perception. Translated by Colin Smith, New York and London, 1962.

Mora, José Ferrater, Being and Death. Berkeley and Los Angeles: University of California Press, 1965.

Murray, Michael, (ed.) Heidegger and Modern Philosophy. New Haven and London: Yale University Press, 1978.

Natanson, Maurice, The Journeying Self: A Study in Philosophy and Social Role. Philippines: Addison Wesley Publishing Co., 1970.

Nedoncelle, Maurice, Love and the Person. Translated by Sr. Ruth Adelaide, S.C. New York: Sheed and Ward, 1966.

Norton, David L., and Kille, Mary F., Philosophies of Love. San Francisco: Chandler Publishing Co., 1971.

Ochs, R. The Death in Every Now. New York: Sheed and Ward, 1969.

Ott, Heinrich, Denken und Sein: Der Weg Martin Heideggers und der Weg der Theologie. Zollikon: Evangelischer Verlag, 1959.

Owens, Joseph, St. Thomas and the Future of Metaphysics. Milwaukee: Marquette University Press, 1957.

Perotti, J.L. Heidegger on the Divine. Ohio: Ohio University Press, 1974.

Richardson, W.J. Heidegger: Through Phenomenology to Thought. The Hague: Martinus Nijhoff, 1963.

Ricoeur, Paul, Fallible Man: Philosophy of the Will. Translated by C. Kelbley. Chicago: Henry Regnery Co., 1967.

Robinson, J.M., and Cobb, J.B. The Later Heidegger and Theology. New York: Harper and Row, 1963.

Sallis, John, Heidegger and the Path of Thinking. Pittsburgh, Pa.: Duquesne University Press, 1970.

Sartre, Jean-Paul, Being and Nothingness. Translated with an introduction by Hazel E. Barnes. New York: Washington Square Press, 1971 (1966).

Shneidman, Edwin S. Death: Current Perspectives. California: Mayfield Publishing Co., 1980.

Schulz, Walter, Der Gott der neuzeitlichen Metaphysik. Pfüllingen, 1957.

Seidel, G.J. Martin Heidegger and the Presocratics. Lincoln: University of Nabraska Press, 1964.

Shibles, Warren, Death: an Interdisciplinary Analysis. Whitewater, Wisconsin: The Language Press (University of Wisconsin), 1974.

Starr, David E. Entity and Existence: An Ontological Investigation of Aristotle and Heidegger. New York: Burt Franklin and Co. Inc., 1975.

Sternberg, Adolf, Der Verstandene Tod. Leipzig, 1934.

Strodack, George K. The Philosophy of Epicurus. Evanston, Ill:
    Northwestern University Press, 1963.

Thévenaz, Pierre, What is Phenomenology?   Edited by J.M. Edie.
    Chicago: Quadrangle Books, 1962.

Tolstoi, L. Anna Karenina.   Oxford: Oxford University Press,
    1977 (1918).

Toynbee, A. et. al., Man's Concern with Death.   London: Hodder
    and Stoughton, 1968.

Van Kaam, A., The Emergent Self. Pennsylvania: Dimensions Books
    Inc., 1968.

Versényi, L. Heidegger, Being and Truth.   New Haven: Yale Univer-
    sity Press, 1965.

Vycinas, V. Earth and Gods.   The Hague: Martinus Nijhoff, 1961.

Wach, Joachim, Das Problem des Todes in der Philosophie unserer
    Zeit. Tübingen, 1934.

Williams, John R. Martin Heidegger's Philosophy of Religion.
    Canadian Corporation for Studies in Religion, 1977.

B. Articles:

Arendt, Hannah,   "Martin Heidegger at Eighty", in New York Review
    of Books, October 1971. p. 50-54.

Biemel, Walter,   "The Development of Heidegger's Concept of the
    Thing", in Southwestern Journal of Philosophy, 11, Fall
    1980, pp. 47-66.

Bollnow, Otto Friedrich, "What Does It Mean to Understand a
    Writer Better than He Understood Himself?" in Philoso-
    phy Today, Vol. 23, Spring 1979. No. 1/4, pp.16-28.

Borgmann, A. "The Transformation of Heidegger's Thought", in The
    Personalist. (Los Angeles). Vol. 47, 1966. pp. 484-499.

Bouckaert, Luk, "Ontology and Ethics: Reflections on Levinas'
    Critique of Heidegger", in International Philosophical
    Quarterly. Vol. 10, September 1970. pp. 402-19.

Bryson, K.A. "Being and Human Death", in New Scholasticism.
    Vol. 48, Summer 1974, pp. 343-350.

Bukala, C.R. "Heidegger Plus: A Dialectic of Living, Dying,
    Living", in Philosophy Today, Vol. 27, Summer 1983, pp. 154-
    168.

Caputo, John, "Meister Eckhart and the Later Heidegger: The
    Mystical Element in Heidegger's Thought", Part II, in The
    Journal of Philosophy, Vol. 13, January 1975, pp. 61-80.

--------. "The Presence of the Other: A Phenomenology of the
    Human Person", Address presented to the Association of
    Catholic Philosophers of America Conference, held in the
    Park Plaza Hotel, April 22, 1979, Toronto, Canada.

Callaghan, B., "Léger and the Lepers", in Weekend, April 28,
    1979. pp. 13-19.

Dallmayr, Fred R., "Heidegger on Intersubjectivity", in Human
    Studies, Vol. 3, July 1980, pp. 221-246.

Dauenhauer, B.P., "On Death and Birth", in The Personalist,
    Vol. 57, Spring 1976. pp. 162-170.

Dillon, Martin C., "Love, Death and Creation", in Research in Phenomenology, Vol. 11, 1981. pp. 190-210.

Edwards, Paul, "Heidegger and Death: A Deflationary Critique", in The Monist, Vol. 59, No. 2, April 1976, pp. 161-186.

--------. "Heidegger and Death as 'Possibility'", in Mind, Vol. 84, October 1975, pp. 548-566.

Ehman, R.R., "Temporal Self-Identity", in Southern Journal of Philosophy, Vol. 12, Fall 1974, pp. 333-341.

Friedman, H.R., "Intimidations of Immortality", in Monist, Vol. 59, April 1976, pp. 234-248.

Gallagher, K.T. "Gabriel Marcel: Death as Mystery", in Humanitas, Vol. 10, Fall 1974, pp. 75-86.

Gaunon, Edward, "Eschaton and Existence: a Phenomenological View", in The Eschaton: A Community of Love. Edited by Joseph Papin. Villanova, Pennsylvania: Villanova University Press, 1971. pp. 173-202.

Gerber, Rudolph, "Focal Points in Recent Heidegger Scholarship", in New Scholasticism, Vol. 42, Fall 1968, pp. 561-577.

Goldstein, Jeffrey, "Buber's Misunderstanding of Heidegger", in Philosophy Today, Vol. 22, No. 2/4, Summer 1978, pp. 156-167.

Gray, J. Glenn, "Martin Heidegger: on anticipating my own death", in The Personalist, Vol. 46, 1965, pp. 439-458.

--------. "The idea of death in existentialism", in The Journal of Philosophy, Vol. 48, 1951, pp. 113-127.

Grimm, R., "Introduction: Being as Appropriation", in Philosophy Today, Vol. 19, Summer 1975. pp. 146-151.

Hall, Harrison, "Love and Death: Kierkegaard and Heidegger on Authentic and Inauthentic Human Existence", in Inquiry, Vol. 27, July 1984, pp. 179-197.

Harries, K. "Heidegger's Conception of the Holy", in Personalist, Vol. 47, 1966. pp. 169-184.

Hirsch, Elisabeth, "Remembrances of Martin Heidegger in Marburg", in Philosophy Today, Vol. 23, No. 2/4, Summer 1979, pp. 160-169.

Johnstone, Henry W. Jr., "Sleep and Death", in The Monist, Vol. 59, No. 2, April 1976. pp. 218-233.

--------. "Toward a Phenomenology of Death", in Philosophy and Phenomenological Research, Vol. 35, March 1975. pp. 396-397.

Jung, Hwa Yol, and Jung, Petee, "To Save the Earth", in Philosophy Today, Vol. 19, No. 2/4, Summer 1975, pp. 108-117.

Krong, Wolfgang, "Das Sein zum Tode bei Heidegger und die Probleme des Könnens und der Liebe", in Zeitschrift für philosophisches Forschung, Vol. 7, 1953. pp. 392-415.

Lackenman, Daniel M., "Philosophic Truth and the 'Existentiell'", in Journal of the British Society for Phenomenology, Volume 12, January 1981, pp. 55-73.

Langan, Thomas, "A Note in Response to Rukavina's Comment", in New Scholasticism, Vol. 33, 1959. pp. 358-9.

--------. "Formal Insight into Material Natures", in Phenomenology in America. Edited by J. Eddie, Chicago: Quadrangle Books, 1967. pp. 109-124.

--------. "Heidegger and the Possibility of Authentic Christianity", in Proceedings of the American Catholic Philosophical Association, Vol. 46, 1972. pp. 101-112.

--------. "Heidegger Beyond Hegel", in Filosofia. 10th Fascicolo internazionale, Vol. XIX, No. 4, November 1968, Torino. pp. 735-746.

--------. "Is Heidegger a Nihilist?", in The Thomist, XXI, No. 3, July 1958. pp. 302-319.

--------. "Transcendence in the Philosophy of Heidegger", in New Scholasticism, Vol. 32, 1958. pp. 45-60.

Lawton, Philip N. Jr., "Love and Justice: Levinas' Reading of Buber", in Philosophy Today, Vol. 20, Spring 1976. pp. 77-83.

Leonard, Linda, "The Belonging-together of Poetry and Death", in Philosophy Today, Vol. 19, No. 2/4, Summer 1975. pp. 137-145.

Levinas, Emmanuel, "God and Philosophy", in Philosophy Today, Vol. 22, No. 2/4, Summer 1978. pp. 127-145.

Lonergan, Martin J., "Gabriel Marcel's Philosophy of Death", in Philosophy Today, Vol. 19, Spring 1975. pp. 22-28.

Löwith, Karl, "M. Heidegger and F. Rosenzweig, or temporality and eternity", in Philosophy and Phenomenological Research, Vol. 3, 1943. pp. 53-77.

Maly, Kenneth, "Toward Ereignis", in Research in Phenomenology, Vol. 3, 1973. pp. 63-93.

Mason, D.R. "Time in Whitehead and Heidegger", in Process Studies, Vol. 5, Summer 1975. pp. 106-113.

Matthis, Michael J., "The Social in Kierkegaard's Concept of the Individual", in Philosophy Today, Vol. 23, No. 1/4, Spring 1979. pp. 74-83.

McCormick, Peter, "A Note on Time and Being", in Philosophy Today, Vol. 19, No. 2/4, Summer 1975. pp. 95-99.

Mijuskovic, Ben, "Loneliness and Time-consciousness", in Philosophy Today, Vol. 22, No. 4/4, Winter 1978. pp. 276-286.

Mirfenderesky, Jamshid, "Concerning Paul Edwards' 'Heidegger on Death'", Journal of the British Society for Phenomenology, Vol. 13, May 1982, pp. 120-128.

Mullen, John D., "Between the Aesthetic and the Ethical: Kierkegaard's 'Either/Or'" in Philosophy Today, Vol. 23, No. 1/4, Spring 1979, pp. 84-94.

Murphy, Jeffrie G. "Rationality and the Fear of Death", in The Monist, Vol. 59, No. 2, April 1976. pp. 187-203.

Nicholson, Graeme, "Disclosure in Heidegger", in Studies of International Philosophy, Fall 1974. pp. 139-154.

--------. "Heidegger on Thinking", in Journal of the History of Philosophy, Vol. 13, October 1975. pp. 491-503.

Paskow, Alan, "The Meaning of My Own Death", in International Philosophical Quarterly, Vol. 14, March 1974. pp. 51-69.

--------. "What Do I Fear in Facing My Death?", in Man and World, Vol. 8, No. 2. May 1975. pp. 146-156.

Pattrica, N.A. "Martin Heidegger's Understanding of Theology", in Listening, Vol. 10, No. 1. Winter 1975. pp. 59-72.

Pegis, Anton C., "After Seven Hundred Years: St. Thomas Aquinas in 1974", in Eglise et Théologie, Vol. 5, 1974. pp. 137-153.

Pöggeler, Otto, "Being as Appropriation", in Philosophy Today, Vol. 19, No. 2/4, Summer 1975. pp. 152-178.

Puccetti, Roland, "The Conquest of Death", in The Monist, Vol. 59, No. 2, April 1976. pp. 249-263.

Richey, C.W. "On the Intentional Ambiguity of Heidegger's Metaphysics", in Journal of Philosophy, (NY), Vol. 55, 1958. pp. 1144-1148.

Rosenstein, Leon, "Heidegger and Plato and the Good", in Philosophy Today, Vol. 22, No. 4/4, Winter 1978. pp. 332-354.

Rukavina, I.F. "Being and Things in Heidegger's Philosophy: A Rejoinder", in New Scholasticism, Vol. 33, 1959. pp. 184-201.
--------. "Kant and the Problem of Metaphysics", in New Scholasticism, Vol. 39, 1965. pp. 547-550.

Ryle, Gilbert, "Critical Notice of 'Sein und Zeit'", in Mind, Vol. XXXVIII, 1929.

Sabatino, Charles J., "Faith and Human Meaning", in Listening, Vol. 10, No. 1, Winter 1975. pp. 51-57.

Schmitz, K. "Embodiment and Situation", in Journal of Philosophy, Vol. 73, November 1976. pp. 710-22.

--------. "Father Richardson on Heidegger", in Modern Schoolman, Vol. 44, March 1967. pp. 247-259.

Sharp, Ann Margaret, "Simone Weil on Friendship", in Philosophy Today, Vol. 22, No. 4/4, Winter 1978. pp. 266-275.

Sherover, C.M. "Kant's Transcendental Object and Heidegger's Nichts", in Journal of the History of Philosophy, Vol. 7, October 1969. pp. 413-422.

Silverman, Hugh J., "Man and the Self as Identity of Difference", in Philosophy Today, Vol. 19, No. 2/4, Summer 1975. pp. 131-136.

Smoot, W., "The Social Dimension of Death - Anxiety", in Philosophy Today, Vol. 21, Spring 1977. pp. 84-89.

Stambaugh, Joan, "Time and Dialectic in Hegel and Heidegger", in Research in Phenomenology, Vol. 4, 1974. pp. 87-97.

Sturm, Fred Gillette, "Authenticity and Other Persons", in Christian Century, Vol. 80, 1963. pp. 340-342.

Van de Pitte, F.P. "The Role of Hölderlin in the Philosophy of Heidegger", in The Personalist, Vol. 43, 1962. pp. 168-179.

Van de Water, L. "Being and Being Human: An Impasse in Heidegger's Thought?" in International Philosophical Quarterly, Vol. 13, Spring 1973. pp. 391-402.

Watson, James R., "Being...there: the Neighbourhood of Being", in Philosophy Today, Vol. 19, No. 2/4, Summer 1975. pp. 118-130.

Weber, Renée, "A Critique of Heidegger's Concept of Solicitude", in New Scholasticism, Vol. 42, Fall 1968. pp. 537-560.

White, Carol J., "Dasein, Existence and Death", in Philosophy Today, Vol. 28, Spring 1984, pp. 52-65.

Williams, John R. "Heidegger and the Theologians", in Heythrop Journal, Vol. 12, No. 3, July 1971. pp. 258-280.

Wyschogrod, Edith, "Death and Some Philosophies of Language", in Philosophy Today, Vol. 23, No. 4/4, Winter 1978. pp. 255-265.

Zimmerman, Michael E., "Heidegger's New Concept of Authentic
    Selfhood", in The Personalist, Vol. 57, Spring 1976, pp. 198-
    212.

--------. "The Foundering of 'Being and Time'", in Philosophy
    Today, Vol. 19, No. 2/4, Summer 1975. pp. 100-107.

--------. "The Unity and Sameness of Self as Depicted in 'Being
    and Time'", in Journal of British Phenomenology, Vol. 6,
    October 1975. pp. 157-167.

-o0o-

KEY TO ABBREVIATIONS

SZ   Sein und Zeit

EM   Einführung in die Metaphysik

GP   Grundprobleme in der Phänomenologie

WG   Vom Wesen des Grundes

KM   Kant und das Problem der Metaphysik

WIM   Was ist Metaphysik?

WM   Wegmarken

ID   Identität und Differenz

HW   Holzwege

FD   Die Frage nach dem Ding

WW   Vom Wesen der Warheit

VA   Vorträge und Aufsätze

US   Unterwegs zur Sprache

ZD   Zur Sache des Denkens

WD   Was Heisst Denken?

HD   Erläuterungen zu Hölderlins Dichtung

All texts are by Martin Heidegger.

Within this volume, all references to "e.t." are to the English translation.

MARTINUS NIJHOFF PHILOSOPHY LIBRARY

Series ISBN 90-247-2344-2